THE SAVIOUR GOD

EDWIN OLIVER JAMES

THE SAVIOUR GOD

COMPARATIVE STUDIES
IN THE CONCEPT OF SALVATION
PRESENTED TO

Edwin Oliver James

Professor Emeritus
in the University of London

by

COLLEAGUES AND FRIENDS

to commemorate
his seventy-fifth birthday

edited by

S. G. F. BRANDON

Professor of Comparative Religion in the
University of Manchester

GREENWOOD PRESS, PUBLISHERS
WESTPORT, CONNECTICUT

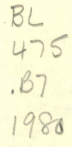

Library of Congress Cataloging in Publication Data

Brandon, Samuel George Frederick, ed.
The saviour god.

Reprint of the ed. published by Manchester University Press, Manchester, England.
English, Italian, or French.
"A list of the principal published writings of E. O. James": p.
Includes bibliographical references and index.
1. Salvation--Comparative studies--Addresses, essays, lectures. 2. James, Edwin Oliver, 1886- --Addresses, essays, lectures. I. James, Edwin Oliver, 1886- II. Title.
BL475.B7 1980 291.2'2 80-14924
ISBN 0-313-22416-1 (lib. bdg.)

Reprinted in 1980 by Greenwood Press, a division of
Congressional Information Service, Inc.
88 Post Road West, Westport, CT 06881

Printed in the United States of America

10 9 8 7 6 5 4 3 2 1

EDITOR'S FOREWORD

BRITISH scholarship may fairly claim that it had its part, and no mean part, in laying the foundations of the comparative study of religion. Two names will suffice to attest the calibre of its pioneers in this field. In 1871 Edward Burnett Tylor, in his magisterial work entitled *Primitive Culture*, demonstrated the scope of the comparative method in propounding his thesis of a primaeval animism. Two decades later saw the commencement of the mighty corpus of *The Golden Bough*, which abides as both a memorial to the learning and imagination of James George Frazer and a landmark in the study of human culture and its significance. But the great promise of those early years was, strangely, not fulfilled in this country as the twentieth century developed towards its middle decades. Teaching appointments in the subject at the universities remained few, and theological circles seemed increasingly to turn from it as though uneasy about the significance of its findings. In Europe and America, fortunately, interest in the objective study of the religions of mankind continued to grow, and its importance for humanistic studies in the universities has been recognized by the establishment of professorial chairs and research foundations. However, in England during these fallow years one scholar, with foresight and devotion, manfully maintained the cause of the comparative study of religion. Gradually making his name known by a steady stream of publications, Edwin Oliver James, by his own studies and through the succession of teaching appointments which he held in various universities, has truly carried this particular torch of learning almost alone until recent years. It is in deep appreciation of this devoted and effective service that a group of his friends and colleagues now pays tribute to him. With them, in this act of respect and affection, they are happy to have the company of a representative body of scholars of other lands. The presence of these distinguished scholars rightly gives an international aspect to this tribute; for Dr James has laboured not only to foster the study of his subject in this country, but he has consistently sought to promote the co-operation of scholars of all lands in a field of such universal interest and importance—indeed the British Section of the International Association for the History of Religions, of which all the British contributors of this volume are members, owes its establishment to his enterprise and energy of action.

The selection of the 'Saviour God' as the subject of this volume was influenced by two considerations. In the first place, it was felt that it would constitute a theme that would please Professor James by being one with which, in its various aspects, he has so often concerned himself. Secondly, it seemed a fruitful theme for a symposium, since soteriology is a topic of both wide and diverse significance. In view of the essential complexity of the idea of Salvation and of the Saviour God, no attempt has, however, been made to define the subject, and to ask the contributors to write with such a definition in mind. The decision would seem to be justified by the variety of topics, and of their treatment, revealed in the following essays, which surely attests both the basic nature of man's aspiration for security and the catholicity of its expression.

I should like to record my thanks to Professors C. J. Bleeker, M. Eliade, H. D. Lewis, M. Simon, and R. C. Zaehner, who, with myself, formed the Sponsoring Committee. I have also been greatly obliged by the ready co-operation of the contributors. Ill health unfortunately precluded contributions from Professors M. Eliade, H.-C. Puech and Dr Margaret A. Murray, and other factors regrettably prevented Professors D. W. Gundry: they all desire, however, to associate themselves warmly with this tribute to Professor James.

To Miss Linda Shepherd, I am especially grateful for her efficient handling of the clerical work involved in this undertaking, for typing some of the manuscripts and helping with the index.

On behalf of the members of the Sponsoring Committee, I wish to thank the Manchester University Press for so readily undertaking the publication of this volume, and to its Secretary, Mr T. L. Jones, I am indebted for his kind advice and co-operation.

S. G. F. BRANDON

The University of Manchester,
November 1962

CONTENTS

EDWIN OLIVER JAMES

by

S. H. HOOKE

TO the eminent subject of this essay in appreciation the words of Horace are happily relevant: 'Sunt quos curriculo pulverem Olympicum collegisse juvat.' The Olympic dust which Professor James's glowing chariot wheels have collected during his long and distinguished course, still in full sweep, has been the dust of ages, dust of the ancient gods, dust of Magdalenian man, dust of British folklore, dust from many a dark and secret recess of the mind of primitive man; all these and more mark his trail.

It has been my privilege to be academically associated with Professor James, and to enjoy his friendship for more than thirty years; hence I rejoice that such a representative body of distinguished scholars will combine in the production of this tribute to his long and fruitful career in the unwearied pursuit of truth in the kindred fields of anthropology, archaeology, and the comparative study of religion.

It is my pleasant task and privilege to record the course of Professor James's long career and to enumerate the achievements and honours with which it is crowded.

He was educated at University College School and Exeter College, Oxford. He was initiated into the mysteries of anthropology by the genial high-priest of that discipline, Dr R. R. Marett, who, as rumour has it, was known in Exeter as the Seigneur of Jersey, and in Jersey as the Rector of Exeter, and whose influence on British anthropology cannot be overestimated. At Oxford James was a contemporary of a number of brilliant scholars whose names are now household words, such as J. L. Myres, Lewis Farnell, and E. T. Leeds. After Oxford he studied for his Ph.D. at University College, London, under Professor Flinders Petrie who had built up there a flourishing school of Egyptology. At that time he came into contact with Professor

Elliot Smith and W. J. Perry who had founded a lively department of anthropology at University College, and round whom the stormy Diffusionist controversy was then raging. The Pan-Egyptian theories of Elliot Smith and Perry were anathema to Flinders Petrie, and E. O. James had to steer a cautious middle course between Scylla and Charybdis. After the first World War ended, when travel was again possible, Professor James embarked on a long series of archaeological expeditions to the decorated caves of Spain, the Dordogne, Ariège and the Pyrenees. He also visited pre-historic sites and excavations in the Aegean, the Eastern Mediterranean, and the megalithic littoral, Brittany, the Seine-Oise-Marne region, and nearer home the pre-historic sites in the British Isles, the Channel Islands, and Ireland. In the course of these expeditions he collected much of the data subsequently published in the many books and articles enumerated in the bibliography appended to this book.

In 1918 his connection with the British Folklore Society began as a member of the Council of that Society, of which he became President in 1930, and for 25 years he was editor of its Journal. His services to British folklore were recognized in 1955 by the award of the Coote Lake Research Medal. In 1932 he was invited to join the team of scholars responsible for the production of *Myth and Ritual*, a book which has had no small influence on the study of the religions of the ancient Near East. In 1933 he became the first occupant of the newly created chair of the History and Philosophy of Religion in the University of Leeds, where he built up from the foundations a flourishing school in that important department of anthropology. During the busy years before the outbreak of the second World War he was engaged in multifarious activities. He was examining chaplain to a succession of Bishops of Wakefield; in 1934 he presided over the Religious Section of the Congrès International des Sciences Anthropologiques et Ethnologiques, and in 1939 he was appointed Wilde Lecturer in Natural and Comparative Religion in the University of Oxford; in the same year he received the honorary degree of D.D. in St Andrews University. The war years caused a reduction of academic activities everywhere, but Professor James performed a valuable service by lecturing twice a week at University College, Bangor, where the war had brought about a depletion of staff, as it had in many other universities.

Immediately after the war he was appointed to the Chair of the History and Philosophy of Religion in the University of London, which he held until his retirement in 1955, when he was made Professor Emeritus. In 1946 he was made a Fellow of University College, London, where he had carried on his post-graduate studies, and four years later he was made a Fellow of King's College, London, which extended its hospitality to him as a University Professor. In 1950 he delivered the Forwood Lectures in Liverpool University, and was appointed visiting lecturer in the University of Amsterdam. It was at this time that his association with the International Congress for the History of Religions began, and as the British representative on the International Executive Board he successfully carried out the organization of the British section. He has been closely connected with its work and with the organization of its Congresses at Amsterdam (1951), Rome (1956), and Marburg (1960). In 1951 Professor James presided over Section H at the Belfast Meeting of the British Association, and since 1956 he has been its representative on the Council. In 1950 he gave the Henry Myres Lecture, under the auspices of the Royal Anthropological Institute, at the Royal Society, in 1952 the Im Thurn Memorial Lecture at Edinburgh, and in 1958 he had the honour and pleasure of delivering the Marett Lecture at Exeter College, Oxford, where he was able to pay an eloquent tribute to Professor Marett and to acknowledge his debt to one who had been his tutor and to whom he owed more than to anyone else. At present Professor James is working on the course of Jordan Lectures which he is to deliver at the School of Oriental and African Studies in the University of London after Easter, 1962. Since 1960 he has occupied the post of Chaplain at All Souls College, Oxford, a source of satisfaction and stimulation to him. After such a full and distinguished career, most men would feel justified in sitting back and enjoying a well-earned leisure, but Professor James with unwearied activity continues to promote those anthropological studies which he has done so much to advance. He is one of the advisory Editors of *Chambers' Encyclopaedia* and the *Encyclopaedia Britannica*, involving labours which might well daunt a much younger man. He is also editing the Hutchinson and Weidenfeld Series on the History of Religions, to the latter of which he has just contributed a splendid volume under the title of *The Ancient Gods*.

The length of the bibliography which follows bears eloquent testimony to Professor James's prodigious industry. It is perhaps worthwhile referring to a book of marked originality which has not received the acclaim it deserves; it is *Christian Myth and Ritual*. In view of the widespread interest in the Liturgical Movement, attention might well be called to a book whose approach to the significance of Christian liturgy is so original and stimulating.

Of Professor James it may truly be said, *Si monumentum requiris, circumspice*. The external record of his career, happily still unfinished, speaks for itself. Here is the Olympic dust, but what about the rider in the chariot? Perhaps the most notable thing to be said about Professor James is that he has never cultivated the gentle art of making enemies. Anyone who has moved much in academic circles knows that *irae saevae* often stir and breed under the surface, and that odium anthropologicum can be as bitter as odium theologicum. But from his first experience of academic feuds when he found himself surrounded by the flames of the great Diffusionist controversy, now happily extinct, Professor James has never allowed himself to become a partisan. Urbane, tolerant and charitable, always able to see both sides of a question, always looking for the best in every man, never making a parade of his great learning, but humble and unaffected in spirit, he has passed through all the vicissitudes of his long and distinguished career untouched by any breath of envy, malice or uncharitableness.

His many friends all over the world on the occasion of his seventy-fifth birthday will wish him a long continuance of good health and many more years of fruitful activity in those studies which he has done so much to adorn.

S. H. HOOKE

A LIST OF THE PRINCIPAL PUBLISHED WRITINGS OF E. O. JAMES

ABBREVIATIONS

C.Q.R.	*Church Quarterly Review*
C.T.	*Church Times*
E.R.E.	*Encyclopaedia of Religions and Ethics* (Hastings)
E.T.	*Expository Times*
F.L.	*Folk-Lore*
H.J.	*Hibbert Journal*
J.R.A.I.	*Journal of the Royal Anthropological Institute*
J.T.S.	*Journal of Theological Studies*

1917

Primitive Ritual and Belief (London, Methuen), pp. 243, with an introduction by R. R. Marett.

1918

'Rain', *E.R.E.* X.

1919

An Introduction to Anthropology (London, Macmillan), pp. 259.

1920

'Sacrifice' (Introductory and Primitive); 'Sieve'; 'Smoking'; 'Staff', *E.R.E.* XI.

1921

'Tutelary Gods and Spirits'; 'Water, Water-Gods (Primitive)'; 'Yawning', *E.R.E.* XII.

'The Origin of Man', *Theology*, III.

Review of *From Ritual to Romance* (J. L. Weston), *Theology*, III.

1922

'Science and Theology', *Theology*, IV.

Review of *Epilogemena to the Study of Greek Religion* (J. Harrison), *Theology*, IV.

1926

'The Emergence of Religion', *Essays Catholic and Critical* (ed. G. Selwyn).
'Magic and Religion', *Theology*, XII.
Reviews of *The Children of the Sun* (W. J. Perry), *Theology*, XII; *The Worship of Nature* (J. G. Frazer), *C.T.*

1927

The Stone Age (London, The Sheldon Press), pp. 202.
'The Concept of the Soul in North America', *F.L.* LXXXVII.
'The Idea of God in Early Religions', *Anthropos*, XXII.

1928

The Beginnings of Man (London, Hodder & Stoughton), pp. 260.
'Cremation and the Preservation of the Dead in North America', *American Anthropologist*, *N.S.* 30, No. 2.
'Evolution and the Christian Faith', *Theology*, XVI.
'Magic and the Sacramental Principle', *C.Q.R.* CVI.
'A Comparative Study of the Old Testament in the Light of Anthropological and Archaeological Research', *A New Commentary on Holy Scripture* (ed. Gore, Goudge and Guillaume).
Reviews of *Le Non-Civilisé et Nous* (R. Allier), *C.Q.R.* CVI; *The Circle and the Cross, Vol. I* (A. Allcroft), *C.Q.R.* CVI; *The Pilgrimage of Buddhism* (J. B. Pratt), *C.T.*

1929

Reviews of *Ur-Entwicklung des Menschen* (D. Artur Neuberg), *C.Q.R.* CVII; *The Travels and Settlements of Early Man* (T. S. Foster), *C.Q.R.* CVII; *Biblical Anthropology* (H. J. D. Astley), *C.Q.R.* CVII and *F.L.* XL; *Forschungsreise zu den Kagaba* (K. T. Preuss), *F.L.* XL; 'The People of the Veil', *F.L.* XL; *Roseel Island* (W. E. Armstrong), *F.L.* XL.

1930

The Christian Faith in the Modern World (London, Mowbray), pp. 259.
Reviews of *Bella Bella Texts* (F. Boas), *F.L.* XLI; *The Origin and Growth of Religion* (W. Schmidt) (*E.T.* by H. J. Rose), *F.L.* XLI; 'Jubilee Congress of the Folk-Lore Society', *F.L.* XLI; *Myths of the Origin of Fire* (J. G. Frazer), *C.T.*; *The Flood* (Harold Peake), *C.T.*

1931

'The Approach to the Study of Folklore' (Presidential Address to the Folk-Lore Society, 1931), *F.L.* XLII.
'The Dawn of Civilization', *Scientia*, CCX.
Reviews of *The Circle and the Cross, Vol II* (A. Allcroft), *C.Q.R.* CXI; *From Savagery to Commerce* (T. S. Foster), *C.Q.R.* CXI; *Joshua, Judges* (J. Garstang), *C.T.*

1932

'The Function of Folklore' (Presidential Address to the Folk-Lore Society, 1932), *F.L.* XLIII.

'Folklore and Archaeology in North-West Spain and Portugal', *F.L.* XLIII.

Reviews of *Atlantis in Andalucia* (E. M. Whishaw), *F.L.* XLIII; *Osiris: A Study in Myths, Mysteries and Religion* (H. P. Cook), *F.L.* XLIII; *Buddha's Teachings* (Lord Chalmers; Harvard Oriental Series), *C.T.*; *Israel* (A. Lods) (*E.T.* by S. H. Hooke), *C.T.*; *Animal Lore in English Literature* (P. A. Robin), *C.T.*; *Faith, Hope and Charity in Primitive Religion* (R. R. Marett, Gifford Lectures), *C.T.* and *Christendom.*

1933

The Origins of Sacrifice (London, John Murray), pp. 259. American edition, 1962.

'Initiation Rites', *Myth and Ritual* (ed. S. H. Hooke).

'The Mystery Religions', *C.Q.R.* CXV.

Review of *Sacraments of Simple Folk* (R. R. Marett, Gifford Lectures), *The Observer.*

1934

Christian Myth and Ritual (London, John Murray), pp. 345, American edition, 1962.

'The Place of History and Philosophy in the Study of Religion' (Inaugural Lecture, University of Leeds), *C.Q.R.* CXVI.

Reviews of *High Gods in North America* (W. Schmidt), *Man,* XXXIV, *F.L.* XLV; *Der Ursprung der Gottesidee,* vols. IV and V (W. Schmidt), *Man,* XXIV; *Archaeology and Folk Tradition* (H. J. Fleure), *F.L.* XLV; *The Fear of The Dead in Primitive Religion* (J. G. Frazer), *C.T.*; *Phases in the Religion of Ancient Rome* (C. Bailey), *C.Q.R.* CXVI.

1935

The Old Testament in the Light of Anthropology (London, S.P.C.K.), pp. 146.

'The Sources of Christian Ritual', *The Labyrinth* (ed. S. H. Hooke).

'Primitive Monotheism', *The Sociological Review,* XXVII, No. 3.

Reviews of *Head, Heart and Hands in Human Evolution* (R. R. Marett), *Oxford Magazine*; *Cecil Sharpe* (A. H. F. Strangeways), *F.L.* XLVI; *Orpheus and Greek Religion* (W. K. C. Guthrie), *The New Statesman and Nation.*

1936

In the Fulness of Time: The Historical Background of Christianity (London, S.P.C.K.), pp. 182.

'Ethical Monotheism', *Occident and Orient* (Gaster Anniversary Volume).

Reviews of *Ancient Hebrew Social Life and Custom* (R. H. Kennett), *Man,* XXXVI; *Der Ursprung der Gottesidee,* VI (W. Schmidt), *Man,* XXXVI; *We Europeans: A Survey of Racial Problems* (J. S. Huxley and A. C. Haddon), *Man,* XXXVI; *The Origins of Religion* (R. Karsten), *F.L.* XLVII; *Custom is King: Essays Presented to R. R. Marett, F.L.* XLVII; *The Fear of the Dead in Primitive Religion* (J. G. Frazer), *C.T.*; *The Early Buddhist Theory of Man Perfected* (I. B. Horner), *C.T.*

1937

The Origins of Religion (London, The Unicorn Press), pp. 159.
'Religion in the Graeco-Roman World', *Judaism and Christianity* (ed. W. O. E. Oesterley).
Reviews of *Religion and History* (J. C. McKerrow), *Man*, XXXVII; *The Hero: A Study in Tradition, Myth and Drama* (Lord Raglan), *Man*, XXXVII; *Volk und Volstum*, vol. II (ed. G. Shreiber), *J.T.S.* XXXVIII; *Foundation of Faith and Morals* (B. Malinowski), *F.L.* XLVIII.

1938

Comparative Religion: A Text Book (London, Methuen), pp. 374. New edition, 1961.
Reviews of *Pyrenean Festivals* (V. Alford), *Man*, XXXVIII; *A Primitive Philosophy of Life* (J. H. Hutton, The Frazer Lecture), *F.L.* XLIX; *The Buddhist Sects of Japan* (E. Steinilber-Oberlin), *C.T.*; *The National Faith of Japan* (D. C. Holtom), *C.T.*

1939

'Comparative Religion', *The Study of Theology* (ed. K. E. Kirk).
'Aspects of Sacrifice in the Old Testament', *E.T.* 50.
'Harold Coote Lake', obituary notice, *F.L.* L.
Reviews of *The Origins of Early Semitic Ritual* (S. H. Hooke, the Sweich Lectures), *Man*, XXXIX; *A History of Roman Religion* (F. Altheim), *Man*, XXXIX; *From Religion to Morality* (W. G. de Burgh), *J.T.S.* XL; *Religion in Essence and Manifestation* (G. Van der Leeuw), *C.Q.R.* CXXVII; *The Original Gita* (R. Otto), *C.T.*; *Analects of Confucius* (A. Waley), *C.T.*; *Cylinder Seals* (H. Frankfort), *C.T.*

1940

The Social Function of Religion (University of London Press), pp. 312. 2nd ed. 1948. French translation 1950 (Editions Payot).
Reviews of *Anthropology and Religion* (P. A. Buck), *Man*, XL, *F.L.* LI; *Christianity and Morals* (E. Westermarck), *Man*, XL; *The Jewish World in the Time of Jesus* (G. Guignebert), *Man*, XL; *Eastern Religions and Western Thought* (S. Radhakrishnan), *J.T.S.* XLI; *The Lady of the Hare* (J. Layard), *The Listener*; *Taboo* (A. R. Radcliffe-Brown, The Frazer Lecture), *Religions*; *Witchcraft* (C. Williams), *F.L.* LII.

1941

Reviews of *Holy Images* (Edwyn Bevan), *Man*, XLI; *Ethnologische Studien an Indonesischen Schöpfungsmythen; ein Beitrag zur Kultur-analyse Sudotasius* (W. Münsterberger), *Man*, XLI; *Religion in Science and Civilization* (R. Gregory), *J.T.S.*; *Ideals of Religion* (A. C. Bradley, The Gifford Lectures), *Religions*; *Living Religions and a World Faith* (W. E. Hocking, The Gifford Lectures), *J.T.S.* XLII.

1942

'Sir J. G. Frazer', obituary, *Man*, XLII and *The Guardian*.
Review of *Good and Evil Spirits* (E. Langton), *Oxford Magazine*.

1943

'Dr R. R. Marett', obituary, *F.L.* LIV.
Reviews of *Bhagwam the Supreme Deity of the Bhils* (W. Koppers), *Man*, XLIII; *Lamps of Anthropology* (J. Murphy), *Man*, XLIII; *Submission in Suffering* (H. H. Rowley), *Theology*.

1944

Review of *Science, Religion and the Future* (C. E. Raven), *Man*, XLIV.

1945

Reviews of *Anthropomorphism and Miracle* (E. Ehnmark), *Man*, XLV; *What is Christian Marriage?* (A. T. Macmillan), *The Listener*.

1947

'The Influence of Christianity on Folklore', *F.L.* LVIII.
'Artificial Human Insemination (Sociological)': Public Morality Council Report.
Review of *Personality and Religion* (W. Brown), *Man*, XLVII.

1948

The Beginnings of Religion (London, Hutchinson University Library), pp. 159. Spanish translation, 1955, new edition, 1958.
'The Social Function of Religion', *Man*, XLVIII.
'World Religions—a Summing Up' (a broadcast), *The Listener*.
Reviews of *The Vedantic Buddhism of the Buddha* (ed. J. G. Jennings), *Man*, XLVIII; *Papago Indian Religion* (R. M. Underhill), *F.L.* LIX.

1949

A History of Christianity in England (London, Hutchinson University Library), pp. 184.
Review of *Ancient Egyptian Religion* (H. Frankfort), *Man*, XLIX.

1950

The Concept of Deity (The Wilde Lectures, Oxford) (London, Hutchinson University Library), pp. 200.
'Religion and Reality' (Henry Myers Memorial Lectures, R.A.I.), *J.R.A.I.* LXXX, 1950.
'Sir James Frazer', *Dictionary of National Biography*.
'Myth and Ritual', *Eranos-Jahrbuch*, XVII.
'Animism'; 'Animal-cults'; 'Ancestor-worship'; 'Bull-roarer'; 'Calendar Customs'; 'Comparative Religion'; 'Images and Image-worship'; 'Magic'; 'Mana and Fetichism'; 'Mystic and Symbolic Numbers'; 'Plant-lore'; 'Sacrifice'; 'Superstitions', *Chambers' Encyclopaedia*; advisory editor, *Religions* section.

'The VIIth International Congress for the History of Religions at Amsterdam', report, *Man*, L, and *F.L.* LXII.

Reviews of *Man, Mind and Music* (F. Howes), *Man*, L; *Der Ursprung der Gottesidee*, VIII (W. Schmidt), *Man*, and *Bulletin of School of Oriental and African Studies*; *Magic, Science and Religion and Other Essays* (B. Malinowski), *Man*, L; *White Magic* (C. G. Loomis), *F.L.* LXI; *Oxford in Brush and Pen* (E. Canziani), *F.L.* LXI.

1951

Reviews of *The Problem of Similarity in Ancient Near Eastern Religion* (H. Frankfort), *H.J.* XLIX; *Essays Presented to Sarvepalli Radhakrishnan*, *H.J.* XLIX; *Tammuz, der Unsterblichkeitsglaube in der Altorientalischen Bildkunst* (von Anton Moorgate), *J.T.S.*; *Magic: A Sociological Study* (H. Webster), *F.L.* LXII; *Living Country Customs in Salzburg* (P. C. Plott-Flatz), *F.L.*, LXII; *The Growth of the Old Testament* (H. H. Rowley), *F.L.* LXII.

1952

Marriage and Society (London, Hutchinson University Library), pp. 215. American edition, 1955.

'A Study of Anthropology and Folklore' (The Im Thurn Memorial Lecture), *Proceedings of the Scottish Anthropological and Folklore Society*, IV, No. 3.

'Archaeology, Folklore and Sacred Tradition' (Presidential Address, Section H, British Association Meeting at Belfast, 1952), *The Advancement of Science*, No. 34.

Reviews of *Essays in Applied Psycho-Analysis* (Ernest Jones, *Folklore and Religion, Vol. II*), *Man*, LII; *The Origin of Death: Studies in African Mythology* (Hans Abrahamsson), *Man*, LII; *Notes and Queries on Anthropology*, *F.L.* LXIII.

1953

'Historical Theology and the History of Religions' (Presidential Address), *Proceedings of the Oxford Society of Historical Theology*, 1953–4.

'The Dunmow Flitch', *F.L.* LXIV.

Reviews of *Religion, Science and Human Crises: A Study in China in Transition* (F. L. K. Hsu), *Man*, LIII; *Divine Horsemen: The Living Gods of Haiti* (Maya Deren), *F.L.* LXIV; *The Oldest Stories in the World* (T. H. Gaster), *F.L.* LXIV.

1954

Reviews of *Myth and Ritual in Christianity* (A. W. Watts), *Man*, LIV; *The Shi'a of India* (J. N. Hollister), *Man*, LIV; *Mythos und Kult bei Naturvölkern* (Ad. E. Jensen), *Man*, LIV; *The Christian Attitude to Other Religions* (E. C. Dewick), *J.T.S.*, *N.S.* V; *Das Himmlische Buch in Antike und Christentum* (L. Koep), *J.T.S.*, *N.S.* V; *Saint Bridget of Sweden* (Johannes Jorgensen 2 vols.), *The Listener*; *The Nazarene Gospel Restored* (R. Graves and J. Podro), *The Listener*; *The Bible: Historical, Social and Literary Aspects* (*The Times*), *F.L.* LXV.

1955

The Nature and Function of Priesthood (London, Thames & Hudson), pp. 336. American edition, 1956. German translation, 1956 (Rheinische Verlags-Anstalt, Wiesbaden).

'Allan Gomme', obituary notice, *F.L.* LXVI.

'An Anthropological and Biological Analysis of the Nature, Place and Function of Monogamy in the Institution of Marriage', *The Church and the Law of Nullity of Marriage.*

'The History, Science and Comparative Study of Religion', *Numen* I, Fasc. 2.

Reviews of *The Fate of the Soul* (R. Firth, The Frazer Lecture), *F.L.* LXVI; *Myth or Legend?* (G. E. Daniel and D. Boyd), *F.L.* LXVI.

1956

History of Religions (London, English Universities Press), pp. 237.

'P. F. Heather', obituary notice, *F.L.* LXVII.

Reviews of *Prophecy and Religion in Ancient China and Israel* (H. H. Rowley, The Jordan Lectures in Comparative Religion), *Bulletin of the School of Oriental and African Studies*; *Water into Wine* (E. S. Drower), *Bulletin of School of Oriental and African Studies* and *Man*, LVI; *Life of Muhammad* (A. Guillaume), *C.Q.R.* CLVII; *Nuer Religion* (E. E. Evans-Pritchard), *Times Literary Supplement* and *J.T.S.*; *The Mysteries: Papers from the Eranos Year-Books* (ed. J. Campbell), *H.J.* LIV; *Sacred Books of the World* (A. C. Bouquet), *The Philosophical Quarterly*; *Rock Paintings of the Drakensberg* (A. R. Willcock), *Times Educational Supplement*; *Essays on the History of Religions* (R. Pettazzoni), *F.L.* LXVII; *Motif-Index of Folk Literature* (Stith Thompson), *F.L.* LXVII.

1957

Prehistoric Religion (London, Thames & Hudson), pp. 300, with illustrations. American edition, 1958. Translations: French and German, 1959, Italian, 1961, Spanish, Dutch and Swedish, 1962.

'The Sacred and the Secular in Primitive Religion', *The Modern Churchman.*

'The Nature and Function of Myth', *F.L.* LXVIII.

Reviews of *The Siege Perilous* (S. H. Hooke), *H.J.* LV, and *F.L.* LXVIII; *Order and History: Vol. I, Israel and Revelation* (E. Voegelin), *H.J.* LV; *All Things Made New* (J. Ferraby), *E.T.*; *The All-Knowing God* (R. Pettazzoni), *F.L.* LXVIII, *N.S.* VIII.

1958

Myth and Ritual in the Ancient Near East (London, Thames & Hudson), pp. 352. American edition, 1959. Translations: French and German, 1959, Italian 1960.

A Comparative Study of Religions in the East, C.U.P. for the National Book League.

'The Threshold of Religion' (The Marett Memorial Lecture, Exeter College, Oxford), *F.L.* LXIX.

Reviews of *The Eye-Goddess* (O. G. S. Crawford), *Nature*, vol. 181; and *Oxford Magazine*; *From the Stone Age to Christianity* (W. F. Albright), *C.Q.R.* CLIX; *Religions: A Historical and Theological Study* (D. W. Gundry), *C.Q.R.* CLIX and *E.T.*; *The Buddhist Wisdom Books: The Diamond Sutra and Heart Sutra* (E. Conze), *C.Q.R.* CLIX and *E.T.*; *Patterns in Comparative Religions* (Mircea Eliade), *F.L.* LXIX; *Gaster Centenary Publications* (ed. B. Schindler), *F.L.* LXIX; *Lamb to the Slaughter* (G. Every), *J.T.S.*, *N.S.* IX; *King Arthur's Avalon: The Story of Glastonbury* (G. Ashe), *F.L.* LXIX.

1959

The Cult of the Mother Goddess (London, Thames & Hudson), pp. 300. American edition, French and German translations, 1960.

'Some Editorial Reminiscences', *F.L.* LXX.

'The Sacral Kingship and the Priesthood', *Studies in the History of Religion IV: La Regalita Sacra* (Brill).

Reviews of *The Phenomenon of Man* (Pierre Teilhard de Chardin), *The Listener*; *Jesus in his own Times* (S. E. Johnson), *C.Q.R.* CLX; *The Comparative Study of Religions* (Joachim Wach), *C.Q.R.* CLX; *Myth, Ritual and Kingship* (ed. S. H. Hooke), *H.J.* LV; *The Sacral Kingship* (VIIIth International Congress for the History of Religions, Rome, 1955), *F.L.* LXX; *At Sundry Times* (R. C. Zaehner), *H.J.* LV; *Les rites de la condition humaine* (Jean Cazeneuve), *Man*, LIX; *Avicenna: His Life and Works* (S. M. Afnain), *E.T.*; *Prophecy in Islam* (F. Rahman), *E.T.*; *Muhammad and the Islamic Tradition* (E. Dermenghem), *E.T.*

1960

The Ancient Gods (London, Wiedenfeld & Nicolson), pp. 359. 96 illustrations. American edition, 1961. Translations: Italian, Spanish and Polish, 1961, French and German, 1962.

'Raffaele Pettazzoni', obituary notice, *F.L.* LXXI.

Reviews of *Folkways: A Study of the Sociological Importance of Usages, Manners, Customs, Mores and Morals* (W. G. Sumner), *Man*, LX; *Le Milieu Divin* (Pierre Teilhard de Chardin), *The Listener*; *The Masks of God: Primitive Mythology* (J. Campbell), *H.J.* LVIII; *The Ancient Near East: An anthology of Texts and Pictures* (J. B. Pritchard), *C.Q.R.* CLXI; *Christianity among the Religions of the World* (Arnold Toynbee), *C.Q.R.* CLXI; *Reasons and Faiths* (Ninian Smart), *C.Q.R.* CLXI; *St James in Spain* (T. D. Kendrick), *F.L.* LXXI.

1961

Seasonal Feasts and Festivals (London, Thames & Hudson), pp. 336.

'Confucianism and Taoism', *American Oxford Encyclopaedia.*

'Christianity', *Grolier Encyclopaedia*, New York.

'The Religions of Antiquity', *Numen*, VII, Fasc. 2, 3.

'Superstitions and Survivals', *F.L.* LXXII.

'Primitive Religion: Past and Present' (Essays in honour of Margaret A. Murray), *F.L.* LXXII.

Reviews of *The Gods of Prehistoric Man* (J. Mariner), *Oxford Magazine*; *Hindu and Muslim Mysticism* (R. C. Zaehner), *Oxford Magazine*; *Mambu: A Melanesian Millennium* (K. O. L. Burridge), *C.Q.R.* CLXII; *Worship in the World's Religions* (G. Parrinder), *E.T.*; *Encyclopaedia of Superstitions* (ed. C. Hole), *F.L.* LXXII; *Culture in History: Essays in Honour of Paul Radin* (ed. S. Diamond), *F.L.* LXXII; *Easter and Its Customs* (C. Hole), *F.L.* LXXII; *Animals and Man in Bible Lands* (F. S. Bodenheimer), *F.L.* LXXII.

1962

Sacrifice and Sacrament: A Comparative Study (London, Thames & Hudson), pp. 319.

The Worship of the Sky-God: A Comparative Study in Semitic and Indo-European Religion (The Jordan Lectures, School of Oriental and African Studies), (London, The Athlone Press, 1963).

'The Influence of Folklore on the History of Religion', *Numen*, IX, Fasc. 2.

Introduction to *Greek Myths and Christian Mysteries* (H. Rayner).

'The Withdrawal of the High God in West African Religion', *Man*, LXII.

'Altar', 'Creation, Myths of', 'Christmas Folk Customs', 'Easter Customs', 'Hallowe'en', 'Incense',' Magic', 'Prayer', 'Priesthood', 'Human Sacrifice', 'Sacrifice', 'Sin-Eater', 'Wake', 'Theurgy', 'Lycanthropy', *Encyclopaedia Britannica*; advisory editor, 'Religions' section.

'Herbert Jennings Rose', obituary notice, *Man*, LXII.

Reviews of *Encyclopaedia of Superstitions* (E. and M. A. Radford), *F.L.* LXXIII; *Notes on the Slavic Religio-Ethical Legends* (M. P. Dragonanov), *F.L.* LXXIII; *Epilogomena to the Study of Greek Religion and Themes* (J. E. Harrison), *F.L.* LXXIII; *Le Démon et son image* (E. Reisner), *Man*, LXII; *Man and His Destiny in the Great Religions* (S. G. F. Brandon), *History Today* and *H.J.* LX; *Eleusis and the Eleusinian Mysteries* (G. E. Mylonas), *The Antiquaries Journal*, XLII, Part 2; *Divinity and Experience* (G. Lienhardt), *Oxford Magazine*; *Crossing the Equator: Baptismal Initiation Rites* (H. Hennington), *F.L.* LXXIII; *Everyman's Dictionary of non-Classical Mythology* (E. Sykes), *F.L.* LXXIII.

ABBREVIATIONS

ASAE	*Annales du Service des Antiquités de l'Égypte*, Cairo.
ASV	American Standard Version.
AV	Authorized Version.
BJRL	*Bulletin of the John Rylands Library*, Manchester.
BSOAS	*Bulletin of the School of Oriental and African Languages*, London.
CT	*Coffin Texts.*
EI	*Encyclopédie de l'Islam*, Leiden/Paris.
Enc. It.	*Enciclopedia Italiana.*
ERE	*Encyclopaedia of Religion and Ethics*, ed. J. Hastings, Edinburgh.
GALS	Supplement to C. Brockelmann, *Geschichte der arabischen Literatur.*
H.Th.R.	*Harvard Theological Review.*
IC	*Islamic Culture*, Hyderabad, India.
JA	*Journal Asiatique.*
JNES	*Journal of Near Eastern Studies*, Chicago.
JRAS	*Journal of the Royal Asiatic Society of Great Britain.*
NEB	New English Bible.
Pyr.	*Pyramid Texts.*
Reallexikon	*Reallexikon der ägyptischen Religionsgeschichte*, by H. Bonnet, Berlin, 1952.
RB	*Revue Biblique.*
RGG	*Die Religion in Geschichte und Gegenwart*, 3 Aufl., 1957–.
RSV	Revised Standard Version.
RV	Revised Version.
RV	*Rig-Veda.*
Wörterbuch	*Wörterbuch der ägyptischen Sprache*, hrg. A. Erman und G. Grapow.
ZfA	*Zeitschrift für Assyriologie und verwandte Gebeite.*
ZDMG	*Zeitschrift der Deutschen Morgenländischen Gesellschaft.*
ZfE	*Zeitschrift für Ethnologie.*
ZThK	*Zeitschrift für Theologie und Kirche.*
ZNTW	*Zeitschrift für die neutestamentliche Wissenschaft und die Kunde der älteren Kirche.*

I

ISIS AS SAVIOUR GODDESS

by

C. J. BLEEKER

IN his comprehensive study on 'The Cult of the Mother-Goddess' Dr E. O. James also devotes a few pages to the Egyptian goddess Isis. He calls her 'Isis of Many Names' and typifies her as follows: 'The most popular and important of all the maternal goddesses (in Egypt), however, was Isis, the prototype of motherhood and the embodiment of wifely love and fidelity.' This undoubtedly is a correct characterization: Isis is a typical maternal goddess. Yet this function does not fully express her nature. She is at the same time a Saviour Goddess. It would not be too much to contend, that of all Egyptian gods and goddesses she can best claim this title of honour—indeed even to a higher degree than Osiris, however strange this may sound. Osiris has got the name of being the typical Egyptian Saviour-God. It is not my intention to deprive him of his renown. However, in my opinion there are solid arguments for defending the thesis, that though Isis is not 'officially' a saviour-goddess, she did actually play that part. This contribution to the *Festschrift*, published in honour of my very learned and distinguished colleague Dr E. O. James, is designed to show the grounds for this thesis and to shed thereby new light on Isis herself.

In order to clear the ground for the following argument, it is desirable to define the concept of the saviour-god. For, only by the aid of a clear description of the nature of this type of gods can it be decided, whether Isis belongs to the category. A saviour-god is, as the word says, a god who acts as a saviour. Not all gods play that part. In the polytheistic religions there are many gods who, in exalted majesty, keep at a distance from the world and do not care for what happens to men. They demand to be adored and grant few favours. Other gods have done a beneficial piece of work by creating the world. They are continuously honoured as creators, but they cannot be called saviour-gods. For, a saviour is a religious figure with a special character and function.[1] The saviour is an essential factor in religion, because many religious people are convinced that the domain of men and the world of the gods are separated by a deep cleft. In order to link up these two worlds a bridge must be laid across the cleft. Man is unable to perform this act. It should be done by a creature who unites the two worlds by his nature. That is the saviour. He is a divine or semi-divine being, who descends from the domain of the gods to the dwelling-places of men, or who operates through other gods for the benefit of men. The figure of the saviour shows many varieties. As he combines in himself a human and a divine element, the emphasis may alternatively be put on the one or the other side of his nature. Saviours, in whom the human factor dominates, are the sacral king, the hero, the prophet, the sage and the saint. It is evident that in the saviour-god, i.e. the god who functions as saviour, the divine nature fully prevails. Yet the human factor is not absolutely absent. It finds its expression on the one hand in the human feelings which the god displays and on the other side in his interest in the destiny of men. Moreover, he often passes a severe trial, so that he is a consolating example to suffering humanity, and he conquers death, so that in man the hope of immortality awakens. The saviour-god thus shows two striking and nearly related features: he is a dynamic personality and he cares for the well-being of men, indeed he sometimes takes part in human sufferings.

In my opinion the character and the activities of Isis correspond to this definition of the saviour-god. Among Egyptian gods as Re, Ptah, Thoth and Min, who are personifications of cosmic forces and who make the impression of aloofness, Isis is a colourful personality and a very human figure. This she owes to her function as the faithful wife of Osiris and the loving mother of Horus. In these capacities she displays great activity. She is truly an energetic goddess. Her action means salvation, not only for Osiris, but also for men, both for the individual and society.

In the Egyptian language the goddess is called *ś.t*, i.e. her name is written in hieroglyphics by a sign, of which the consonant element is *ś.t*. It needs hardly to be recalled, that the vowels of the Egyptian words are unknown. In Coptic Isis is named Èse or Èsi, from which the Greek form of the name Isis originates. These linguistic facts provide the key to the original character of Isis. For, *ś.t* means: 'chair', 'throne', and it is in hieroglyphic writing represented by a simple, high seat with a short, straight back and a small footstool. Isis wears this hieroglyph on her head and is recognized by it. Originally the hieroglyphs were a pictographic form of writing. It may, therefore, be assumed that the name of Isis is not accidentally written by the sign of a seat. This hieroglyph must express her original nature and function.

There are actually sound reasons to suppose that Isis represents the throne, the holy seat of the pharaoh.[2] This in itself is not surprising. It is a well-known fact that the peoples of antiquity took important objects of daily use for divine beings. Primarily cultic instruments enjoyed that honour. Egyptian religion provides several instances of the practice. The royal sceptre was a kind of fetish.[3] Hymns were directed to the crowns, which the king wears.[4] It is in such a religious context that Isis, the holy royal seat, has significance. A throne is a highly important sacral piece of furniture. The king receives his dignity from sitting on the throne. The throne 'makes' the king. The throne is, so to say, his mother. These conceptions in Egypt date from time immemorial, as the texts indicate. The texts also show that Isis' beneficial function in regard to the king belonged to her original nature. That she in ancient times only served the king is the consequence of the fact that the pharaoh as son of the sun-god, was a sacral king and kept an all-dominating position. What Isis does for the king, she at the same time performs for society.

The Egyptians understood the idea that Isis, the holy throne, is the mother of the pharaoh not symbolically but literally. This is evident from a relief in the temple of Abydos, showing Seti I seated on the lap of Isis, who in turn sits on the typical Egyptian throne.[5] Since the first dynasties the Egyptian kings called themselves sons of Isis.[6] This conception is elaborated in the *Pyramid Texts* in a realistic way. It is said that Isis gave birth to the king, that she suckled him and that she attended to him as a mother.[7] This conception of the relation between Isis and the pharaoh has its mythical prototype. That is a well-known feature of the myth of Osiris, i.e. the initiative taken by Isis in order to have her son Horus recognized by the tribunal of the gods as the legal heir of Osiris and as the ascendant to the throne. What Isis once did for Horus, she further does for each king. One of the official sacral titles of the pharaoh was Horus. It is evident that this title originally indicated the so-called elder Horus, a sky-god. This Horus clearly differs in typological respect from Horus, the son of Isis.[8] However, the two Horus-Gods have already in ancient times been mixed. No wonder, therefore, that Isis, the throne, could be conceived of as the mythical mother of the pharaoh who bore the Horus-name.

Isis is characterized by her wisdom. The Egyptians called her 'great in magic power'. This amounts to the same thing, but it emphasizes better her dynamic character. According to the religious notions of antiquity, real wisdom consists in insight into the mystery of life and death. This knowledge is creative: it evokes life from death. As this wisdom furthers life, it is utterly beneficial. Thus wisdom was to the Egyptians equivalent to the capacity of exerting magic power. Isis possessed this gift to a high degree. This appears, e.g. from a curious text, telling how Isis got to know the secret name of Re.[9] According to the religious conceptions of antiquity, the name expresses the nature of the person who bears the name. Therefore, the secret name of Re contained the mystery of his creative power. By her cunning Isis managed to master the secret. That she thereby also rendered a service to men, appears from the wording of the text, which shows that it was used against the bite of a scorpion—in other words it was a spell. The myth relates how Re was cured from the bite of a snake. The same effect was expected from the recital of the text in a similar situation in the world of men. According to the myth, Re grew old. His mouth trembled and his spittle dropped on the ground. Isis mixed this with a bit of earth and formed therefrom a snake, which she concealed at the side of the path along which Re used to walk. When Re came that way, together with his retinue, the snake bit him. Re cried out for pain and his legs trembled. He said: 'Something has stung me; my heart does not know it and my eyes have not seen it; I have never felt such pain; it is no fire, it is no water, but my heart burns and my body shudders.' The gods pitied him, among them Isis. She offered to cure him by her magic art, but on the condition that he should mention his real name. Thereupon Re enumerated a series of impressive names, all of them expressing his creative activity. However, Isis was not deceived thereby. She spoke: 'Thine real name is not among those which thou hast mentioned. Give me thine name and the poison will recede.' As the poison burned more violent than fire, Re surrendered. He said: 'Lend me thine ear, so that my name passes from my body to thine.' And so it happened: Re whispered his name in the ear of Isis.

The end of the story expresses the profound idea that no creature, not even a god, but Isis only, knows the secret name, i.e. the real nature of Re. The creator-god is unknowable. Isis alone, the wise goddess, has insight into his being. This is the reason why in ancient Egypt spells were invariably ascribed to Isis.[10] It was assumed that Isis knew every spell which could avert danger and make life prevail over death.

Isis became famous as the wife of Osiris. It is possible that she originally was an independent goddess, who patronized a certain city or province, as most Egyptian gods did. Two places, Buto and Behbet, both in the Nile delta, claimed the honour of being the original home of Isis. Because Busiris, one of the centres of the cult of Osiris, was situated in the neighbourhood, it has been suggested that Isis became associated from a very early period with this god.[11] The theory is, however, built on suppositions which cannot be proved. It is very hard to establish whether Isis in prehistoric times was the patroness of a city, and what function she exerted in that capacity. When she enters history, Isis is already the wife of Osiris, and as such great was her achievement and saving power.

After the murder of Osiris by Seth, Isis immediately became

active. She went out to seek the corpse of her dead husband. Sometimes she was alone in her searchings; but mostly she was helped by her sister Nephthys. The *Pyramid Texts* already allude to the wanderings of the two sisters and to the way in which they found the corpse of Osiris. As the death of Osiris was considered to be a dreadful mystery, it is only alluded to in profound awe. It is said that Seth cast Osiris to the ground in Ndjt (*Pyr.* 1256), or that Osiris was drowned and that he lay on his side on the bank of Ndjt (*Pyr.* 1008). There Isis and Nephthys found him: 'Isis and Nephthys have seen thee, they have found thee' (*Pyr.* 584). Cheerfully they cry to one another: ' "I have found", says Isis; "I have found", says Nephthys, when they saw Osiris on his side on the bank (of Ndjt)' (*Pyr.* 2144). Ndjt is the mythical place, where the drama of the murder of Osiris occurred. An Osiris hymn from the 18th century B.C. commemorates this search of Isis for her husband in a beautiful way: 'Isis who sought for him without tiring, passing through the country in sorrow; she did not take rest until she had found him; she made shadow with her feathers, she produced air with her wings (i.e. she waved refreshing, vivifying air to him), she who rejoiced when she brought her brother to the bank.'[12] Plutarch has elaborated this theme. He tells us that Isis, on receiving the sad news of the death of her beloved husband, cut off one of her curls and put on a mourning dress. After having made inquiries, she learned that the sarcophagus in which Seth and his helpers had put Osiris, had drifted off through one of the mouths of the Nile and been cast ashore at Byblos. Thereupon she made her way to the city. After an adventurous course of events, which need not be related, she got hold of the coffin, containing the dead body of Osiris. In the possession of this treasure she returned to Egypt.[13]

Plutarch also tells that, as soon as she was alone with the coffin, Isis opened it, laid her face on that of the dead one and kissed it, weeping.[14] This means that, after having found the dead body of Osiris, Isis lamented over it. This lamentation had special significance for Egyptian mortuary belief. It was not only a natural expression of sorrow; but it possessed also the power of a spell: it raised Osiris from the death. Already in the *Pyramid Texts* mention is made of the lamentation for the dead. It is said: 'his sister it is, the lady of Buto, who weeps over him' (*Pyr.* 309). In another text one reads: '"I am thy sister, who loves thee," says Isis, says Nephthys; "(thy sisters who) weep over thee"' (*Pyr.* 2192). As is natural, Isis is often described as lamenting her dead husband alone—such is the case in the first quotation from the *Pyramid Texts*. The *Book of the Dead* also mentions 'the night in which Isis lay down to keep vigil, bewailing her brother' (19:11, 20:5). Here it is evident that a lamentation for the dead is referred to, it being performed by Isis alone. However, already in ancient times Nephthys was also thought to have assisted her sister in this sad duty.

Isis and Nephthys play, as wailing women, an important part, both in the myth and the cult of Osiris, and in the funeral rite which was celebrated for the human dead.[15] There is a close connection between the cult of Osiris and the cult of the dead. This is not surprising, for in ancient Egypt it was hoped that the dead would participate in what occurred to Osiris, i.e. resurrection. Therefore, rites of the cult of Osiris were also used in the cult of the dead, among them a special form of lamentation. From time immemorial two figures took part in the funerary procession, usually distinguished as 'the big wailing-woman' and 'the small wailing-woman', who were identified with Isis and Nephthys.[16] In the cult of Osiris also two wailing-women appear, who represent the two mythical wailing-women. This is attested by two papyri, called 'The songs of Isis and Nephthys' and 'The Lamentations of Isis and Nephthys'.[17] That these two wailing-women actually represented the divine sisters appears from the opening passage of 'The Songs of Isis and Nephthys', which reads: 'Two women should be fetched, pure of body, virgins, the hair of whose bodies has been shaved off, round whose heads braids have been plaited, whose hands hold a tambourine and on whose upper arms their names have been written, viz. Isis and Nephthys.' Though the language of the ritual lamentation is stylized, it has passages expressing the feelings of affliction and mourning so directly and intensely that they sound as though a wife is lamenting over the recent loss of her dear husband. Thus the wailing-woman Isis says: 'Come to thine house; for a long, long time I have not seen thee;

my heart suffers for thee; my heart seeks thee; I cry for thee, under tears, so that it reaches the high skies; but thou dost not hear my voice, though I am thine sister, who loved thee on earth: my heart is hot, because thou art unjustly separated from me.' In a similar text it is said: 'Over thee weeps the sister in Abydos, the "lamenting one", sick for misery; moisture is in my eyes; she is ill for mourning over her husband.'[18]

The two sisters do more than merely to sit passively at the bier of the deceased Osiris, giving free play to their sorrow. They take care of the ill-treated body of Osiris and thereby rouse him to new life. The *Pyramid Texts* speak of Osiris: 'Thou art washed by Isis, thou art cleaned by Nephthys, thy two great sisters, who join together thy flesh, who raise thy legs' (*Pyr.* 1981). In one of the texts quoted, Isis says of Osiris: 'I gave wind to his nose, so that he should live.' In this instance Isis is thought of as winged. The reason for this is that Isis and Nephthys, in their capacity of wailing-women, were often identified with birds. They, accordingly, bear the name of a high-soaring bird of prey, a falcon or a kite. This identification is probably due to the fact that the cry of this bird is said to possess the same pitch as the shrill sound of the ancient Egyptian lamentation.[19] However this may be, the wings serve in the text concerned to fan to Osiris the fresh air which revives him. It has already been mentioned that in the Osiris hymn of the eighteenth dynasty Isis is described performing this act: 'she made shadow with her feathers, she produced air with her wings'. In the hot Egyptian climate fresh air was equivalent to the breath of life. Therefore, the text concerned says: 'Isis provides thee with life.' Together the wailing-women exclaim: 'Raise thyself, thou art risen, thou shalt not die, thine soul will live.' The chorus of this text runs: 'Thou dost triumph, O Osiris, king of the westerners (i.e. the dead).'[20] These exclamations prove that the lamentation over Osiris not only expresses sorrow and grief, but also possesses the force of the magical word. The litany is a spell which raises Osiris from death. Osiris rises by the powerful word of Isis.

Isis performed an act of still greater saving power. She provided the dead Osiris with offspring. She gave birth to Horus. In the Osiris-hymn of the eighteenth century, the line which tells how

Isis brought the drowned Osiris ashore is followed by the sentence: 'She who raised the slackness of the weary (i.e. the phallus of the dead), who received his seed, who formed an heir.' Thus Isis took the initiative in this act of procreation. In a late Osiris-ritual, used at the mourning over Osiris in the month Choiak, Isis takes pride in this 'manly' deed in the following words: 'O Osiris, the first of the westerners, I am thine sister Isis, there is no god who has done what I have done, nor a goddess: I made myself to a man, though I was a woman, in order to make thy name live upon earth. Thy divine seed, which was in my body, I put it on the back of the earth so that it should partake in thy nature, that it should cure thy suffering and that it should retaliate the deed of violence to him who has committed it.'[21] The act is frequently depicted, showing Isis in the form of a bird descending on the phallus of Osiris in order to impregnate herself.

Finally, Isis took care that justice prevailed. After educating her son Horus in a hidden place so that he was protected against the evil designs of Seth, she brought him, as soon as he was mature, to the hall in which the court of justice of the gods resided. Before this tribunal she opened a lawsuit against Seth, which resulted in his condemnation. The details of this lawsuit are in this connection of no special interest. It may suffice to quote the Osiris-hymn of the eighteenth dynasty:

> She who educated the child in a secret place, one did not know where he was; she who introduced him into the hall of Geb, when his arm was strong; the Ennead rejoices: "welcome Horus, son of Osiris" . . . the court of *Ma.a.t* gathered for him, the Ennead and the lord of the universe himself, the lords of truth, who turn their back to the lie . . . it appeared that Horus was righteous; the office of his father was allotted to him . . . he received the rule over the two parts of the country . . . the two lands are satisfied; wickedness has disappeared . . . *Ma.a.t* is established for her lord and the back has been turned to the lie.

Ma.a.t is restored and Egypt revives by the condemnation of Seth and by the recognition of Horus as the heir of Osiris, i.e. as the legal sovereign. Thanks to the energetic intervention of Isis justice, peace and prosperity return.

As appears from her name, Isis was originally closely related to the symbols of royalty. She was not directly connected with any part of the cosmos. However, by her function in the Osiris myth, she was directly linked with cosmic events and natural phenomena. Accordingly, her significance grows and diversifies. She becomes a beneficial goddess of nature. She is identified with Thermuthis, the goddess of the harvest and with Hathor, the great goddess of Dendera. The Egyptians connected her with Sothis, the goddess of the star Sirius. She was looked upon as the eye of Re, the sun-god. The main centre of her worship was Philae, at the southern border of Egypt. From there her influence extended to Nubia and to more southern regions. In the last period of the Egyptian civilization, when the traffic with the surrounding countries became frequent, she also acquired popularity in the countries about the Mediterranean Sea. Already in the fourth century before Christ she possessed a sanctuary in Piraeus near Athens.[22] Her cult spread also to the Greek islands. Next she conquered the western parts of the Roman empire. Traces of her cult are found, e.g. in Sardinia, in North Africa, Switzerland, Germany and Spain, and particularly in Rome.[23] As the goddess of the harbour of Alexandria, she became the patroness of sailors. Being a Saviour Goddess, she protected all sea-going people. In her honour the *πλοιοφέσια*, the *navigium Isidis* was yearly celebrated, during which a small ship was launched to open a favourable season for journeys over the sea. Apuleius has given a colourful description of this festival at Corinth. A gay company marched out to the seashore, where a ship was launched, dedicated to the goddess: at the front of the procession there walked a group of oddly dressed people; next came women in white clothes who strew flowers; thereafter stolists with the requisites of the toilet of the goddess, dadophors with torches, hymnods, who sang with flute and sistra and at last a group of initiated and of priests, who bore images and symbols, e.g. the golden jar, containing water of the Nile. At the seashore the procession stopped. There the ship of Isis was consecrated by certain rites and was loaded with good gifts. Accompanied by good wishes, the ship put to sea.[24]

In process of time Isis became in many respects Hellenized. This appears from her images of that period, which show the Greek style.[25] Moreover, she was identified with goddesses like Demeter and Kybele. This is not surprising, since these two goddesses were also saviour-goddesses. Thus Isis became a goddess of universal significance. In the *Asinus Aureus*, written by Apuleius, she extols herself in this manner:

'I am she that is the natural mother of all things, mistress and governess of all the elements, the initial progeny of worlds, chief of the powers divine, queen of all that are in hell, the principal of them that dwell in heaven, manifested alone and under one form of the gods and goddesses . . . For the Phrygians, who are the first of all men, call me Mother of the gods of Pessinus; the Athenians, who are sprung from their own soil, Crecropian Minerva; the Cyprians, who are girt about by the sea, Paphian Venus; the Cretans, who bear arrows, Dictynnian Venus; the Sicilians, who speak three tongues, infernal Proserpine; the Eleusians their ancient goddess Ceres; some Juno, others Bellona, others Hecate, others Rhamnusia, and principally both sort of the Ethiopians who dwelt in the Orient and are enlightened by the morning rays of the sun, and the Egyptians, who are excellent in all kinds of ancient doctrine, and by their proper ceremonies accustomed to worship me, do call me by my true name, Queen Isis.'[26]

This eulogy portrays a universal saviour-goddess.

By the Hellenistic period Isis had become a saviour-goddess in the essential meaning of the term, in that she redeems individuals. This redemption was accomplished in the mysteries of Isis, which were apparently founded under Ptolemaeus I, probably after the example of the Eleusinian mysteries, because, next to the Egyptian Manetho, Timotheus from Eleusis served as an adviser to the king.[27] According to the myth, Isis herself had instituted the mysteries. In a hymn, in which she extols herself, the goddess says: 'I have taught the mysteries to men.'[28] Plutarch reveals the motive which induced Isis to found the mysteries. He writes:

When the sister and wife of Osiris, as his avenger, had tempered and extinguished the fury of Seth, she desired that the struggle, the dangers and the wanderings, which she passed through, being so many acts of courage and wisdom, should not be forgotten. Therefore, she wove into the most secret initiations the images, indications and imitations of previous sufferings, and she instituted a doctrine of piety and a consolation to men and women, who find themselves in the same misfortune.[29]

The last sentence here is particularly noteworthy in that it makes clear the character of Isis as a saviour-goddess: she is the comforting example to the faithful who are in distress. She is able to redeem them, because she herself, through the courage with which she bore her suffering, had once obtained salvation.

The best information about the character of the mysteries, and the part that Isis played therein, is to be drawn from this novel of Apuleius. It is a curious book that combines comical and scabrous stories with deep and profound ideas, in the course of relating the adventures of Lucius, who by the misuse of a magical unguent was changed into an ass. From this animal form, in which he underwent much hardship, Lucius was ultimately released by the favour of Isis. At her direction he ate from the wreath of roses which the high-priest bore in the procession of the *navigium Isidis*, when it was being celebrated at Corinth. By so doing he assumed the obligation to become a follower of Isis and to be initiated into her mysteries. The initiation is accomplished after due preparations. Lucius, in whom one easily recognizes the author, is required to undergo three initiations, a demand which rouses not only his surprise but also his suspicion.

These initiations have repeatedly been the subject of penetrating studies. However, no satisfactory explanation of the veiled words in which Lucius describes his experiences has yet been found. This is not surprising, because Lucius was not allowed to divulge the esoteric wisdom which he acquired by the initiation. It is not the purpose of the present study to seek a new solution of the problem, but to focus the attention on the meaning of the mysteries and on the part which Isis plays therein, so that her function as saviour-goddess may be illuminated.

It is well-known that the people of antiquity expected that initiation into the mysteries would afford insight into esoteric wisdom and the hope of immortality. The decisive act apparently was the *epopteia*, i.e. the vision of the highest truth, which was probably a dramatized representation of some crucial event of the mystery. This conception of the gist of what happened in the mystery finds support in the explanation of the dwelling place of Osiris given by Plutarch on the authority of the Egyptian priests. He says that Osiris does not dwell in or under the earth, in which the dead bodies of men are buried,

but he lives at a long distance from this earth, undefiled, untouched and pure from all that is subjected to decay and death. The human souls, which are bound to bodies and passions, have no communion with the god, except that they may by philosophic thinking obtain a vague shadowy idea of it. But, when by redemption, they are allowed to pass into the eternal, invisible, quiet and holy sphere, Osiris is their leader and king. They love him and they continuously behold, with longing, the unspeakable beauty which is invisible to mortal beings. As the old myth relates, Isis longs for this beauty (i.e. Osiris) with loving desire. She follows him and consorts with him in order to complete all that on earth is subjected to generation with what is good and beautiful.[30]

From these words it becomes clear, that the dead rejoice in the *epopteia* in the realm of Osiris and that Isis also takes part therein. Consequently she is able to offer a higher beauty and goodness to mortal beings, who are involved in the process of birth and transmutation. This occurs during initiation into the mysteries, and it offers a foretaste of the vision, that is revealed to the dead. In accordance with the Greek saying, *τελεῖσθαι τελευτᾶν*, to be initiated means to die, the priest who prepares Lucius for the initiation, declares that the initiation is 'like a voluntary death and a difficult restoration to health', and that the goddess possesses the power 'to let the initiated, as it were, be reborn and to bring them back on the path of salvation'.[31] Lucius tells that he celebrated the initiation as his birthday by arranging a banquet. It is quite natural that Lucius keeps silence about the nature of the salvation which Isis offered him. Nevertheless, he alludes to what happened during the initiation in the following passage: '*Accessi confinium mortis et calcato Proserpinae limine per omnia vectus elementa remeavi, nocte media vidi solem candido coruscantem lumine; deos inferos et deos superos accessi coram et adoravi de proxumo.*'[32] It is not superfluous to quote once more these famous words; for they affirm the idea that the initiation was a symbolic death. Though the quoted words probably reflect the emotions which Lucius underwent rather than describe the actual procedure of the initiation, they at least clearly testify to the significance of that which Isis as saviour-goddess had to offer to the devotee.

The initiation took place during the night. The next morning Lucius appeared, dressed in twelve stoles, having a precious cope on his shoulders, whereon beasts in various colours were wrought —it was a garment commonly called the Olympian stole. He carried a lighted torch in his right hand, and a garland of flowers was upon his head. Thus he was adorned like the sun (*ad instar solis exornatus*). This means that the initiation apparently brought about a kind of *deificatio*. Lucius was commanded to stand upon a platform of wood, which was placed in the middle of the temple in front of the figure of the goddess. The curtains were drawn aside and all people flocked together to behold him in his glorified shape.

In this connection we need not digress on the curious fact, that Lucius had to undergo a second and even a third initiation. The second initiation took place in Rome. The goddess warned him in his sleep to receive a new order and consecration. This new initiation was required, because Lucius had become an adherent of Isis, but was not yet a minister of Osiris. Though there was a religious concord and even unity between the two gods, there was a difference of order and ceremony.[33] The reason for the third initiation was the fact that he had left the stola, in which the goddess dressed him in Corinth, behind in this city.[34] The significance of this garment of initiation may be inferred from a passage of Plutarch, in which he tells that 'the dead followers of Isis are dressed in the holy garment, as a sign that they enter the hereafter with nothing else than this doctrine'.[35]

In these three cases the initiation is performed at the command of the goddess. This fact provides occasion for a few final remarks on the part which Isis plays in the mysteries. Isis proves to be a gracious goddess, but also a severe one. Her austerity appears from the strict regulation that nobody can be initiated before he was deemed worthy and was called by the goddess.[36] Moreover, Isis demanded abstinence during the preparation for the initiation. Lucius must fast ten days, i.e. he must abstain from animal food and wine, before he is allowed to be initiated. Also in other respects Isis keeps her followers under severe discipline. If the *Satura* of the cynical Juvenal can be trusted, Isis demanded from the Roman ladies, who served her, that they in midwinter should cut an ice-hole in the Tiber and should plunge therein three times or that they should creep with bloody knees on the field of Mars, where her temple was situated.[37] She also demanded that people should openly confess the offences against her regulations at the entrance of the temple.[38] From these facts it is evident that Isis kept her adherents under discipline. At the other hand, she acted as a gracious saviour-goddess, and she knew how to obtain the devotion of the initiated. This appears from the prayer which Lucius says after his initiation. This article may be closed by quoting its first sentences:

Tu quidem sancta et humani generis sospitatrix perpetua, semper fovendis mortalibus munifica, dulcem matris affectionem miserorum casibus tribuis. Nec dies nec quies ulla ac ne momentum quidem tenue tuis transcurrit beneficiis otiosum, quin mari terraque protegas homines et depulsis vitae procellis salutarem porrigas dexteram, qua fatorum etiam inextricabiliter contorta retractas licia, et Fortunae tempestates mitigas et stellarum noxios meatus cohibes.[39]

NOTES

1 C. J. Bleeker, *De phaenomenologie van de Heilandsfiguur* (Christologische Studiën, 1943).

2 H. Frankfort, *Kinship and the Gods*, 1948, p. 43 sq.

3 H. de Buck, *Egyptische godsdienst* (*Godsdiensten der Wereld*, II, 1956), p. 7.

4 A. Erman, *Hymnen an das Diadem der Pharaonen* (Abh. d. Preusz. Ak. d. Wiss., 1911).

5 H. Frankfort, *Ancient Egyptian Religion*, 1948, picture opposite title-page.

6 W. H. Flinders Petrie, *The Royal Tombs of the first Dynasty*, 1901, II, pl. II: 13, 14.

7 *Pyr.*, 371, 379, 556, 734, 1154, 1375, 1703.

8 C. J. Bleeker, *Die Geburt eines Gottes*, 1956, p. 15 sq.

9 A. Erman, *Aegypten und aegyptisches Leben im Altertum*, 1923, p. 301 sq.

10 H. Bonnet, *Reallexikon der ägyptischen Religionsgeschichte*, 1952, p. 328.

[11] Bonnet, *Reallexikon*, p. 326 sq.; J. Vandier, *La religion égyptienne* (Mana, I, 1949), pp. 62/3, 67/9.

[12] Chabat, *Rev. arch.*, 14.

[13] Plutarch, *de Iside et Osiride*, chaps. 15–16.

[14] Ibid., chap. 17.

[15] C. J. Bleeker, 'Isis and Nephthys as wailing women' (*Numen*, V, 1).

[16] E. Lüddekens, *Untersuchungen über religiösen Gehalt, Sprache und Form der ägyptischen Totenklagen* (Mitt. d. Deutsch. Inst. f. äg. Altertumskunde in Kairo, Band II, Heft 1, 2, 1943), p. 15.

[17] Bleeker, op. cit., p. 3 sq.

[18] H. Junker, *Stundenwachen in den Osirismysterien nach den Inschriften von Dendera, Edfu und Philae* (Denkschriften d. kais. Ak. der Wiss. in Wien, phil.-hist. Klasse, Band LIV, 1910), p. 45.

[19] Lüddekens, op. cit., p. 15.

[20] Junker, op. cit., p. 35, 45, 120, 84.

[21] H. Kees, *Aegypten* (*Religionsgeschichtliches Lesebuch*, no. 10), p. 30/1.

[22] A. Erman, *Die Religion der Aegypter*, 1934, chap. 22.

[23] W. H. Roscher, *Ausführliches Lexikon*, II, I, 359–457.

[24] Apuleius XI, 8–16.

[25] H. Haas, *Die Religionen in der Umwelt des Urchristentums* (*Bilderatlas zur Religionsgeschichte*, 9–11), p. 23 sq.

[26] Apuleius, XI, 4, 5.

[27] Tacitus, *Historiae*, IV, 83, 84; Plutarch, *De Iside et Osiride*, 28.

[28] W. Peek, *Hymnus in Isim Andrius.*

[29] Plutarch, 27, 35.

[30] Plutarch, 79.

[31] Apuleius, XI, 21.

[32] Apuleius, XI, 23.

[33] Apuleius, XI, 27/8.

[34] Apuleius, XI, 30.

[35] Plutarch, 3.

[36] Apuleius, XI, 21.

[37] Juvenalis, VI, 522 sq.

[38] J. Leipoldt, *Die Mysterien—Das Christentum* (*Handbuch der Religionswissenschaft*, 1948), p. 26.

[39] Apuleius, XI, 25.

II

THE RITUAL TECHNIQUE OF SALVATION IN THE ANCIENT NEAR EAST

by

S. G. F. BRANDON

IT is natural that each contributor to such a volume as this should look back to the time when he first became acquainted with the work of the scholar whom it commemorates. The present writer recalls how he first met the name of E. O. James when, as a student, he read his essay on 'The Emergence of Religion' in the symposium entitled *Essays Catholic and Critical* (1926). It then opened to him a new field of thought, in which his interest has ever since remained. A few years later he was introduced to that aspect of the work of Professor James that is surely most characteristic of him and which is aptly denoted by the titles of two publications that appeared in 1933–4, 'Initiatory Rituals' in *Myth and Ritual* (ed. S. H. Hooke) and *Christian Myth and Ritual.* In these writings Dr James gave impressive evidence of his interest in the myth and ritual complex that surrounded the sacral king and the saviour-god in the ancient Near East. That interest has found recurrent expression in his later works, and it is hoped that he will find in the following essay evidence of the extent to which his interest, and his devotion to it, have stimulated the thought of a younger scholar, who thereby seeks to acknowledge his debt to him.

The concept of salvation is clearly one of very wide and diverse connotation. Even if kept within the context of religion, its application ranges from the idea of safety from disease and misfortune, engendered by demoniac agency, to that of deliverance from some form of eternal damnation. And the means by which such various kinds of salvation have been thought to be effected are equally diverse—indeed from the magical amulet to the divine saviour. This complex diversity, however, can be conveniently simplified to reveal what is surely the quintessence of the idea of salvation.

Human consciousness, inhering essentially in awareness of the three temporal categories of past, present and future, causes man to know that he is mortal. Hence in each individual there is a fundamental sense of insecurity; for, whatever be his present fortune, each knows that he is subject to time that brings old age, decay and death. The realization that such is the nature of human destiny has provoked from mankind a varied pattern of reaction which has found expression in its many religions. With a few exceptions, in this reaction there has been a common factor, namely, the quest for the assurance of *post-mortem* security by attaching oneself to, or associating with, some eternal of life-giving entity.[1] This disposition already reveals itself in the dawn of human culture, during the Upper Palaeolithic period, when the dead were sometimes covered with a red pigment in burial with the apparent intention of revivifying them by contact with a substance having the colour of blood.[2] More notable, however, is the evidence which comes from ancient Egypt; for it provides our earliest, as well as the most remarkable, instance of an endeavour to secure *post-mortem* salvation which was destined in time to find its most significant expression in one of the greatest of world-religions. The intention discloses itself in a veritable technique based on the principle of ritual assimilation, and as such it represents the translation of a human aspiration for eternal well-being into practical action.

The *Pyramid Texts*, so-called because they are inscribed on the walls of royal pyramidal sepulchres dating from about 2500 B.C., are doubly unique, since they constitute the earliest corpus of written documents so far known and afford the earliest insight through the medium of writing into the human mind when faced with its greatest challenge—death. These texts, which evidently incorporate many diverse cultic traditions, are designed to secure for the dead pharaohs some form of *post-mortem* well-being and are consequently greatly concerned with death and its consequences. The means adopted to win this salvation for each of the deceased kings are of several kinds, and as such they clearly stem from different types of practice and belief. There are simple assertions to the effect that the pharaoh is not really dead, or that he could not die because he had existed before death appeared.[3] Other texts are designed to enable the king, or his *ba*, to join the circumpolar stars or the sun-god on his daily journey across the heavens[3a] —here salvation is evidently to be achieved by association with cosmic entities that were apparently unchangeable or eternal. Another rather primitive device for securing desired immunity from decay and death was the solemn identification of the dead monarch with some god, and a consequent declaration of his relationship to a number of gods *seriatim*.[4] Such identification or assimilation was apparently thought to be effected by virtue of the mere assertion that it was so, and as such it differed notably from another form of assimilation that constitutes the major praxis of the soteriology of the *Pyramid Texts*.

This latter form of assimilation, which, as we shall see, expressed itself in a variety of ways, involved the dead king with a deity, whose origin and nature have long been the subject of expert discussion. Osiris, the deity concerned, appears in the *Pyramid Texts* as the central figure of what was obviously a complex ritual, the *rationale* of which was evidently provided by a legend of a very distinctive kind that was conceived in essentially anthropomorphic terms and envisaged an historical event.[5] This legend, which is generally well known from the later accounts of Greek writers, is nowhere described in the *Pyramid Texts*, a fact which surely attests its well-established familiarity at that period, although constant and essential reference is made to its various episodes. For the purpose of the present study it will be best to approach the issue concerned by noticing first its most crucial episode, although as we shall see, it actually constituted the climax of a consequential ritual series.

In what would appear to be a critical stage of the funeral liturgy of king Unas[6] the following invocation is addressed to Atum, the patron god of Heliopolis who was associated with the sun-god Re: 'Recite: O Atum, it is thy son—this one here, Osiris, whom thou hast caused to live (and) to remain in life. He liveth (and) this Unas (also) liveth; he (i.e. Osiris) dieth not, (and) this Unas (also) dieth not. He (Osiris) *nhp* not; this Unas (also) *nhp* not. He (Osiris) *nhp*; this Unas (also) *nhp*.'[7] The invocation is then addressed in turn to a number of other deities, the parallelism between the fate of Osiris and that of the king being carefully maintained.[8] This series of invocations is followed by another series addressed to Osiris, who is requested to direct his attention to the dead king: 'Osiris, turn around thy face (that) thou mayest see this Unas.'[9] Having thus obtained this deity's attention, after further addresses and a repetition of the formulae quoted above, the parallelism contained in the formulae between Osiris and the deceased is transformed into identification: 'Thy (i.e. Osiris') body is the body of this Unas. Thy flesh is the flesh of this Unas. Thy bones are the bones of this Unas. (If) thou walkest, this Unas walks; (if) this Unas walks, thou walkest.'[10]

The ritual situation implied here is one of profound significance for understanding both Egyptian mortuary belief and the fundamental pattern of a soteriology that centres on a saviour-god of the so-called 'dying-rising' type. In the first place, it must be noted that the very logic of the formulae implies a belief that Osiris had either been prevented from dying or had been restored to life after having died. The prevention or revivification had been achieved by divine agency. Further, it may be inferred that the efficacy of this restoration of Osiris, which had apparently happened once in the past, could be recreated or in some way made available for the benefit of the dead pharaoh by imploring some deity to make the situation of the deceased like that of Osiris, or by actually identifying the deceased with Osiris. In the texts concerned here we have no indication of what ritual action accompanied the solemn recitation of the formulae; but there is reason for thinking, as we shall presently see in other connections, that the parallelism between, or the identification with, the deceased and Osiris was commemorated by some ritual action of an imitative kind.

As we have noted, this act of ritual assimilation seems to have constituted the climax or perhaps rather the most critical stage in a ritual process, since reference is here made to what was surely the most critical juncture in the history of Osiris, namely, his resurrection or revivification after death. It would appear, however, that the assimilation of the dead king to Osiris was not only made at this point and in this manner, for a series of texts assures the deceased that, as Osiris did not in death suffer physical corruption and that his body was reconstituted, such would also be his experience. Thus the assurance is given, in terms of the experience of Osiris: 'Recite: the Great One has fallen on his side. He moves himself, he who is in *Ndỉ.t*. His head is raised by Re. His abhorrence is to sleep; he hates to be tired. The flesh of this Teti, let it become not foul, not decay. Let not thy odour be bad.'[11] Other texts evidently envisage a ritual of embalmment, which is also conceived in terms of the history of Osiris:

Isis comes and Nephthys; the one from the right, the other from the left . . . They find Osiris, as his brother Set laid him low in *Ndỉ.t*. Then speaks Osiris Pepi: 'Hasten thou to me!', and thus he exists in his name Sokaris. They prevent thee from perishing in thy name *ỉnpw* (Anubis); they prevent thy putrefaction from flowing on the earth according to thy name *sꜣb šmʿ*; they prevent the odour of thy corpse from being evil for thee in thy name of *Ḥrw ḫꜣtỉ* . . .[12]

Other parts of the process of securing the body against decomposition are similarly described: 'Isis brings a libation to thee, Nephthys cleanses thee; thy two great sisters restore thy flesh, they reunite thy members, they cause thy two eyes to appear in thy face.'[13] That this ritual of embalmment also involved the wrapping of the corpse in linen bandages is attested by a significant invocation of *Tait*, the personification of such wrappings: 'Recite: Hail *Tait*. . . . Protect the head of Teti, so that it becomes not detached. Bind together the bones of Teti, so that they do not fall apart. . . .'[14]

At other points of the mortuary liturgy it would appear that the dead king was called upon to rise from the immobility of death, the invocation once more being based on an assimilation of the deceased with Osiris: 'Recite: Wake up, Osiris, wake up! O Pepi, stand up, be seated, shake the dust from thee!'[15] 'Recite: Wake up, Osiris, stand up thou Weary One! Raise thyself, O God! The God hath power over his body. Wake up, *Nfr-kȝ-rʿ* stand up, thou Weary One! Raise thyself, O God! The God hath power over his body.'[16] And resurrection, when achieved, is envisaged similarly in terms of the fortune of Osiris: 'This *Nfr-kȝ-rʿ* comes; he is equipped as a god; his bones reunited as [Osiris].'[17] 'Recite: Raise thyself (*nomina*)! Hasten, thou who art great in power. Sit thou before the gods; do that which Osiris did in the House of the Prince, which is in Heliopolis.'[18]

Other texts indicate other features of this mortuary ritual. Most notably is the libretto which evidently accompanied a ritual action which is well-known in later times as that of the 'Opening of the Mouth', and which is often illustrated in copies of the so-called *Book of the Dead*.[19] Here again the ceremony is intended to reproduce what was believed once to have been done to revivify Osiris:

Recite four times: Osiris *Nfr-kȝ-rʿ*, I open for thee thy mouth with the thigh, the eye of Horus. One thigh. [Recite: how well is thy mouth, after I have adjusted for thee thy mouth to thy bones! I open for thee thy mouth; I open for thee thy (two) eyes, O *Nfr-kȝ-rʿ*. I open for thee thy mouth] with the *nwz*[3] (of Anubis), the *mśḫtiw* hook of metal, which opens the mouth of the gods. Horus opens the mouth of this *Nfr-kȝ-rʿ*. [Horus opens the mouth of this *Nfr.-kȝ-rʿ*]. [Horus has opened the mouth of this *Nfr-kȝ-rʿ*. Horus has opened the mouth of this *Nfr-kȝ-rʿ*] with that whereby he opened the mouth of his father; with that whereby he opened the mouth of Osiris, with the metal that comes forth from Set, the *mśhtiw* hook [of metal, which opens the mouth of the gods]. [He opens the mouth of *Nfr-kȝ-rʿ* therewith, (that) he may go], (that) he may speak before the Great Ennead in the residence of the prince, which is in] Heliopolis, (that) he may bear away the *wrr.t* crown that is with Horus, lord of men.[20]

Another important feature of this mortuary ritual was clearly the purification of the deceased, which was effected mainly by washing with water. It is evident that the purpose of the rite was not primarily that of cleansing the corpse, but of re-animating it.

This ritual bath or washing, as many references attest, was regarded as having the efficacy of that by which it was believed that Re, the sun-god, was reborn or rejuvenated each day. The ceremony was, moreover, as the following passage shows, significantly associated with the reconstitution of the corpse, and it was also designed to re-present or reproduce an essential part of the action that had revivified Osiris:[21]

> Recite: O Pepi, stand up! Thou art pure (*wʿb*). Thy *ka* is pure. Horus purifies thee in (*m*) *ḳbḥw*. Thy purification (*ʿbw*) is the purification of Shu; thy purification is the purification of Tefnut. Thy purification is the purification of the four spirits (*ȝḫw*) of the houses, (who) rejoice in Buto (because) thou art pure. Thy mother Nut, the great protectress, purifies thee, protects thee. 'Take to thee thy head; unite to thee thy bones!', says Geb. 'Destroyed is the evil which attaches to this Pepi; destroyed is the evil that is his!', says Atum.[22]

We see, then, what appear to be the basic constituents of the mortuary ritual employed about the middle of the third millennium B.C. to accomplish, as it was believed, the *post-mortem* salvation or well-being of the deceased pharaoh. This ritual was apparently founded on two presuppositions, which were naturally *de fide* for those who performed it and those on behalf of whom it was performed. The first of these presuppositions was that a divine hero, Osiris, had once, after being killed, been raised to life again by certain specific actions performed on his behalf by certain deities. The *post-mortem* life, to which he was thus raised, was not, however, identical with that which he had lived before dying; it was a *Jenseits*-existence, but none the less conceived of in completely materialistic terms, involving the use of a reconstituted physical body. The death of Osiris does not seem to have had any special significance *per se*, beyond its being the result of a wicked act on part of Set, although no reason is mentioned for Set's presumed enmity.[23] The death was certainly not regarded soteriologically, i.e. that it was in some way a substitutionary sacrifice made by Osiris, or through Osiris, on behalf of the dead king. This brings us to the second presupposition, namely, that Osiris, in his death and resurrection, was evidently regarded as one by whom, or through whom, other men could obtain a similar state of *post-mortem* well-being. But such salvation was not to be achieved by worshipping Osiris or by making offerings to him, after the manner in which the favour of other deities was sought. It was done, as we have seen, by assuming the efficacy of acts of ritual simulation, whereby what were deemed to have been critical episodes in the experience of Osiris were recreated or re-presented in terms of the person of the dead king.[24]

These episodes, as we have noted them, seem to have been focussed on the revivification of the deceased by means of solemn declarations of his identity with Osiris and the invocation of certain deities to aid him as they had aided Osiris. This climax was anticipated and prepared for by the embalmment of the corpse to prevent its corruption. As is well known, the mummification of the dead became a very elaborate process, technically and ritually, in Egypt. To what extent the practice had been developed by the time of the *Pyramid Texts* is not certainly known; but the evidence of these documents reveals, as we have seen, the use of mummy bands to hold the corpse together, and two ritual actions of considerable significance, both of which were related to the preservation of the body of Osiris. The ceremony of the Opening of the Mouth, best known in the elaborate form in which it was practised during the New Kingdom period (*c.* 1575–1087), was designed to restore to the corpse, after its embalmment and prior to burial, the ability to see, to breathe, and to receive food, so that it might be ready for its life in the tomb, its 'eternal house'.[24a] The ritual lavation of the body, as we have also seen, was an established part of the revivification process, inspired undoubtedly by the primitive regard for water as a life-giving substance and equated with the rejuvenating bath by which the sun-god was renewed each day.

The relation that undoubtedly exists between the texts inscribed on the interior walls of the pyramids concerned, the layout of the corridors and chambers of these pyramids, and the actual recitation of the texts at the funeral ceremony of the pharaoh, constitutes an important problem, but one that is perhaps intrinsically insoluble. A notable attempt to provide a solution has recently been made by Professor J. Spiegel, who regards the inscribed texts as perpetuating the efficacy of their original recitation and of the performance of the related ritual.[25] He concentrates his study on the texts and the layout of the pyramid of king Unas, and he believes that they describe a true 'Mysterienspiel' or 'Ritualdrama' which was enacted in the tomb at the time of the king's burial.[26] According to his thesis, the *ba* of the dead pharaoh was the chief subject of the ritual, which was designed to release it from the body, enclosed in its coffin, so that it might pass through the 'Unterwelt der Sargkammer' and finally take up its abode in the *ba*-statue in the *serdab*, which represented heaven.[27] The interpretation is an intensely interesting one, and pregnant with suggestion; but the present writer finds it difficult to accept the idea that in the crucial passage, 167a ff. (Utterance 219), the reference is exclusively to the *ba* of the deceased king.[28] The destiny of the *ba* was certainly an issue of profound concern to the ancient Egyptian; but just as profound was the concern for the fate of the body, since, according to Egyptian anthropology, man was a psycho-physical organism, of which the body, the *ba*, the *ka* and some other constituents were all essential for a proper *post-mortem* life.[29] As we have seen, the mortuary ritual, documented by the *Pyramid Texts*, represented the practical implementation of a soteriology that envisaged *post-mortem* salvation as essentially dependent on the mystical or magical assimilation of the deceased to Osiris at each crucial stage in the process of his legendary resuscitation, which was primarily conceived in physical terms.

The ritual pattern of assimilation to Osiris, which the *Pyramid Texts* attest, concerns only the pharaoh at his death; that pattern must at the time of the inscription of the *Texts* have been already well established, and some formulae also indicate that they must originally have been used for private persons. However that may be, it has long been recognized that what, in the *Pyramid Texts*, was exclusively a royal mortuary ritual was gradually democratized, so that in process of time its benefits could be enjoyed by all who could afford the minimum essentials of the Osirian obsequies. Such adaptation inevitably brought many changes as the ritual continued to be practised throughout some twenty-six or more centuries—indeed until the forcible suppression of paganism in favour of Christianity in the fourth century A.D.[30] However, despite such consequent changes, the fundamental pattern of ritual assimilation was maintained, a fact which is surely of the greatest significance for the study of religious phenomenology. This continuity of tradition may be briefly illustrated by a chronological sequence of examples.

In the *Coffin Texts*, which document Egyptian mortuary faith and practice during the Middle Kingdom period (*c.* 2160–1575), the identification of the deceased with Osiris has become so complete that the earlier parallel formulae disappear and the deceased is directly addressed as Osiris in the various ritual situations involved. Thus the dead person is directly called upon, as Osiris, to resurrect himself: 'Raise thyself to life, (for) thou diest not! Raise thyself from thy left side, lay on thy right side (and) receive all the goods with which thy father Geb has endowed thee and with which Hathor has invested thee.'[31] Then this text which obviously relates to the ritual lamentation and embalmment of the deceased:

O thou Weary One, O weary Sleeper, in that abode which thou knowest not. Take thought concerning it! (*rḫs*). Behold, I found thee lying there. Weary is the Great One . . . Then speaks Isis to Nephthys: 'This is our brother! Come! Let us raise his head, gather together his bones—to protect his limbs! Come let us protect him! In our presence he should no more be tired!' Vivifying water, which flows from this Glorified One, thou fillest the seas and createst the rivers! O Osiris, live! stand up, thou Unfortunate One who liest there! I am Isis; I am Nephthys. . . .[32]

The same ritual pattern is still being observed many centuries later as the following passage from the *Book of the Dead* graphically witnesses:

Speech for not letting the body perish . . . (the speaker impersonates Anubis) 'Hail to thee, my father Osiris! I come to embalm thee.' (Osiris speaks) 'Thou embalmest my body. I am perfect as my father Kheper—imperishable as he' . . . (Anubis speaks at the conclusion of the embalming process) 'Hail to thee, my father Osiris, thou art (secure) in thy body; thou decayest not; worms did not take possession of thee;

thou corruptest not (and) stinketh not. Thou putrifiest not, nor hast thou become the prey of worms.' (Osiris) 'I am Kheper, whose body endureth eternally.'[33]

Coming down the centuries, we may next notice how a papyrus, dating from the late Ptolemaic era, witnesses to the continuance of this ritual pattern. The document concerned has illustrations which are intimately connected with the accompanying texts. These illustrations, as do many of those in the *Book of the Dead*, depict the deceased as standing in the presence of Osiris as a separate being, although in the texts he is assimilated with the deity.[34] This assimilation, set forth in the traditional Osirian terminology, is notably represented in a passage concerning the process of embalmment: (Anubis speaks) 'I lay my hands upon thy body, as I did for my father Osiris. I cure thy limbs as (the god) "who dwells on his mountain", in my first form of the embalmer (demotic text: of the Cheri-heb). I make the way (by cutting the stomach) for thy effluence to the Great Green (i.e. the ocean, as a form of infinity), so that it may unite itself with the effluence of the god' (demotic text: Osiris).[35] Of the illustrations we may note particularly one in which the dead man begins to rise from his bier, preparatory to appearing in the next scene before Osiris.[36] In another the deceased is shown, very significantly, under streams of water, which are being poured by two Anubis-figures, while Osiris, with Isis and Nephthys, looks on.[37] As our last link in this long tradition of soteriological assimilation or identification, we may notice some painted shrouds dating from the present era, which have been the subject of a masterly study by Professor S. Morenz.[38] The shrouds have each a scene in which there are three main figures. The central figure is that of a man (or woman) in contemporary Graeco-Roman costume. To the right of this figure is depicted the typical Osirian figure in mummiform, as represented at this period. On the left of the central figure stands that of Anubis, who plays so important a role in the Osirian mortuary ritual.[39] About these three figures, and as it were in the background, a number of other smaller figures are depicted, each having some Osirian significance. The significance of the three main figures has been convincingly interpreted by Professor Morenz as that of 'Das Werden zu Osiris'—in other words, it is an attempt to re-present pictorially the supposed process of the Osirian mortuary ritual. Thus Anubis, who has his right arm around the shoulder of the central figure, i.e. the deceased, is represented as leading him towards the Osirian figure, into which he has been ritually transformed.[40]

We see, then, in the Osirian mortuary ritual a most impressive tradition, preserved throughout almost three millennia, of the means adopted to give practical effect to a belief that the *post-mortem* salvation, to which a divine hero had once attained, could be enjoyed by other men, generation after generation. The principle of ritual assimilation or identification involved is undoubtedly the product of a primitive logic; but on reflection it appears to be also the most natural form of implementation of such soteriological belief. As we shall see, the ritual pattern of assimilation, pioneered by those Egyptians whose ideas first found literary expression in the *Pyramid Texts*, was so natural, and therefore necessary, that it occurs in the practice of other later religions. Before evaluating these other forms, we must, however, briefly note here, since space forbids a proper exposition of so important a topic, that the Osirian mortuary ritual came to include belief in a *post-mortem* judgement of the dead. At first adumbrated in the *Pyramid Texts*, the idea grew in importance and dramatic expression, and was still an effective force in the early centuries of the present era. This conception of a *post-mortem* judgement also incorporated the *motif* of the assimilation of the deceased to Osiris, since the title *mꜣʿ ḫrw* ('true of voice') given to those buried according to the Osirian rites, was derived from the legend of Osiris. However, the *motif* operated rather illogically, although the Egyptians never seem to have noticed it; for, while he was regarded as assimilated to Osiris, the deceased was also thought of as being judged by Osiris.[41]

There is some evidence in the sister civilization of Mesopotamia of the practice of ritual assimilation in the cult of Tammuz. The nature of Mesopotamian eschatology, however, precluded this deity's becoming a saviour-god in the sense in which Osiris was, namely, as one who could provide *post-mortem* salvation for his devotees.[42] Consequently, although substitution rituals existed based upon assimilation to Tammuz, the salvation obtained was from sickness in this life, not eternal well-being after death.[43] Although the death and resurrection of a deity was apparently ritually re-presented in the cults of Adonis and Attis, there does not seem to have been in these cults any effective assimilation of devotees, living or dead, with these deities in their deaths and resurrections.[44] The *drōmena* of the Eleusinian Mysteries might seem to afford a better example of ritual assimilation with soteriological intent. Unfortunately, despite the research of several generations of scholars, we are still uncertain of the nature of these *drōmena*. It would seem likely that they included some representation of Demeter's search for her lost daughter and the subsequent reunion of the two goddesses, and it would also seem probable that by participation in such representation the *mystae* were given a sense of communion with Demeter in both her sorrow and her exultation; but it would appear doubtful whether such ritual action and its effect were being described by Themistios when he wrote: 'The soul [at the point of death] has the same experience as those who are initiated into the great mysteries. . . .'[45] Participation in the rites must surely have given a sense of spiritual comfort and exaltation; however, so far as can be known, the *drōmena* at Eleusis did not relate to a death and resurrection *mythos* of immediate personal significance as did that concerning Osiris.

For the study of the phenomenology of religion it is Christianity that provides the only real parallel to Osirian soteriology. In what way and to what degree, if at all, the Christian conception of a saviour-god was influenced by the ancient Egyptian view of Osiris has been the subject of a long and continuing debate. It is not within the terms of reference of this essay to discuss the issue; instead we shall seek to trace out the earliest ritual means by which individual Christians obtained, or partook of, the salvation that was believed to be available through Christ. This task, however, necessarily involves an incursion into one of the most fundamental issues of the study of Christian Origins which can only be adequately discussed in an extended and fully documented monograph; this being so, the present writer will take the liberty of drawing on certain conclusions which he has already published elsewhere.

In interpreting the death by crucifixion of Jesus of Nazareth soteriologically, the Apostle Paul had to draw on concepts which were alien to Jewish religion. The original community of the disciples had probably seen in the death of Jesus a martyrdom for the sake of Israel, although the fact of that death by crucifixion constituted a serious objection to Jesus' being the promised Messiah. The Jewish disciples had surmounted this objection by finding prophetic warranty for such a death, particularly in terms of the figure of the Suffering Servant in *Isaiah*; but beyond this they had no essential interest in the death, for their hopes were centred upon the imminent return of Jesus in power and glory to 'restore the kingdom again to Israel'. It was Paul who, not learning the faith from those who were apostles before him, had seen in the death of Jesus not just a martyrdom for Israel, but a divinely ordained act to accomplish the salvation of mankind. Such a conception, however, was completely foreign, and indeed offensive, to current Jewish thought, so that Paul was obliged to employ other concepts in formulating his 'gospel', which he recognized as differing from that of his Jewish Christian opponents. He had in particular to construct a doctrine of Man which would explain how the death (and resurrection) of Jesus could effect human salvation. This was done by representing men and women as being in a state of perdition and subject to daemoniac forces. The crucifixion of Jesus, accomplished in ignorance of his true character by these daemons, had broken their hold over mankind and thus had potentially achieved the salvation of its members from the consequences of such bondage. Paul is never explicit as to the exact nature of such consequences, but he obviously regarded them as involving some form of (spiritual?) death or eternal damnation.[46] In whatever form he may have conceived of such a *post-mortem* state, Paul was, however, necessarily faced with the question, how could the salvation won by Christ be mediated or made available to those who accepted him as their saviour?

So far as our evidence permits us to know, Paul found the

means in baptism. Now, it would appear that some form of ritual lustration was already being practised in the Christian communities, both Jewish and Gentile. The origin and purpose of such a practice is uncertain, but it was clearly regarded as an essential initiatory rite which conferred a new spiritual character or status upon the neophyte. Since Paul's writings provide our earliest information about Christian faith and practice as he knew it or conceived it to be, an incidental reference to what were then surely recognized as the consequences of baptism is illuminating. Writing to his Corinthian converts in admonition, Paul adds, after reminding them of the corruption of pagan life, of which they had partaken: 'But ye were washed (*ἀπελούσασθε*), but ye were sanctified (*ἡγιάσθητε*), but ye were justified (*ἐδικαιώθητε*) in the name of the Lord Jesus Christ, and in the Spirit of our God.' It would, accordingly, appear that baptism was already regarded as effecting some kind of purification, undoubtedly from past sin, and, consequent upon it, a hallowing and vindicating of the neophyte. Such an effect is intelligible in the light of what is known of contemporary Jewish usage of ritual lustrations, of which that practised by John the Baptist is the most notable.[47] But, although this pre-Pauline form of baptism associated the neophyte with Jesus Christ, it would seem that the chief *motif* of the rite was that of purification, undoubtedly in an ethical sense. Such a view of baptism is completely intelligible in terms of what we know of the 'gospel' of the Jerusalem Church, and in this sense the rite must have been known and practised by Paul at the beginning of his ministry. However, at some time later he came to interpret baptism in a fundamentally different way, attributing to it an efficacy which is only intelligible in the light of his soteriological evaluation of the death of Christ. Accordingly, he transformed baptism from a purifactory rite into a ritual of mystical assimilation whereby the neophyte was united to Christ in both his death and his resurrection. When Paul first propounded this new interpretation of baptism is not known; in his notable statement of it in his *Epistle to the Romans* (6:3–9) it is not clear whether he is reminding his readers of an aspect of baptism of which they were already informed, or whether it occurs to him to draw out this significance for the first time by virtue of his theme that acceptance of Christ means a dying to sin. On balance the former situation seems the more likely when he writes: 'Or are ye ignorant that all we who were baptized into Christ Jesus were baptized into his death?' He continues:

We were buried therefore with him through baptism into death; that like as Christ was raised from the dead through the glory of the Father, so we also might walk in newness of life. For if we are become united (σύμφυτοι) with *him* by the likeness (τῷ ὁμοιώματι) of his death, we shall be also *by the likeness* of his resurrection; knowing this, that our old man was crucified with *him* (συνεσταυρώθη), that the body of sin might be done away, that we should no longer be in bondage to sin; for he that hath died is justified from sin. But if we died with Christ, we believe that we shall also live with him (συζήσομεν αὐτῷ); knowing that Christ being raised from the dead dieth no more; death no more hath dominion over him.[48]

Quite clearly, in conceiving of this assimilation of the Christian neophyte with Christ in his death and resurrection, Paul must have been inspired to see in what was hitherto a simple rite of lustration a ritual potentiality capable of mediating the new life of the saviour to the initiate. It would appear also that he envisaged this effect as the consequence of the enactment of the ritual *ex opere operato*, since no mention is made of any *a priori* condition—in view of his emphasis elsewhere on the essentiality of faith in Christ, it is, however, unlikely that this would really have been Paul's considered opinion as to the nature of the operation of the rite. However that may be, the fact is nevertheless of profound significance that in teaching the soteriological efficacy of the death and resurrection of Christ, Paul was led to invoke that same principle of ritual assimilation that had for so many centuries operated in the Osirian mortuary cult. Whether or not Paul was aware of this feature of the Egyptian faith is not an issue for our consideration here.[49] What is important phenomenologically is that, when he sought to make the salvation won by Christ practically available to his converts, Paul resorted to the principle of ritual assimilation, which in its practice constituted so remarkable a parallel to the ritual pattern so long observed in Osirianism. Moreover, although the subject cannot be pursued here, we may note that this Pauline invocation of the principle of ritual assimilation found dramatic expression in the baptismal ceremonies which were subsequently developed in the Church.[50]

One final observation is necessary. The Osirian ritual was designed to secure *post-mortem* salvation for the dead: the Christian baptismal ritual was performed to place the living in a state of salvation. But each was concerned with a common task, namely, of mediating new life that had been won by a divine saviour.[51] To accomplish that task each ritual was significantly based upon the principle of mystical (or magical) assimilation.

NOTES

[1] Cf. S. G. F. Brandon, *Man and his Destiny in the Great Religions* (Manchester, 1962), pp. 6–7, chap. xii; 'The Origin of Religion', in *The Hibbert Journal*, vol. lvii (1959); 'Time, Man and Society', in *Essays on Time* (U.S.A., forthcoming); *Time and History in Religion* (Manchester, forthcoming).

[2] Cf. E. O. James, *The Origins of Sacrifice* (London, 1937), pp. 27–34, *Prehistoric Religion* (London, 1957), p. 28; Brandon, *Man and his Destiny*, pp. 11–12.

[3] *Pyr.* 167, 775, 1453, 1477; 1466d. Cf. C. E. Sander-Hansen, *Der Begriff des Todes bei den Aegyptern* (Copenhagen, 1942), pp. 18–20.

[3a] *Pyr.* 656, 365–8. Cf. Brandon, *Man and his Destiny*, p. 38; H. Frankfort, *Ancient Egyptian Religions* (New York, 1948), pp. 100, 103, 106–8.

[4] *Pyr.* 135a–135c, 703a–705a (for identification with Osiris see below); 167a–179a. See also *Pyr.* 397a–412a.

[5] 'Eine Fülle von Texten legt Zeugnis davon ab, dass die Aegypter den Osiris und sein Schichsal als geschichtliche Gestalt gesehen und geglaubt haben. Wer Mythus und Kultform des Osiris mit dem vergleicht, was in der alten Mittelmeerwelt von Sterbenden und auferstehenden Göttern überliefert ist, empfindet die Ebene der Geschichte als die besondere Basis des Osiris. Politische Dinge sind erzählt, politische Termini prägen die Kultsprache im Osirisdienst,' S. Morenz, *Die Zauberflöte* (Münster/Köln, 1952), p. 74. Cf. H. Bonnet, *Reallexikon der aegyptischen Religionsgeschichte* (Berlin, 1952), pp. 570b–571a.

[6] Unas was the last king of the fifth dynasty.

[7] *Pyr.* 167a–d (text in K. Sethe, *Die altaegyptischen Pyramidentexten*, I, pp. 93–4). According to Erman u. Grapow, *Wörterbuch d. aeg. Sprache*, II, p. 283, *nhp* is 'Verbum (neben "leben" und "nicht sterben")'. S. A. B. Mercer (*Pyramid Texts*, I, p. 63), translates *nhp* as 'judged' or 'judges': he does not give his reasons in his commentary, op. cit., II, p. 88. L. Speleers (*Les Textes des Pyramides égyptiennes*, I, p. 16) renders it as 'engendre'.

[8] *Pyr.* 168a–180c.

[9] *Pyr.* 186b.

[10] *Pyr.* 193a–c. Cf. *Mercer*, II, p. 90–2.

[11] *Pyr.* 721a–722b. The 'Great One' signifies Osiris. *Ndi.t* was the place where Osiris was killed; it was located near Abydos: cf. Bonnet, *Reallexikon*, p. 508b; Mercer, II, p. 120. *Ḳd* ('to sleep') is equated with death; cf. J. Zandee, *Death as an Enemy according to ancient Egyptian Conceptions* (Leiden, 1960), p. 85. Teti was the first pharaoh of the sixth dynasty.

[12] *Pyr.* 1255c–1257d. Cf. G. Thausing, *Der Auferstehungsgedanke in ägyptischen religiosen Texten* (Leipzig, 1943), p. 116, n. 3, 4; Brandon, *Man and his Destiny*, p. 37.

[13] *Pyr.* 1981a–c.

[14] *Pyr.* 738a, 739a–b. Cf. Thausing, p. 21.

[15] *Pyr.* 1068a–b. Pepi was the second king of the sixth dynasty.

[16] *Pyr.* 2092a–2093b. The epithet *bꜣgj* ('weary one') applied to Osiris denotes the condition of death, see n. 11 above; cf. Erman u. Grapow, *Wörterbuch*, I, p. 431; Zandee, p. 82. *Nfr-kꜣ-rʿ* was the fourth pharaoh of the sixth dynasty.

[17] *Pyr.* 2097a.

[18] *Pyr.* 622a–b. Note the equation in *post-mortem* action: *ỉr.k nw ỉr.n Wsỉr.*

[19] Cf. Bonnet, *Reallexikon*, p. 487 ff, ('Mundöffnung'); J. Vandier, *La religion égyptienne* (Paris, 1949), pp. 113–14; Mercer, IV, pp. 36–7.

[20] *Pyr.* 12c–14d, cf. 1329a–1330b. See Mercer's note (II, p. 13) on *nwꜣ*; he takes the sign for Anubis as a determinative.

[21] Cf. Mercer, IV, pp. 54–6; Bonnet, *Reallexikon*, pp. 635a–636a.

[22] *Pyr.* 841a–843b. On the symbolism of *ḳbḥ.w*, which means 'cool water', see Mercer, IV, pp. 53–4.

[23] In a very real sense Osiris, in his death and resurrection, became a type of 'Everyman' for the Egyptians; cf. Brandon, *Man and his Destiny*, pp. 66–7. On the origin of Set's role as the murderer of Osiris see H. Kees, *Totenglauben und Jenseitsvorstellungen der alten Aegypter* (Berlin, 1956^2), p. 141.

[24] Bonnet, *Reallexikon*, p. 350a, thinks that assimilation to Osiris was essentially of a magical, not a mystical, character: 'Denn es bedeutet keineswegs eine irgendwie geartete Gemeinschaft mit dem Gott im Sinne einer Osirismystik; es ist nur magische Fiktion, die den Toten den Durchgang vom Tod zum Leben, den Osiris erfuhr, zu Sichern zum Ziele hat, und steht damit im letzten den Identifikationen mit anderen Göttern gleich.' The efficacy of the assimilation was certainly *ex opere operato*; but it is very difficult to draw the line between the 'mystical' and the 'magical'. The 'Everyman' theme (see n. 23 above) is very evident in the pathos of many references to and laments for Osiris. Cf. Morenz, *Aegyptische Religion* (Stuttgart, 1960), pp. 58, 220; Thausing, pp. 21–2.

[24a] To the references in n. 19 add E. A. W. Budge, *The Mummy* (Cambridge, 1925), pp. 336–51.

[25] 'Das Auferstehungsritual der Unaspyramide', in *A.S.A.E.*, LIII (1956), pp. 344–5: 'Dies muss in besonderem Masse für Kulthandlungen gelten, die ihren Wesen nach (und zugleich aus technischen Gründen) *nur einmal* vollzogen werden können während ihre Bedeutung *eine bleibende* sein soll.'

[26] Op. cit., p. 405.

[27] Op. cit. pp. 408–9.

[28] Op. cit., pp. 363–4: 'Auch das Personalpronomen "er" in den Sätzen des Refrains *Er lebt und es lebt dieser Unas usw* geht zunächst auf den Ba, um dessen Wesensidentität mit dem Toten sich der ganze Spruch 219 dreht (s.u.). Nur mittelbar betreffen die Aussagen des Refrains zugleich Osiris, weil der Ba während seines Weges durch die Unterwelt dessen Gestalt und Wesenheit angenommen hat. Die Wesenidentität des Ba mit dem Toten muss hier so besonders betont werden, weil es noch unsichtbar ist.' This identification of the *ba* only with the new Osiris is clearly made impossible by the statement in *Pyr.* 186b, which objection Spiegel is hard put to explain away (p. 365). Cf. Brandon in *Numen*, VI (1959), p. 117, n. 17.

[29] Cf. Brandon, *Man and his Destiny*, pp. 39–48.

[30] For an interesting indication of Christian preoccupation with the significance of Osiris, see the Coptic document, dating from about the beginning of the fifth century, concerning the death of Joseph, as edited by S. Morenz, *Die Geschichte von Joseph dem Zimmermann* (Berlin, 1951), pp. 112, 123–7.

[31] *C.T.*, 44 (A. de Buck, *The Egyptian Coffin Texts*, I (Chicago, 1936), p. 191. The left side was the 'Todesseite', through which the 'Todeshauch' entered; cf. Thausing, p. 103, n. 4, see also p. 143. Cf. Kees, p. 268.

[32] *C.T.* 74 (de Buck, I, pp. 306–7), *sꜣb rḏw* ('vivifying water') in some versions of the text has the sign of a jackal (Anubis) as a determinative. Cf. Thausing, pp. 156–7; Kees, pp. 269–70.

[33] *Book of the Dead*, cap. 154, 1–3, 15–16 (text ed. E. A. W. Budge, London, 1898, pp. 398–401). Cf. Thausing, pp. 175–6.

[34] *Rhind Papyrus*, I. See reproductions of the illustrations in G. Roeder, *Die ägyptische Religion in Text und Bild*, Band IV (Zürich/Stuttgart, 1961), Abb. 26, 27, 28, 29, 31.

[35] Cf. Roeder, p. 336.

[36] Roeder, Abb. 31.

[37] Roeder, Abb. 28. See also J. Leipoldt in *Bilderatlas zur Religionsgeschichte* (Leipzig/Erlangen, 1926), 9–11. Lieferung, Abb. 2, and p. iii.

[38] 'Das Werden zu Osiris (Die Darstellungen auf einem Leinentuch der römischen Kaiserzeit (Berlin 11651) und verwandten Stücken)', in *Staatliche Museen zu Berlin: Forschungen und Berichte*, I (1957), pp. 52–70.

[39] Op. cit., Abb. 1, see also Abb. 7 (the deceased is a female; Anubis is replaced by a goddess, probably Hathor), Abb. 8, 9.

[40] 'der Tote werde hier zugleich zu seiner eigenen Mumie hingeleitet, die ja ihrerseits durch ihre ritualgerechte Herrichtung, also ex opere operato, mit Osiris gleich wird. Kurz gesagt: Es ist hier in knapper und wesentlicher Form das Werden zu Osiris dargestellt', op. cit., p. 59.

[41] Cf. Brandon, 'A problem of the Osirian judgment of the dead', in *Numen*, V (1958), pp. 110–27; *Man and his Destiny*, pp. 50–7.

[42] Cf. S. N. Kramer in *Mythologies of the Ancient World* (New York, 1961), pp. 10, 11; Brandon, *Man and his Destiny*, pp. 101–5.

[43] Cf. E. Ebeling, *Tod und Leben nach den Vorstellungen des Babylonier*, I (Berlin/Leipzig, 1931), pp. 47–56; S. H. Hooke, *Babylonian and Assyrian Religion* (London, 1953), pp. 42–3.

[44] Cf. G. Wagner, *Das religionsgeschichtliche Problem von Römer 6, 1–11* (Zürich/Stuttgart, 1962), pp. 276–80.

[45] Cf. G. E. Mylonas, *Eleusis and the Eleusinian Mysteries* (Princeton, N. J., 1961), pp. 261–72; Brandon, *Time and Mankind* (London, 1951), pp. 121–3.

[46] For a fully documented discussion of the issues involved here see Brandon, *The Fall of Jerusalem and the Christian Church* (London, 1957²), chaps. iv and v, *Man and his Destiny*, pp. 194–224.

[47] I Cor. 6:11. Cf. E. Dinkler in *Religion in Geschichte und Gegenwart* (3. Aufl. 1962), VI, 629a–630.

[48] 'Die Taufe ist nicht so sehr Initiationsakt und Abwaschung der Sünden, sondern Aktualisierung des ein für allemal (6, 10: ἐφάπαξ) geschehenen Heilsereignisses, sie bedeutet ein Mitsterben mit Christus, eine Gewissheit der kommenden Auferstehung und den sofortigen Beginn eines neuen Lebens', Dinkler, op. cit., p. 631. Wagner, p. 293, in his desire to refute any suggestion of an Osirian parallel here, overlooks the fact that the actual death and resurrection was not (indeed could not) be represented ritually in the Osirian mortuary ritual any more than it could be in the baptismal ritual: he also seems to forget the evidence of the recited formulae for bringing out the meaning of symbolic acts of assimilation.

[49] Wagner, op. cit., pp. 98–145, 272–4, has recently published a long and valuable discussion of the subject. It would seem that his concern with the 'Mystery-cult' aspect of the issue has caused him, however, to underestimate the significance of the fact that the ancient mortuary assimilation of the deceased with Osiris continued into the Christian era, as the evidence of the shrouds studied by Morenz (see above) so graphically shows.

[50] Cf. M. Werner, *Die Entstehung des christlichen Dogmas* (Berne, 1941²), pp. 420–31, *The Formation of Christian Dogma* (E. T., London, 1957), pp. 177–9.

[51] E.g. Rom. 6:8–11; Col. 2:20, 3:2–4.

III

POLITEISMO E SOTERIOLOGIA

by

ANGELO BRELICH

L'OCCASIONE di poter contribuire alle onoranze di E. O. James cui tanto deve la cultura storico-religiosa odierna, mi ha indotto ad affrontare un tema di cui finora non mi ero occupato; ma, per evitare ogni deteriore improvvisazione, ho mantenuto le seguenti pagine nei limiti di uno sguardo, per cosí dire, laterale, gettato sul tema centrale del presente volume dal mio campo abituale di ricerche, e su un piano di considerazioni di portata prevalentemente teorica, che forse potranno utilmente esser sottoposte ad ulteriori discussioni.

Il problema accennato nel titolo sorge dai seguenti dati di fatto. Tutti sanno che le religioni piú caratteristicamente soteriologiche —quali p.es. il Cristianesimo e il Buddhismo[1]—non sono religioni politeistiche.[2] Tuttavia, nelle ricerche sulle origini dell'idea giudaica, cristiana e gnostica[3] della salvezza, sono state costantemente coinvolte le religioni politeistiche dell'ambiente storico, anche largamente inteso, del mondo giudaico-cristiano. Tali ricerche, infatti, si muovevano soprattutto su due linee ora polemicamente opposte ora conciliate: quella che si orientava verso retaggi indo-iranici[4] e quella che, invece, dava maggior importanza al filone babilonese-egiziano.[5] Sotto l'influsso di queste ricerche, oggi è del tutto corrente parlare di 'dèi salvatori' nelle religioni politeistiche del mondo antico. Il problema che ci vogliamo porre è, dunque, il seguente: come si spiega che le principali religioni soteriologiche non siano quelle politeistiche, e, anzi, in queste ultime gli elementi soteriologici debbano essere oggetto di faticose ricerche, e come si spiega, d'altra parte, che tali ricerche si siano susseguite per decenni onde scoprire nelle religioni polietistiche almeno i germi della soteriologia giudaico-cristiana? In altri termini: qual'è il reale rapporto tra politeismo e soteriologia?

Anzitutto, se già fu necessario un chiarimento sull'uso del termine 'politeismo', non sembra meno necessario precisare che cosa si debba intendere per 'soteriologia', per 'salvezza', 'salvatore', ecc. Oggi non sarà piú da ripetere che questi termini possono esser intesi in un senso assai largo, ma anche in uno o piú sensi specifici: nel senso largo, tutte le religioni sono—come spesso si afferma anche esplicitamente—'soteriologiche', in tutte le religioni (e, in verità, anche al di fuori delle religioni) l'uomo cerca la salvezza, e tutti gli esseri religiosamente venerati sono 'salvatori'.[6] Ma ciò vuol dire proprio che il senso largo dei termini non è 'operativo', in quanto nella sua genericità non distingue e non specifica nulla. Rimane, piuttosto, la questione, se si sia autorizzati a considerare i fenomeni specifici indicati dagli stessi termini come forme particolari del fenomeno generico o se non si cada, anche in questo caso, vittime delle parole: nulla dimostra, infatti—fino a prova contraria—che solo perché noi abbiamo un concetto piú largo e concetti piú stretti di 'salvezza', i fenomeni corrispondenti a questi ultimi siano da considerarsi come sviluppi *storici*—forme particolari prese in determinate situazioni, epoche, civiltà—del fenomeno corrispondente al primo, quasi *Völkergedanken* radicati in un *Elementargedanke*; potrebbe trattarsi di un preconcetto evoluzionistico o fenomenologico o, semplicemente, dell'ingenua proiezione delle nostre classificazioni concettuali nella realtà storica.[7]

L'inoperatività del termine in senso largo appare anche dal punto di vista del nostro problema, in quanto 'in senso largo' anche il politeismo (ma anche ogni altro tipo di religione) è soteriologico, e tutti gli dèi[8] (ma anche gli antenati, i 'feticci', gli spiriti tutelari, ecc.) sono salvatori: altrimenti perché si indirizzerebbero preghiere ad essi? un essere che non servisse ai fini di una qualsiasi 'salvezza', non sarebbe nemmeno venerato.

E' già una questione lievemente diversa, perché *determinate* divinità, nelle religioni politeistiche, appaiono *piú particolarmente* salvatrici di altre. Nella religione greca p.es.—cui dobbiamo anche il termine *soter*—le divinità che occasionalmente o in determinati loro culti portano l'epiteto *soter* o *soteira* sono tante e cosí varie[9] da far pensare che a qualsiasi divinità si potesse attribuire quella qualifica e che se qualche divinità non appare mai esplicitamente come 'salvatrice' ciò possa dipendere anche dal capriccio della conservazione dei documenti. Tuttavia, alcune divinità si distinguono, tra le altre, sia per la frequenza sia per l'enfasi della loro qualificazione di *soteres*. Una semplice analisi dei casi mostra che—a parte le divinità implicate in culti a carattere di mistero, caso in cui l'epiteto assume un nuovo significato[10]—si tratta di quelle divinità da cui ci si attendeva un pronto e immediato intervento in particolari situazioni di crisi acuta: cosí, p.es., quando si tratta dei Dioskuroi che, per concorde tradizione,[11] salvavano i navigatori in pericolo, o di Asklepios e Hygieia che salvavano gli ammalati. In questo quadro rientra anche l'uso dell'epiteto per i sovrani ellenistici[12] che salvavano le città nelle acute crisi politiche e militari.

Ma questa differenza di sfumatura tra divinità 'salvatrici' in quanto divinità (anzi, in quanto oggetti di venerazione in generale, v. sopra p. 38) e divinità *piú particolarmente* 'salvatrici' in quanto tradizionalmente messe in rapporto con singole e concrete situazioni pericolose, non autorizzerebbe ancora a parlare di soteriologia come di forma religiosa ben distinta e definita: in tutte le religioni, infatti, ci si attende l'intervento—ora piú costante e meno appariscente, ora immediato e concreto—delle potenze sovrumane.

La distinzione tra salvezza '*da ogni sorta* di male' e salvezza '*dal* male '[13] può forse esser precisata nel senso che vi è un'idea della salvezza che presuppone il male insito nell'esistenza stessa: non si tratta, cioè, di cercare rimedio contro i mali o pericoli contingenti che possono capitare a chiunque, bensí la salvezza da ciò che è un connotato fondamentale della normale condizione umana. La 'soteriologia' intesa in questo senso particolare presuppone, cioè, un guidizio negativo sulla realtà quale appare all'esperienza di una società. Con una di quelle generalizzazioni che, pur essendo soggette a infinite riserve e bisognose di precisazioni, sono tuttavia atte ad illustrare, in grandi linee, una situazione, si potrebbe dire che, mentre la maggior parte delle civiltà c.d. primitive e di quelle arcaiche si fondano su un'accettazione piú o meno irriflessiva della realtà,[14] alcune civiltà—ciascuna per processi storici particolari—sono arrivate ad opporsi ad essa e a contrapporle una condizione desiderata, quella della salvezza. In India, p.es., a cominciare dal periodo delle piú antiche Upanishad, la realtà empirica tende ad esser svalutata: lo scorrere sempre vario dell'esistenza (*saṃsāra*) appare privo di valore, frutto di illusione (*māyā*), fonte di incessante dolore: non si tratterà piú di cercare solo la salvezza dai 'lacci di Varuna' in cui singole trasgressioni possono precipitare l'individuo,[15] bensí di cercare la salvezza da tutta l'esistenza empirica falsa e dolorosa: quali che siano le vie della salvezza indicate dai vari orientamenti religiosi che sorgono da questa posizione, esse concordano nel rinnegare la realtà 'data'. Nell'Iran, Zarathustra ha interpretato la realtà come prodotto di una lotta in atto tra forze positive e forze negative, ponendo la salvezza nell'avvenire in cui il bene avrebbe definitivamente sconfitto e annientato il male. In Israele, sulla tradizione mitica, diffusa presso numerosi popoli, di uno stato paradisiaco iniziale e di una trasgressione primordiale, causa degli aspetti negativi della condizione umana, s'innestava, con l'affermarsi del monoteismo e della credenza in un particolare rapporto tra il popolo ebraico e Dio, nonché sotto l'incalzare di eventi storici catastrofici, una nuova ideologia secondo cui il 'peccato originale' sarebbe stato riscattato, in avvenire, da un Messia che avrebbe ricondotto il popolo alle condizioni paradisiache. Non è qui, naturalmente, il luogo di voler ricostruire i processi di formazione di queste credenze soteriologiche, né di porre la questione di eventuali rapporti storici tra di essi: solo dal punto di vista del nostro problema va osservato che in Israele l'idea soteriologica si forma nel segno del monoteismo, nell'Iran è legata a una riforma anti-politeistica, mentre in India scaturisce dalla disgregazione del classico politeismo vedico.[16]

Non è, del resto, difficile capire perché le religioni politeistiche siano in generale prive di orizzonti soteriologici. Le divinità del politeismo sono *immanenti* alla realtà dell'esperienza: esse *sono* la realtà, anche se non, naturalmente, 'parti', 'elementi' o 'fenomeni' di essa come l'ingenuo naturismo immaginava; nell'insieme delle figure divine personali, complesse e suscettibili di rapporti reciproci, si organizzano gli aspetti esistenzialemente importanti della realtà, che altrimenti sfuggirebbero al controllo umano. Immortali come sono, le divinità garantiscono la stabilità del mondo. Visto dall'altro lato, ciò significa che la realtà, tale qual'è, è divina e perciò non solo è stabile, ma anche si vuole che *sia* stabile. Nelle religioni politeistiche la realtà viene accettata, ivi compresa la normale condizione umana—anche ove se ne avverta la durezza (si pensi al mondo di Zeus contapposto al pre-cosmo di Kronos[17])—quale permanente manifestazione della volontà e della natura degli dèi: perciò essa non richiede salvezza. Anche da questo punto di vista appare importante la differenza tra l'idea politeistica e quella monoteistica di 'dio': il dio unico è trascendente e perciò i valori religiosi non si fissano necessariamente sulla realtà che, sebbene opera di dio, è essenzialmente distinta da lui.

Se quanto si è detto finora rende sufficientemente comprensibile perché le religioni politeistiche, in generale, non sono orientate verso idee soteriologiche, non offre, tuttavia, una soluzione esauriente del problema dei rapporti tra politeismo e soteriologia. Non era, certo, un capriccio di generazioni di studiosi che cercavano nelle religioni politeistiche antiche i germi della soteriologia giudaico-cristiano-gnostica; d'altronde, sta di fatto che, almeno nella fase della loro disgregazione, le religioni politeistiche offrono concreti spunti a sviluppi soteriologici: in India, Viṣṇu, già presente, sia pure in secondo piano, alla piú antica cosmogonia vedica, diventa piú tardi un vero dio salvatore;[18] le divinità salvatrici dei misteri ellenistici provengono da religioni politeistiche come quella egiziana, quella siriana, ecc., a parte gli stessi dèi greci. Tutto ciò mostra che la constatazione, pur giusta, del carattere fondamentalmente non-soteriologico del politeismo lascia sussistere una sottile e complessa problematica che richiede ancora di esser esaminata.

Si è detto che il mondo retto dalle divinità politeistiche è un mondo stabile. Anche se, però, la stabilità essenziale e positivamente valutata dell'ordine garantito dagli dèi è uno dei cardini della concezione politeistica del mondo, resta ovvio che anche l'umanità politeista ha una sua esperienza del *tempo*, cioè del continuo mutamento della realtà. Come si conciliano, dunque, l'esigenza della stabilità, realizzata sul piano religioso nell'immortalità divina, e l'esperienza del cambiamento continuo, essenza del tempo? M. Eliade[19] ha mostrato con la piú incisiva chiarezza come la concezione *ciclica* del tempo miri alla periodica eliminazione delle conseguenze dei mutamenti continui: il tempo progressivo, lineare, 'profano' porta logorio, impurità, squilibri nell'ordine permanente che, perciò, ha bisogno di essere, di tanto in tanto, ritsabilito mediante un'abolizione di quanto è avvenuto e un ritorno al punto di partenza. Si conosce anche la 'tecnica' tradizionale che porta a questo periodico ritorno dell'ordine: riti di purificazione e di eliminazione, una realizzazione rituale del disordine concepito come 'anteriore' all'ordine e suo presupposto dialettico, e infine la ripetizione del processo di formazione dell'ordine: schema comune a molteplici rituali di 'capodanno' o, comunque, di rinnovamento.[20] La stabilità non significa, dunque —e non *può* significare—immobiltà, ma perpetuo rinnovamento. Perciò le religioni orientate—come, ma non soltanto, quelle politeistiche—verso una valutazione positiva della realtà e della sua perennità, danno necessariamente una grande importanza all''eterno ritorno'.

Il ritorno all'ordine è, dunque, l'iterazione del primo formarsi dell'ordine: eventualmente della *cosmogonia* che, nelle religioni politeistiche, può esser intesa come la formazione del pantheon, la distribuzione definitiva delle competenze e delle funzioni tra le divinità.[21] D'altra parte, a questa sistemazione dell'ordine si arriva di solito attraverso una lotta cosmogonica contro le potenze caotiche, e questa lotta è condotta o capeggiata normalmente da un singolo dio destinato ad occupare una posizione particolare nel pantheon: egli ne sarà il sovrano (come Zeus o Marduk) o, comunque, avrà una posizione ben distinta tra gli altri dèi (come Indra.[22]) Ora, è inevitabile che questo dio cosmogonico abbia una parte di primo piano anche nei rituali festivi di rinnovamento ciclico: ogni volta egli ri-fonda l'ordine, trionfando sul caos.

A questo punto s'impone una considerazione che spesso si trascura. Ognuno sa che le feste possono avere un aspetto commemorativo: come nella religione cattolica si celebrano, nel giro dello stesso anno, la nascita, la morte, la risurrezione e altre vicende minori di Gesú, la concezione, la nascita, l'assunzione della Vergine e le date di morte di numerosi santi, e nell'Ebraismo si commemora l'esodo dall'Egitto e la permanenza nel deserto, cosí anche gli indigeni australiani rievocano le vicende dei loro antenati totemici e i Marind-anim quelle dei loro esseri 'dema'. Tali 'commemorazioni'—tra i popoli 'primitivi'—hanno la funzione di rinsaldare periodicamente la coscienza dell'importanza o della sacralità delle istituzioni fondate, nei tempi delle origini, da quegli esseri vissuti e scomparsi al momento della formazione del mondo e della condizione umana. C'è da chiedersi, se nella stessa funzione si esaurisca la festa 'commemorativa' delle vicende mitiche attribuite ad esseri che sono ritenuti esistenti anche nel presente, come le divinità delle religioni politeistiche. Il mito—situato necessariamente nel tempo delle origini—caratterizza la divinità: ciò che essa ha fatto nel tempo del mito, rivela ciò che essa *è* sempre; le sue gesta mitiche sono, almeno potenzialmente, le sue gesta di sempre. E' solo cosí che si può comprendere p.es. ciò che a prima vista ci potrebbe sembrare come un'oscillazione nella concezione religiosa vedica: uccidendo Vrtra, liberando le acque e le vacche rosse, Indra compí atti *cosmogonici* fondamentali[23] nel tempo delle origini: eppure, non mancano passi vedici (p.es. RV 8,89,3 sg.), in cui egli viene esortato a compiere queste medesime azioni, come se esse attendessero ancora di esser compiute: la ragione ne è che Indra *è* sempre colui che uccide Vrtra: si potrebbe dire che lo uccide permanentemente, ma, visto che la perennità è, per le religioni politeistiche (ed altre) un ripetersi ciclico, si può anche dire che lo uccida ripetutamente, ciclicamente.[24] La base mitica del rinnovamento ciclico non è, dunque, soltanto materia da 'commemorare': il protagonista divino della cosmogonia compie ogni volta la propria opera per ri-fondare l'ordine. In ciò le divinità cosmogoniche del politeismo si distinguono dallo *Heilbringer* primitivo.[25] Ma la loro capacità salvifica—in cui gli studiosi dei primi decenni del secolo hanno creduto di trovare le prime manifestazioni dell'idea soteriologica[26]—si situa, d'altra parte, su un piano essenzialmente differente da quello del potere dei veri 'salvatori': esse, infatti, 'salvano' perennemente (o periodicamente) la *realtà*, l'ordine da loro stabilito nel tempo delle origini, le condizioni normali dell'esistenza umana, da quanto li minacci, anziché salvare l'uomo *dalla* realtà e *dalle* condizioni normali. Nulla vi è di piú estraneo al periodico ristabilimento del'ordine, di quello scardinamento radicale della realtà condannata che è alla base di ogni soteriologia. Un dio che operi per il superamento della realtà, non esiste nelle religioni politeistiche.

E' per ragioni analoghe che anche un'altra traccia seguita dagli studiosi in cerca delle origini della soteriologia risulta erronea in partenza: quella della regalità sacra.[27] L'idea che il nuovo re, salendo sul trono, apporti una nuova era di felicità, mettendo fine a una crisi, si riscontra anche a livello etnologico;[28] essa raggiunge sviluppi rigogliosi nelle antiche civiltà orientali in cui non è raro che l'intronizzazione del re sia concepita come una ripetizione della cosmogonia.[29] Ma, appunto, si tratta di *restaurare* l'ordine stabilito all'origine dei tempi, di ripetere il processo nel corso del quale esso è emerso dal caos. Anche questo complesso ideologico è, dunque, di per sé, privo di dimensioni soteriologiche: è un altro conto, se su di esso potesse innestarsi l'idea soteriologica, come, in effetti, è accaduto in Israele e anche altrove.[30]

Un legame tra religione soteriologica e antiche religioni politeistiche del Vicino Oriente, si è creduto di trovare nel 'dio che muore e risorge' di queste ultime, che sembrava esser sostanzialmente identico al 'salvatore salvato'. Dai tempi del *dying god* di Frazer, la critica storico-religiosa ha praticamente smantellato questo presunto tipo di divinità: tipo in cui non rientrano né Osiris (che non risorge, se non nell'al di là, diventando cioè, da morto, re prototipico dei morti) né Tammuz (che non risorge affatto) né Attis (che tutt'al piú non muore completamente), e tanto meno Marduk che dovette il proprio inserimento in questa tipologia a un'interpretazione avventurosa di alcuni testi.[31] Ad ogni modo, bisogna tener presente che 1) il dio morente o morto non è affatto una figura caratteristica delle religioni politeistiche che, se mai, l'ereditano—come ho cercato di mostrare altrove[32]—da civiltà anteriori di agricoltori primitivi (la cui religione conosce i 'dema' nel senso in cui A. E. Jensen[33] ce li ha resi familiari) e lo trasformano, ciascuna a modo suo, per conciliare i suoi caratteri originari con l'esigenza politeistica dell'immortalità divine; 2) che anche ove si trovasse una divinità che veramente muore e risorge (Dionysos? Persephone?), non sarebbe affatto sicuro dover attribuirle una funzione soteriologica: tra l'altro, essa potrebbe esser riferita—nel senso frazeriano o in un senso meno semplicisticamente naturistico-vegetale—anche al rinnovamento ciclico. Con ciò non si vuol negare che nei misteri ellenisticoromani—nell'epoca, cioè, in cui il politeismo antico andava disgregandosi—il dio morente (ed eventualmente risorgente?) abbia potuto assumere un significato soteriologico e che la celebre formula riportata da Firmico Materno (*err. prof. rel.* 22: *θαρρεῖτε μύσται τοῦ θεοῦ σεσωσμένου. ἔσται γὰρ ἡμῖν ἐκ πόνων σωτηρία.*)—di cui non si sa bene a quale culto misterico appartenesse[34]—possa esser interpretato anche nel senso di un'allusione, certo non esplicita, alla risurrezione di una divinità.

Uno dei temi fondamentali degli studi sulle origini della soteriologia è l'equivalenza tra *Urzeit* ed *Endzeit*, cioè tra tempo mitico delle origini e tempo finale della salvezza. H. Gunkel cui si deve l'osservazione di quest'idea religiosa nell'ebraismo, affermò ripetutamente la sua convinzione[35] che essa avesse origine nella religione babilonese, ma non tentò neppure di addurre prove in favore a questa tesi. Nè vi sarebbe riuscito, dato che il politeismo babilonese era completamente privo di orientamenti soteriologici: il suo tempo delle origini era quello in cui Marduk (o i suoi predecessori, prima dell'egemonia di Babele) stabilí, una volta per sempre, l'ordine attuale; e certo esso non agognava a ritornare in quella *Urzeit* anteriore di cui Tiamat e Mummu erano i padroni, come neanche la religione vedica si augurava il ritorno dei tempi in cui Indra non aveva ancora ucciso Vrtra, né la religione greca si sognava di far rientrare, in una *Endzeit* desiderabile, gli dèi olimpici nel ventre di Kronos. Certo, l'*Urzeit* è ambivalente, quale rovescio di quella realtà esistente di cui nessuna civiltà ignora gli aspetti negativi o anche tragici: il tempo anteriore al formarsi di questa realtà può apparire, nello stesso orizzonte culturale, contemporaneamente nei colori dell' 'età aurea' e del caos: perfino i Greci esprimevano una certa nostalgia per il *bios epi Kronou*. Ma una decisa presa di posizione religiosa e culturale in favore del ritorno definitivo dell'*Urzeit* può sorgere solo là dove le condizioni normali dell'esistenza cadono sotto una definitiva e globale condanna: ciò che non accade in una civiltà che vede nella realtà la manifestazione degli dèi.[36]

In conclusione: il politeismo, prima di disgregarsi sotto l'azione di nuovi orientamenti culturali ad esso estranei, ignora la soteriologia. Ma ciò non esclude che, dovunque l'idea soteriologica prenda piede, essa si appropri delle forme d'espressione dell'esperienza politeistica: di modo che ciò che era un rituale ristabilimento ciclico dell'ordine normale, diventi simbolo del ritorno dell'*Urzeit*;[37] ciò che si attendeva da ogni re nuovo—il superamento di una regressione nelle condizioni caotiche—diventi la restituzione delle condizioni paradisiache per opera di un futuro re 'salvatore'; che la risurrezione di un dio in cui, se mai, si affermava l'esigenza politeistica dell'immortalità divina contro una piú antica tradizione su esseri che con la loro morte assicuravano all'umanità i prodotti agricoli, si associno speranze escatologiche; e che—eventualmente[38]—si attenda che un protagonista della cosmogonia (p.es. Viṣṇu?) ritorni come portatore e fondatore di una nuova e diversa realtà.

NOTES

[1] Oppure: il Giudaismo, lo Zoroastrismo; si aggiungano, se si vuole, gl attuali movimenti religiosi 'messianici' dei popoli coloniali o ex-coloniali ugualmente non politeisti.

[2] Per 'politeismo' qui non s'intende una qualsiasi religione che ammetta ed eventualmente veneri una pluralità di esseri sovrumani: in tal caso, infatti, religioni tipologicamente assai differenti (p.es. quelle imperniate sul culto degli antenati o quelle che accanto ad un c.d. Essere Supremo riconoscono l'esistenza di spiriti vari, ecc.) rientrerebbero nella troppo grossa categoria di 'religioni politeistiche' che escluderebbe, dunque, solo le poche religioni monoteistiche. Del politeismo si può, invece, piú utilmente parlare come di un tipo particolare di religione, nel senso in cui ho tentato di farlo in *Numen*, 7, 1960, 123 sgg.

[3] Sulla storia degli studi dal punto di vista delle origini della soteriologia gnostica, v. oggi C. Colpe, *Die religionsgeschichtliche Schule. Darstellung und Kritik ihres Bildes vom gnostischen Erlösermythus* (Forsch. z. Rel. u. Lit. des A. u. N. Testamentes, 78), Göttingen, 1961.

[4] In quest'indirizzo che partiva soprattutto dai problemi storici presentati dalla gnosi, grande fu la parte delle ricerche di R. Reitzenstein (v. soprattutto:

Das iranische Erlösungsmysterium, Bonn 1921). Naturalmente, anche ricerche indipendenti dalle questioni gnostiche si sono susseguite sugli elementi soteriologici delle religioni indiane e iraniche: cfr. p.es. H. Güntert, *Der arische Weltkönig und Heiland*, Halle 1923; E. Abegg, *Der Messiasglaube in Indien und Iran*, Berlin–Leipzig 1928. Sulla sola India: H. W. Schomerus, *Indische und christliche Enderwartung und Erlösungshoffnung*, Göttersloh 1941; S. Rodhe, *Deliver us from evil*, Lund, 1946.

[5] Quest'indirizzo partiva dalla problematica nota sotto l'etichetta "Babel und Bibel"; anticipato, come si vedrà piú avanti, già da H. Gunkel, esso trovava rappresentanti, per la questione specifica, in J. Hehn, *Sünde und Erlösung nach biblischen und babylonischen Anschauung*, Leipzig, 1903; in H. Zimmern, *Keilinschriften und Bibel*, Berlin, 1903 (e in E. Schrader, *Die Keilinschriften und d. A.T.*, Berlin[3], 1903, 377 sgg.; A. Jeremias, *Hdb. d. altorient. Geisteskultur*, Leipzig, 1913, 205 sgg. Ma a questa linea si avvicinano, seppure con maggior indipendenza, anche H. Lietzmann, *Der Weltheiland*, Bonn, 1909, ed E. Norden, *Die Geburt des Kindes*, Leipzig–Berlin, 1924 (con propensione per l'Egitto). In diversi punti, facendo la critica dell'altro indirizzo, a questo filone aderisce anche W. Staerk, *Die Erlösererwartung in den östlichen Religionen* (Soter II), Stuttgart, 1938.

[6] Cfr. F. Bammel in *RGG*[3] s.v. *Erlösung*: '*Ein allen Religionen gemeinsames Anliegen ist die E. von* '*allerlei Übel*'. *Fasst man E. im weitesten Sinne des Wortes, so will alle Religion E.sreligion sein.*' Cfr. anche A. Pincherle in *Enc. It.* s.v. *soteriologia.*

[7] Cosi p.es. per F. Täschner, *Orientalische Stimmen zum Erlösungsgedanken*, Leipzig, 1936, l'idea della salvezza è comune ad ogni religione, ma in Oriente essa assume diverse forme; '*Da haben wir das einfache Schutzsuchen bei den Wesen der übermenschlichen Welt von der Unbilder des Weltgeschehens, das Streben durch Opfer an sie, Erlösung von allerlei Übel zu erreichen*', ecc., fino a '*das Streben nach Erlösung vom Tode*' e alla salvezza '*im Bereiche des Sittlichen*' (p. 4).—Anche la fenomenologia religiosa è spesso vittima delle parole: G. van der Leeuw, *Phänomenologie der Religion*, Tübingen[2], 1956, 100 sgg. (e *passim*) presuppone un'idea universale della salvezza di cui le idee concrete non sarebbero che manifestazioni e sviluppi particolari. V. invece la semplice osservazione di S. Rohde, *op. c.* (in n. 4), p. 26/32: '*Salvation, deliverance, release, such words say nothing in themselves . . . Everything depends on the sense given to the evil from which man seeks deliverance . . .*'

[8] L'affermazione secondo cui *tutte* le divinità sarebbero 'salvatrici' nel senso piú largo del termine, sembra contraddetta dall'esistenza, in diverse religioni politeistiche, di divinità che sembrano rappresentare proprio una minaccia alla 'salvezza' e la cui venerazione ha lo scopo principale di placarle o addirittura di allontanarle, di ottenere, cioè, il loro non-intervento (p.es. Rudra nei Veda: cfr. H. Oldenberg, *Die Rel. des Veda*, Stuttgart 1923, 217 sg.; J. Gonda, *Die Religionen Indiens* I, Stuttgart 1960, 85 sgg.; o p.es. il dio-fuoco distruttore dello shintoimo, Kagudzuchi: K. Florenz in E. Lehmann–A. Bertholet, *Lehrb. d. Rel.-gesch.* 1, 1925, 292 sg.). La contraddizione è solo apparente: forgiando simili figure divine, la società concentra in esse ciò che avverte come minaccia alla propria 'salvezza', precisamente per poter parare la minaccia, allontanando queste divinità; di modo che anche queste hanno la funzione di assicurare la

'salvezza' del soggetto religioso. (Del resto, la concezione religiosa di esseri da allontanare è anteriore al politeismo: cfr. gli spiriti dei morti o altri spiriti pericolosi.)

[9] L'elenco piú abbondante di queste divinità è tuttora quello che si trova nel *Myth. Lex.* di Roscher, sotto le voci *soter* e *soteira*. Dalle grandi divinità come Zeus, Apollon, Poseidon, Hermes, Athena, Hera, Artemis, Aphrodite, ecc. a quelle d'importanza limitata (p.es. varie divinità fluviali), le due voci abbracciano una buona cinquantina di nomi divini.

[10] Cosí p.es. nel caso delle divinità misteriche d'origine orientale come Isis, Sarapis, Harpokrates, Men, Agdistis: ma spesso anche nel caso di divinità classiche bisogna controllare se l'uso dell'epiteto non sia dovuto a un culto misterico (p.es. Kore, Hades, Leukothea e Palaimon, ecc.).

[11] Cfr. *Hom. hymn.* 33, 6 sgg.; Strab. 1, 48; Paus, 2, 1, 9, ecc.

[12] Anche dall'epoca classica si conoscono alcuni casi di sovrani 'salvatori', in base alla stessa concezione: se si può credere a Diodoro (11, 26, 6) già Gelon di Siracusa—vincitore dei Cartaginesi!—sarebbe stato proclamato *euergetes, soter* e *basileus* dai cittadini; Agesilaos, ad ogni modo, fu definito *soter* da coloro che con lui condividevano i pericoli delle guerre: Xenoph. *Ages.* 11, 3.

[13] F. Bammel, l.c. (n. 6).

[14] Il che non significa necessariamente un 'ottimismo', ma solo un 'realismo': i miti delle origini della condizione umana sono fortemente 'pessimistici' presso la maggior parte delle civiltà c.d. primitive e anche nelle tradizioni mitiche di religioni politeiste: la mortalità, le malattie, la vecchiaia, il lavoro ecc. appaiono come tragiche conseguenze di qualche accadimento primordiale.

[15] La citata opera di S.Rodhe (n. 4) mostra anche il passaggio semantico dei termini relativi alla 'liberazione' e 'salvezza' (p.es. del verbo *muñcati* che è alla base di *mokṣa e mukti*) dall'originairio senso 'largo' a quello piú particolarmente 'soteriologico'; altrettanto si potrebbe mostrare per i termini greci *sozein, soter, soteria.*

[16] Sulla disgregazione del politeismo vedico, giunta quasi a compimento nelle Upanishad, cfr. J. Gonda, *op. c.* (n. 8), 174 sgg.

[17] Per il pessimismo greco che tuttavia non ha intaccato l'atteggiamento realistico e positivo dei Greci, cfr. S. G. F. Brandon, *Time and Mankind*, London, 1951, 138, 140.

[18] E. Abegg, *op. c.* (n. 4), 44 sgg.

[19] *Le mythe de l'éternel retour*, Paris, 1949.

[20] Anche pluriennali—p.es. i vari cicli (come quelli penteterici greci) o 'grandi anni', il *saeculum*, ecc.—e occasionali (p.es. feste di incoronazione, ecc.).

[21] Cfr. le *timai* distribuite da Zeus (Hes. *theog.* 885); nell'*enuma elish* Marduk divide gli dèi in due gruppi (tav. 6, 9 sg.), li raduna per conferir loro direttive (6, 17 sg.); nella teologia menfitica è naturalmente Ptah che "pone gli dèi nei loro santuari"; sulla distribuzione delle competenze divine secondo la dottrina di Hermopolis, v. J. Spiegel, *Das Werden der ägyptischen Hochkultur*, Heidelberg, 1953, 196.

[22] Del resto, nella celebre disputa tra Indra e Varuna (RV, 4, 42), anche il primo rivendica una posizione di sovrano. Non è privo d'interesse che di alcuni di questi dèi si dice che siano i piú giovani, o nati altrove (quasi fosse avvertito l'eccezionalità della loro opera cosmogonica rispetto alla stabilità dell'esistenza

degli altri dèi): per Zeus cfr. Hes. *theog.* 478 sg.; per Indra, i dati in A. Hillebrandt, *Vedische Mythologie* 2, Breslau, 1929, 149 sg.; per Marduk: *enuma elish* tav. 1, 79 sgg.

[23] Sull'aspetto cosmogonico dell'impresa di Indra (per molto tempo nascosto agli indologi dalle rozze interpretazioni naturistiche!) cfr. H. Lüders, *Varuna* 1, Göttingen 1951, 183 sgg., e, naturalmente, J. Gonda, *op. c.* (n. 8), 56 sg.

[24] Da tutti gli dèi che hanno compiuto imprese cosmogoniche contro avversari mostruosi, ci si attende che essi continuino ad agire in maniera analoga anche nel presente: cfr. p.es. i testi citati, per Marduk, da J. Hehn, *op. c.* (n. 5), 15 sgg.

[25] Che in una divinità (e perfino nel dio unico di una religione monoteistica) possano conservarsi e trasformarsi i tratti di quegli esseri mitici delle religioni 'primitive', che hanno determinato le origini dell'ordine attuale, è stato visto acutamente già da K. Breysig, *Die Entstehung des Gottesgedankens und der Heilbringer*, Berlin, 1905, che ha peccato soprattutto nella generalizzazione, abituale alla sua epoca, e nell'ingenuo evemerismo. Egli intuisce già (p. 88) la differenza essenziale tra lo *Heilbringer* che agisce solo nel tempo delle origini e il dio che agisce perpetuamente: ma, nel suo evoluzionismo, non riesce a render conto di come si producesse lo scatto qualitativo tra questi due tipi di figure.

[26] Solo questa prospettiva erronea poteva render possibili gli assurdi confronti p.es. tra Marduk e Cristo, come quello tracciato da Zimmern (v sopra, n. 5).

[27] A cominciare da H. Lietzmann, *op. c.* (n. 5), 19 sgg.; A. Jeremias, *op. c.* (n. 5), 205 sgg.; W. Staerk, *op. c.* (n. 5), 218 sgg. Quest'idea è costantemente presente alla mente dei seguaci della scuola '*myth and ritual*'. Giustamente critico: S. Mowinckel, *He that cometh*, Oxford, 1956, 55.

[28] A parte il materiale frazeriano, cfr. p.es., per i Bantu meridionali, i riti d'incoronazione descritti da O. Petterson, *Chiefs and Gods*, Lund, 1953, 214 sg., 334 sgg. Motivo tipico: l'estinzione di tutti i fuochi (rottura con l'ordine precedente, reingresso nel caos) e l'accensione di un fuoco nuovo da cui tutti accenderanno il fuoco proprio.

[29] P.es. in Egitto il re—come Horus dopo la sua vittoria cosmogonica—lascia partire quattro uccelli (verso i quattro punti cardinali), per annunciare il nuovo ordine. Cfr. H. Frankfort, *Kingship and the Gods*, Chicago, 1948, 190.

[30] La quarta ecloga virgiliana tuttavia non parla esplicitamente di un sovrano apportatore della nuova età d'oro.—Su certe profezie egiziane relative all'avvento di un re che riporterebbe l'ordine e il benessere, interpretate in chiave soteriologica, v. H. Lietzmann, *op. c.* (n. 5), 23 sgg. ed E. Norden, *op. c.* (n. 5), 53 sgg.

[31] Cfr. oggi H. von Soden in ZfA 51, 1955, 130 sgg.

[32] In SMSR 31, 1960, 92–8.

[33] E. A. Jensen, *Mythus und Kult bei Naturvölkern*, Wiesbaden, 2, 1960, 103 sgg.

[34] Cfr. il commento di K. Ziegler nella sua edizione (München, 1953, 2, 61 *ad l.*) del *de errore prof. rel.*

[35] *Schöpfung und Chaos*, Göttingen, 1895, 87, 317 sg. e soprattutto 369/3.

[36] Oggi anche l'autore celebrato con il presente volume vede chiaramente che

tra le religioni del Vicino Oriente antico solo lo Zoroastrismo e l'Ebraismo avevano una soteriologia: v. E. O. James negli Atti del *X Internationaler Kongress für Religionsgeschichte*, Marburg, 1961, 61 sgg.

[37] In questo senso, soltanto, può esser accettata la tesi di A. J. Wensinck in *Acta Orientalia* 1, 1923, 158 sgg. secondo cui (p. 171) '*eschatology is nothing but a particular case of cosmology*' e perciò avrebbe la sua origine nell'ideologia del rinnovamento ciclico ritualmente celebrato nella festa del capodanno.

[38] La restrizione è doverosa: nei primi decenni del secolo le ricerche intorno alle origini dell'Anthropos gnostico consideravano ancora quasi come ovvio che all'equivalenza tra *Urzeit* e *Endzeit* corrispondesse anche l'identità del Primo Uomo con il Savatore escatologico (cfr. le speculazioni talmudiche su Adamo); vittima di tale preconcetto fu p.es. l'iranico l'iranico Gayomart, di cui solo la critica recente (cfr. J. Duchesne-Guillemin, *The Western Response to Zoroaster*, Oxford, 1958, 77 sgg., 89; C. Colpe, *op.c.* /n. 3/ 140–64) ha mostra to come la sua comparsa escatologica sia priva di ogni significato soteriologico: egli, primo morto, sarà anche il primo risorto, ma non è lui il salvatore.—Del resto, mentre presso i popoli c.d. primitivi, l'idea del ritorno dello *Heilbringer* primordiale non è del tutto eccezionale (casi ne sono stati segnalati già nel noto articolo di P. Ehrenreich in ZfE, 38, 1906, 536 sgg.), le sole religioni *politeistiche* che prevedano un ritorno delle divinità attive nel tempo delle origini, sono quelle dell'America precolombiana: esse costituiscono, dunque, un problema del tutto particolare che non è il caso di affrontare in questo luogo. Quali processi di trasformazione e, non in ultimo luogo, evemerizzazione, abbia dovuto subíre p.es. un Quetzalcoatl, per diventare da una normale divinità politeistica, un essere di cui si attendesse il ritorno, appare dalle pagine che gli consacra W. Krickeberg, *Altmexikanische Kulturen*, Berlin, 1956, 192 sgg.

IV

'OUR GOD AND SAVIOUR': A RECURRING BIBLICAL PATTERN

by

F. F. BRUCE

I

WHEN the New Delhi Assembly of the World Council of Churches, meeting towards the end of 1961, adopted an amplified basis of membership beginning with the words, 'The World Council of Churches is a fellowship of churches which confess the Lord Jesus Christ as God and Saviour according to the scriptures . . .', it made the most recent documentary contribution to the concept of the Saviour God within the Hebrew and Christian tradition.

The designation of Christ as 'God and Saviour' belongs to the later New Testament books. In Titus 2:13 Christians are taught to wait for 'the appearing of the glory of our great God and Saviour Jesus Christ'; in 2 Pet. 1:1 mention is made of 'the righteousness of our God and Saviour Jesus Christ'. Some versions, indeed, detach 'God' from 'Saviour' in these two passages, rendering the former '. . . the great God, and our Saviour Jesus Christ' and the latter 'the righteousness of God, and our Saviour Jesus Christ' (or 'the righteousness of our God, and the Saviour Jesus Christ');[1] but the fact that in the Greek text of both passages the two substantives 'God' and 'Saviour' come under the regimen of a single definite article[2] strongly suggests that one and the same person is denoted as being both God and Saviour,[3] the Saviour God. In four other passages in 2 Peter reference is made to 'our *Lord* and Saviour

Jesus Christ' (1:11; 2:20; 3:2, 18). A characteristic expression of the Pastoral Epistles is 'God our Saviour' (1 Tim. 1:1; 2:3; Titus 1:3; 2:10; 3:4), where however God the Father is more probably intended (over against 'our Saviour Christ Jesus' in 2 Tim. 1:10; 'Christ Jesus our Saviour' in Titus 1:4, and 'Jesus Christ our Saviour' in Titus 3:6). It is indeed noteworthy that the designation 'Saviour', applied either to God or to Christ, occurs fifteen times in the Pastoral Epistles and 2 Peter as against nine times in the remaining books of the New Testament. The distribution of the derivative *σωτηρία* ('salvation') is quite different; but we naturally ask why the personal substantive *σωτήρ* should appear with such relative frequency in the later books of the New Testament.

One suggestion of recent times is that these documents reflect a body of teaching, called 'the knowledge of the truth', of Essene affinity, in which the idea of Saviourhood played a central part.[4] More probable is the view that we can trace here a Christian reaction to the pagan claims which were being made on behalf of other *θεοὶ σωτῆρες*,[5] not least (especially from the second half of the first century onwards) on behalf of the Roman emperor himself.[6] But if contemporary conditions stimulated the increased application of the title 'Saviour' to the God and Redeemer of the Christians, this application of the title was in itself no innovation. The canticles of Luke's nativity narrative, which belong to the most archaic strata of the New Testament, exult in 'God my Saviour' (Luke 1:47) and proclaim the birth of 'a Saviour, who is Christ the Lord'[7] (Luke 2:11). Such language is derived unmistakably from earlier Old Testament usage, in which the designation 'Saviour' is given alike to the God of Israel and to the king of Israel.

II

The Old Testament portrayal of the Saviour God is sometimes couched in pictorial terms which survive into New Testament times and even into Christian hymnody, and which remind us vividly of the environment in which Israel's faith came to birth and grew up.

In one of his lesser-known hymns on the nativity, Charles Wesley acclaims the infant Christ in these words:

> Gaze on that helpless Object
> Of endless adoration!
> Those infant hands shall burst our bonds
> And work out our salvation;
> Strangle the crooked serpent,
> Destroy his works for ever,
> And open set the heavenly gate
> To every true believer.

We know what Wesley means: he is expressing in poetical language the New Testament teaching that 'the reason the Son of God appeared was to destroy the works of the devil' (1 John 3:8); that the purpose of his incarnation was 'that through death he might destroy him who has the power of death, that is, the devil, and deliver all these who through fear of death were subject to lifelong bondage' (Heb. 2:14 f.). But where does he go for his imagery?

One of his sources, quite plainly, is Greek mythology: the picture of 'infant hands' strangling the serpent recalls the story of the infant Heracles[8] strangling with his hands the two serpents which Hera sent to kill him in his cradle.[9] But it is not only the familiar mythology of Greece that underlies Wesley's language.

The picture of a deity or hero procuring deliverance by fighting and conquering a serpent or dragon is widespread in the ancient Near East, and farther afield as well. The dragon may be the dragon of chaos or of drought, or (and this is specially marked in Old Testament literature) he may symbolize some historical figure. In the Old Testament it is uniformly Yahweh who destroys the dragon, no matter what malign power may be denoted by the dragon from one place to another. The functions which in the Canaanite pantheon are shared out among a wide variety of deities are for the Israelites concentrated in Yahweh; in the Ugaritic texts Asherah walks on the sea and Baal rides on the clouds, but in the Old Testament it is Yahweh who does both:[10]

> He plants his footsteps in the sea,
> And rides upon the storm.[11]

So too it is Yahweh who curbs the forces of chaos and brings the ordered world into being; it is Yahweh who delivers his people from the threat of drought and famine and gives them 'the grain, the wine and the oil' (Hos. 2:8); it is Yahweh who goes forth to war against their human enemies and wins salvation for them.

III

So far as the curbing of the forces of chaos is concerned, it is not to the creation narratives of Genesis that we look for the pictorial representation of this conflict; there is the barest verbal reminiscence of it in Gen. 1: 2, 'darkness was upon the face of the deep'; for *t*^{e}*hôm* ('deep') is probably cognate with Tiamat, the monster destroyed by Marduk in the Babylonian creation myth. But when the creative might of God is described by Job, the ancient conflict imagery comes to clear expression:

> By his power he stilled the sea;
> by his understanding he smote Rahab.
> By his wind the heavens were made fair;
> his hand pierced the fleeing serpent (Job 26: 12 f.).

'Rahab' is the monster of chaos,[12] and the 'fleeing serpent' (*nāḥāš bārîaḥ*[13]) is her dragon associate Leviathan. The smiting of the chaos monster is closely associated here and elsewhere with the curbing of the unruly sea, whose constant threat to overflow the cultivated land and spread havoc and disorder made it a ready symbol of chaos. In the Ugaritic texts Yam ('Sea') is personified as a rival power to the Canaanite pantheon; when he demands the surrender of Baal, Baal attacks him with two clubs, vanquishes him and succeeds to the sovereignty. Baal's victory thus delivers the ordered land from the menace of the sea.[14]

In another passage in Job Yahweh's action against the sea in the course of his creative work is described without mention of the chaos monster:

> Or who shut in the sea with doors,
> when it burst forth from the womb;
> when I made clouds its garment,
> and thick darkness its swaddling band,
> and prescribed bounds for it,
> and set bars and doors,
> and said, 'Thus far shall you come, and no farther,
> and here shall your proud waves be stayed'? (Job 38: 8–11).

But whether personification is prominent or not, the God who restrains the raging of the sea is the Saviour God—not only because one and the same Hebrew term (*yešaʿ* or *yᵉšûʿāh*) does duty for victory and salvation, but also because Yahweh's victory over the sea is the salvation of those who inhabit dry land.

IV

Israel's conception of Yahweh as the Saviour God was mainly dependent, however, not so much on his activity in creation as on his intervention in their interest at the time of the Exodus. 'Yahweh is my strength and my song,' they sang in commemoration of this deliverance, 'and he has become my salvation' (Exod. 15:2).[15] It was their deliverance because it was Yahweh's victory—not only over Pharaoh and his chariotry but over all the gods of Egypt he had 'triumphed gloriously' (Exod. 12:12, 15:1). Moreover, this victory and deliverance became the pattern for all their future experiences of Yahweh's saving power.

But the Exodus itself was portrayed time and again in terms of Yahweh's earlier victory against the forces of chaos. The use of these terms to portray the Exodus was made the easier because in the Exodus, as at the creation, Yahweh manifested his mastery over the sea. If he curbed it at the creation, he divided it at the Exodus. Thus one of the later psalmists, praying for national deliverance in a time of great distress, recalls how Yahweh wrought deliverance for his people at the Exodus, but does so in these words:

Yet God my King is from of old,
working salvation in the midst of the earth.
Thou didst divide the sea by thy might;
thou didst break the heads of the dragons on the waters.
Thou didst crush the heads of Leviathan,
thou didst give him as food for the creatures of the wilderness
(Ps. 74: 12–14).

The language shows plainly that it is drawn from the story of the creation conflict, and there are explicit creation motifs in the context; but it is not the creation that is uppermost in the psalmist's mind.

Another psalmist, at a time when the royal house of David has fallen on evil days, calls upon Yahweh to remember not only his covenanted promises to David but also the display of his power at the Exodus, and describes that display of power in terms of the creation conflict:

O Yahweh God of hosts,
who is mighty as thou art, O Yahweh,
with thy faithfulness round about thee?
Thou dost rule the raging of the sea;
when its waves rise, thou stillest them.
Thou didst crush Rahab like a carcass,
thou didst scatter thy enemies with thy mighty arm (Ps. 89:8–10).

Here the old conflict terminology is transferred to Yahweh's contest on his people's behalf against the power of Egypt. Rahab, the ancient name of the chaos monster, now becomes a name for Egypt; and in fact it appears elsewhere in the Old Testament as a poetic synonym for Egypt, quite apart from this kind of context. Thus in Isa. 30:7 Yahweh exposes the hollowness of promises of aid from Egypt:

For Egypt's help is worthless and empty,
therefore I have called her
'Rahab who sits still.'

And in a psalm which brings foreign nations within the range of his mercy Yahweh says: 'Among those who know me I mention Rahab and Babylon' (Ps. 87:4). Similarly Rahab's dragon associate becomes a figure of the Egyptian king, as in Ezek. 29:3 ff., where Pharaoh Hophra, described as 'the great dragon that lies in the midst of his streams', is told that, Leviathan as he is, he will be dragged out of his river with a hook[16] and thrown into the wilderness to be devoured by beasts and birds of prey—a close parallel to the fate of Leviathan in Ps. 74:14.

When another prophet[17] speaks of Yahweh's end-time victory and the final deliverance of his people, the same imagery is used: 'In that day Yahweh with his hard and great and strong sword will punish Leviathan the fleeing serpent, Leviathan the twisting serpent, and he will slay the dragon that is in the sea' (Isa. 27:1). The dragon in the sea is probably the power of Egypt, while Leviathan may well be Assyria or Babylon. It is noteworthy, however, that the double description of Leviathan as 'the fleeing serpent, . . . the twisting serpent' is paralleled exactly in the Ugaritic text where Môt tells Baal that he will overcome him,

> Though thou didst smite Lotan the fleeing serpent,
> Didst destroy the twisting serpent,
> The accursed one of seven heads.[18]

The Old Testament records establish the many-headed nature of Leviathan, but do not give the exact number of his heads; this the Ugaritic text does, and incidentally supplies a background for the seven-headed dragon of the New Testament Apocalypse.[19]

V

The autumnal equinox was the occasion for the greatest festival of the agricultural year of Israel, the harvest thanksgiving at which they acknowledged the goodness of Yahweh in providing the fruits of the earth during the preceding season and prayed for a continuation of his mercy in this regard throughout the ensuing year. This festival may well have been the setting for the 'prayer of Habakkuk the prophet' which appears in our traditional text as an epilogue to his oracle.[20] The oracle is concerned with deliverance from oppression by human enemies, while the prayer is concerned more with deliverance from pestilence, drought and famine; but in either case the deliverance comes from one and the same God, 'the God of my salvation', as the prophet calls him (Hab. 3:18). The potency of the ancient imagery of Yahweh's victory over the unruly sea appears in the prophet's use of it here to celebrate Yahweh's deliverance of his people from natural calamities; this may indeed reflect the part played by this imagery in the liturgy for the Feast of Tabernacles:

> Was thy wrath against the rivers, Yahweh?
>   Was thy anger against the rivers,
>   or thy indignation against the sea,
> when thou didst ride upon thy horses,
>   upon thy chariot of victory?[21] . . .
>
> The mountains saw thee, and writhed;
>   the raging waters swept on;
> the deep gave forth its voice,
>   it lifted its hands on high.[22] . . .
>
> Thou wentest forth for the salvation of thy people,
>   for the salvation of thy anointed.
> Thou didst crush the head of the wicked,
>   laying him bare from thigh to neck. . . .
> Thou didst trample the sea with thy horses,
>   the surging of mighty waters.

The memory of Yahweh's past victories, especially at the Exodus, to which the worshippers were very much alive at the Feast of Tabernacles, encourages the prophet to expect his intervention afresh for his people's salvation, whether it be by bringing trouble upon the foreign invaders (Hab. 3:16) or by restoring the fertility of the land:

> Though the fig tree do not blossom,
>   nor fruit be on the vines,
> the produce of the olive fail
>   and the fields yield no food,

the flock be cut off from the fold
  and there be no herd in the stalls,
yet I will rejoice in Yahweh,
  I will joy in the God of my salvation (Hab. 3:17 f.).

The salvation which Yahweh's victory had procured in the beginning was a salvation continually renewed—in the order of nature as in the history of Israel—and ultimately to be consummated on the day of Yahweh. This bringing together of past, present and future is celebrated at the end of Ps. 29, perhaps another composition for the Tabernacles liturgy:

Yahweh sits enthroned over the flood;
  Yahweh sits enthroned as king for ever.
May Yahweh give strength to his people!
  May Yahweh bless his people with peace![23]

VI

Even in the celebration of personal deliverances the Exodus deliverance is almost bound to be introduced in the Israelite tradition. In Ps. 66, for example, a private worshipper gathers his friends about him as he enters the temple to give thanks to God for some signal deliverance and fulfil the vows which he had undertaken when he was in distress:

Come and hear, all you who fear God,
  and I will tell what he has done for me.
I cried aloud to him,
  and he was extolled with my tongue (vv. 16 f.).

But before this—before he comes to recount his personal experience of deliverance—he recalls the doings of Yahweh in the past, with special reference to his mighty works at the Exodus:

Come and see what God has done:
  he is terrible in his deeds among men.
He turned the sea into dry land;
  men passed through the river on foot (vv. 5 f.).

Yahweh's character, the psalmist implies, is consistent from age to age; the private salvation which he himself has experienced is all of a piece with the national salvation which his people have experienced at Yahweh's hands from the Exodus onwards.

If a private worshipper can express his praise in terms like these, much more can the king of Israel, the embodiment of his people's welfare, do so. In Ps. 18 the royal worshipper celebrates a great deliverance which he himself has experienced, when Yahweh flew to his relief, riding on a cherub, soaring on the wings of the wind, thundering and lightening as he came:

> Then the channels of the sea were seen,
>   and the foundations of the world were laid bare,
> at thy rebuke, O Yahweh,
>   at the blast of the breath of thy nostrils.
> He reached from on high, he took me,
>   he drew me out of many waters.
> He delivered me from my strong enemy,
>   and from those who hated me;
>   for they were too mighty for me (vv. 15–17).

The theophany here described has elements which recall the creation conflict and others which recall the dividing of the Red Sea and the manifestation of divine power on Mount Sinai. Whether an actual deliverance from foreign foes is being celebrated here (as the general wording of the psalm strongly suggests) or the reference is to the king's ritual combat with the forces of chaos which threatened to overwhelm him and his nation,[24] the intervention of the Saviour God is portrayed in language hallowed by ancestral use. Yahweh is the God who 'makes great the deliverances of his king and performs covenant-loyalty to his anointed' (Ps. 18:50); he is preeminently the Saviour God.

As such Yahweh's name is extolled in the national liturgy; his saving victory in the past, reproduced repeatedly in the present, will have its climax on a day yet future:

> Let the sea roar, and all that fills it,
>   the world and those who dwell in it!
> Let the floods clap their hands;

let the hills sing for joy together
before Yahweh, for he comes
to rule the earth.
He will judge the world with righteousness,
and the peoples with equity (Ps. 98: 7–9).

VII

A day dawned when the language of the national liturgy seemed to have come true in history on a scale unexampled since the Exodus, when Israel's God, by bringing his people back from Babylonian captivity, vindicated his reputation as a Saviour God in a manner that gave the lie to all those who assured them mockingly that he was either unable or unwilling to deliver them:

O sing to Yahweh a new song,
for he has done marvellous things!
His right hand and his holy arm
have gotten him victory.
Yahweh has made known his victory,
he has revealed his vindication in the sight of the nations.
He has remembered his steadfast love and faithfulness
to the house of Israel.
All the ends of the earth have seen
the victory of our God (Ps. 98: 1–3).

This celebration of Yahweh's *ṣᵉdāqāh* and *yᵉšûʿāh* finds a clear echo in the context of the return from exile, in the oracles of Isa. 40–55. In lyric modes drawn from the ancient liturgy[25] the prophet cries:

Sing to Yahweh a new song,
his praise from the end of the earth!
Let the sea roar and all that fills it,
the coastlands and their inhabitants.
Let the desert and its cities lift up their voice,
the villages that Kedar inhabits;
let the inhabitants of Sela sing for joy,
let them shout from the top of the mountains.

Let them give glory to Yahweh,
  and declare his praise in the coastlands.
Yahweh goes forth like a mighty man,
  like a man of war[26] he stirs up his fury;
he cries out, he shouts aloud,
  he shows himself mighty against his foes (Isa. 42:10–13).

If at the Exodus Yahweh saved his people by making 'a way in the sea, a path in the mighty waters,' now he is to save them by making 'a way in the wilderness, and rivers in the desert' (Isa. 43:16, 19). Even the ancient conflict imagery is invoked once again, to link this new deliverance with those which Yahweh wrought in ages past. So, in Isa. 51:9 f., Yahweh's power is apostrophized:

Awake, awake, put on strength,
  O arm of Yahweh;
awake, as in days of old,
  the generations of long ago.
Was it not thou that didst cut Rahab in pieces,
  that didst pierce the dragon?
Was it not thou that didst dry up the sea,
  the waters of the great deep;
that didst make the depths of the sea a way
  for the redeemed to pass over?

This appeal is followed immediately by the assurance:

And the ransomed of Yahweh shall return
  and come with singing to Zion.

As then, so now; as Yahweh once brought his people out of Egypt, so (prays the prophet) let him now bring them out of their captivity in Babylonia.

It is in Isa. 40–55 more than anywhere else in the Old Testament that Yahweh's essential character as the Saviour God is emphasized. He is repeatedly called his people's *gō'ēl*, their kinsman-redeemer;[27] he brings near his righteousness[28] which is at once his own victorious vindication and the deliverance of his people; he alone is Yahweh, 'and besides me', he says, 'there is no saviour' (Isa. 43:11)—

> a righteous God and a Saviour;
> there is none besides me (Isa. 45:21).

'A righteous God and a Saviour'—*ṣaddîq* and *môšîa‘*. Practically the same two epithets are given by a later prophet to the future king whom he describes as coming for the deliverance of Jerusalem from other overlords than the Babylonians:

> Rejoice greatly, O daughter of Zion!
> Shout aloud, O daughter of Jerusalem!
> Lo, your king comes to you;
> triumphant and victorious is he,
> humble and riding on an ass,
> on a colt the foal of an ass (Zech. 9:9).

'Triumphant and victorious is he'—*ṣaddîq w^{e}nôšā‘ hû'* [29]—the description is almost identical with that of Yahweh in Isa. 45:21, although the ordinary reader of the RSV (from which most of the biblical quotations in this article are taken) might not suspect it. The original affinity between the two passages is preserved better in the older translations, from the Septuagint (*δίκαιος καὶ σωτήρ* in Isa. 45:21; *δίκαιος καὶ σῴζων* in Zech. 9:9) to the RV ('a just God and a saviour' . . . 'just, and having salvation'). Zion's king comes in Yahweh's name to accomplish Yahweh's work.

VIII

So, in the Gospel record, Jesus' entry into Jerusalem in fulfilment of Zech. 9:9 presents him as the king who comes in the name of the Lord to fulfil his work of *ṣ^{e}dāqāh* and *y^{e}šû‘āh* for his people[30]—or, in a striking Lukan expression, to accomplish his Exodus at Jerusalem.[31] In him, according to the consensus of New Testament witness, the God of Israel reveals himself supremely as the Saviour God, *δίκαιος καὶ δικαιῶν*, as Paul puts it (Rom. 3:26). The presentation of the redemptive work of Christ in terms of the

Exodus motif in so many strands of New Testament teaching[32] shows how primitive was the Christian use of this motif—going back, quite probably, to the period of Jesus' ministry. Jesus' contemporaries freely identified him as a second Moses—the expectation of a second Moses played an important part in popular eschatology at the time[33]—and with the expectation of a second Moses went very naturally the expectation of a second Exodus. One might have thought, in view of the identity of name, that Jesus would have been more readily thought of as a second Joshua ('Yahweh is salvation'). The second Joshua concept does indeed appear here and there in the New Testament[34]—and the saving significance of the name is made explicit in Matt. 1:21 ('you shall call his name Jesus, for he will save his people from their sins')—but the second Moses concept is much more prominent. The coincidence of Jesus' death with the Passover season no doubt helped the interpretation of his work as a new Exodus, in which the God of Israel had once more 'visited and redeemed his people'.

Traces are not lacking, either, even in the New Testament, of the conflict imagery which was repeatedly used in Old Testament times to set forth the saving act of God. In the teaching of Jesus it finds expression in the parable of the invasion of the strong man's fastness and the plundering of his goods by a stronger than himself.[35] In the Pauline writings we have the picture of the crucified Christ disarming the hostile 'principalities and powers' and driving them in triumph before him.[36]

But above all it is in the Apocalypse, that 'rebirth of images', as Dr Austin Farrer has called it, that the primeval motif of conflict comes into its own again, this time to depict the Christian salvation. The seven-headed dragon, the age-old antagonist of righteousness, is identified with the old serpent of Eden and with the malevolent accuser of God's elect.[37] But the victory over him and his minions is won in a new fashion. The conqueror-in-chief is the Davidic Messiah, 'the lion of the tribe of Judah', who appears however as the sacrificed Lamb restored to life after winning his victory by submission to death;[38] his followers share his victory by similar submission. When the dragon assaults them, 'they have conquered him by the blood of the Lamb and by the word of their testimony, for they loved not their lives even unto death' (Rev. 12:11). This victory is hailed as the final manifestation and vindication of the Saviour God;[39] it is greeted by a loud voice proclaiming in heaven: 'Now the salvation and the power and the kingdom of our God and the authority of his Christ have come' (Rev. 12:10).

NOTES

[1] So AV and ASV.

[2] *τοῦ μεγάλου θεοῦ καὶ σωτῆρος ἡμῶν Ἰησοῦ Χριστοῦ* (Tit. 2:13); *τοῦ θεοῦ ἡμῶν καὶ σωτῆρος Ἰησοῦ Χριστοῦ* (2 Pet. 1:1).

[3] So RV, RSV, NEB.

[4] Cf. H. Kosmala, *Hebräer-Essener-Christen* (Leiden, 1959), pp. 135 ff.

[5] The expression *θεοὶ σωτῆρες* was applied in a formal sense to Roman rulers at an earlier date; thus as early as 166 B.C. Prusias II of Bithynia addressed the Roman senate as *θεοὶ σωτῆρες* (Polybius, *Hist.* xxx. 16); but this is a far cry from a claim to the honours appropriate to a divine saviour.

[6] Cf. E. Stauffer, *Christ and the Caesars* (London, 1955), pp. 138 ff.; C.D. Morrison, *The Powers that Be* (London, 1960), pp. 90 ff., 134 f.; C. F. D. Moule, *The Birth of the New Testament* (London, 1962), pp. 110 f.

[7] *χριστὸς κύριος*, as in Ps. Sol. 17:36.

[8] Cf. W. L. Knox, 'The "Divine Hero" Christology in the New Testament', HTR 41 (1948), 229 ff.

[9] Pindar, *Nem.* i. 35 ff.; Theocritus, *Id.* xxiv. 26 ff., etc.

[10] Cf. Job 9:8; Ps. 77:19; Isa. 19:1; Deut. 33:26.

[11] W. Cowper.

[12] Cf. Job 9:13, 'God will not turn back his anger; beneath him bowed the helpers of Rahab.'

[13] Here *bārîaḥ* is translated 'crooked' in AV, as is *ʿᵃqallātôn* in Isa. 27:1 (see n. 18 below); hence the 'crooked serpent' of Wesley's hymn quoted above.

[14] Texts 137; 133; 68.

[15] Cf. F. M. Cross and D. N. Freedman, 'The Song of Miriam', *JNES* 14 (1955), 237 ff.

[16] Cf. Job 41:1.

[17] In one of the most recent commentaries on Isaiah—*Isaiah 1–39* (London, 1962)—J. Mauchline includes Isa. 27:1 among passages in the 'Isaiah Apocalypse' (Isa. 24–7) which 'may be genuine Isaianic material' (p. 196).

[18] Text 67:I:1–3. The Hebrew adjectives applied to Leviathan in Isa. 27:1 are *bārîaḥ* (as in Job 26:13) and *ʿᵃqallātôn* (not elsewhere in OT); the Ugaritic equivalents in the passage quoted are *brḥ* and *ʿqltn*.

[19] Rev. 12:3.

[20] Cf. J. H. Eaton, *Obadiah, Nahum, Habakkuk and Zephaniah* (London, 1961), pp. 108 ff.; W. F. Albright, 'The Psalm of Habakkuk', *Studies in Old Testament*

Prophecy presented to T. H. Robinson (ed. H. H. Rowley, Edinburgh, 1950), pp. 1 ff.

[21] Heb. *y^e^šû^c^āh*, 'salvation'.

[22] Perhaps the most striking personification of the deep (*t^e^hôm*) in the Old Testament.

[23] Cf. A. R. Johnson, *Sacral Kingship in Ancient Israel* (Cardiff, 1955), pp. 54 ff.

[24] The latter view is maintained by A. R. Johnson (op. cit., pp. 107 ff.).

[25] It must be pointed out that some scholars think it was the language of Isa. 40–55 that influenced the liturgy, and not *vice versa*; so notably N. H. Snaith, according to whom, even if a pre-exilic New Year festival existed in Israel, Pss. 93 and 95–9 'could never have belonged to it, for they are demonstrably dependent upon Second-Isaiah' (*The Psalms: A Short Introduction* [London, 1945], p. 19; cf. his *The Jewish New Year Festival* [London, 1947], pp. 195 ff.).

[26] Heb. *'îš milḥāmāh*, as in Exod. 15:3.

[27] E.g., in Isa. 41:14; 43:14; 44:6, 24; 47:4; 48:17; 49:7, 26; 54:5, 8.

[28] His *ṣ^e^dāqāh*, with which his *t^e^šû^c^āh* stands in synonymous parallelism (Isa. 46:13).

[29] Literally 'righteous and delivered' (i.e. 'blessed with victory').

[30] Cf. F. F. Bruce, 'The Book of Zechariah and the Passion Narrative', BJRL 43 (1960–1), 336 ff.

[31] Luke 9:31.

[32] Cf. 1 Cor. 5:7 f.; 10:1 ff.; Heb. 3:7 ff.; Jude 5.

[33] In terms of Deut. 18:15 ff. (cf. John 6:14; 7:40; Acts 3:22 f.; 7:37). Cf. F. F. Bruce, *Biblical Exegesis in the Qumran Texts* (London, 1960), pp. 46 ff.

[34] Cf. Heb. 4:8. The leader into the earthly rest of Canaan bears the same name as the leader into the 'rest that remains for the people of God'.

[35] Mark 3:27 and parallels.

[36] Col. 2:15.

[37] Rev. 12:9. The dragon's ten horns are derived from Dan. 7:7. The fact that the imperial beast of Rev. 13:1; 17:3 also has seven heads and ten horns indicates that he is an agent of the great dragon.

[38] Rev. 5:5 ff.

[39] It is followed, strikingly enough, by a *ἱερὸς γάμος*—but that is another story.

V

BUDDHIST SAVIOURS

by

EDWARD CONZE

I

IN the interest of terminological precision the Sanskrit terms corresponding to 'save' and 'saviour' must first be ascertained. When the Baptists of Serampore translated the New Testament in 1808, they used *trāṇa* for 'salvation' and *trātur* for 'saviour', the root being *trai*, to protect. Just so the Bactrian coins had translated *sōtēr* as *trātur*. Monier Williams's *A Dictionary of English and Sanskrit* (1851) gives further equivalents derived from the roots *raksh*, *pāl*, *gup*, to guard, defend, protect, *tṛī* cs. to carry across ((*nis*) *tāraka*, etc.), *uddhṛi*, to extricate and *muc*, to liberate ((*pari*) *mokshaka*). In addition we may mention *nātha*, helper, protector and *śaraṇa*, refuge. In fact, however, Buddhist terminology has no exact equivalent to the Christian conception of a 'saviour'. H. A. Jaeschke in his *Tibetan-English Dictionary* tells us that in Tibet Protestant missionaries used *skyabs-mgon* (*śaraṇa* + *nātha*) for 'Saviour, Redeemer, Christ', whereas Catholics seem to prefer *blu-pa-po*, from *blu-ba*, to redeem (a pawn, pledge, or security). Neither of these words was ever used by Buddhists, as the dictionaries of Das and Lokesh Chandra make quite clear.

It will be best to first describe the Buddhist beliefs about 'saviours' in the actual words of the texts themselves. In many ways they are so similar to Christian views that missionaries have often seen them as a counterfeit gospel deliberately created by the

Devil to deceive the faithful. At the same time, when the exact words of the originals are faithfully rendered into English it becomes obvious that there are no precise equivalents to the key terms, that the finer shades of meaning and the emotional flavours and overtones differ throughout, that much of this teaching must seem strange to Christians and that in fact the logic behind it is at variance with all the basic presuppositions of Christianity. From the very start we must be careful to eschew such loaded words as worship, prayer, sin, love, eternal or supernatural, and instead use more neutral terms such as revere (= to regard with extreme respect), vow, evil, devotion, deathless and supernormal, and we must also distrust any description of the Buddhist doctrine which, without many qualifications, attributes to the saviours 'grace', 'mercy' or 'forgiveness'.

(1) The famous 24th chapter of the *Lotus of the Good Law*[1] contains all the main ingredients of our theme. There we read that all those beings 'who experience sufferings will, on hearing the name of Avalokiteśvara, the Bodhisattva, the great being, be set free (*parimucyeran*) from their ills'. What they have to do is 'to learn' (*grahaṇa*) his name and to 'bear it in mind' (*dhārayati*), to 'invoke' or 'implore' him (*ākrandaṃ kuryuḥ*), to 'pay homage' to him, to 'recollect' (*smarato*) and to 'revere' him (*pūjayati*). 'Think of him (*smarathā*), think of him, without hesitation, / Of Avalokiteśvara, the being so pure! / In death, disaster and calamity, / He is the saviour, refuge and resort (*trāṇu bhoti śaraṇaṃ parāyaṇam*).'

The 'merit' derived from bearing in mind his name, or of even once paying homage to him, is 'immeasurable' and lasts through many aeons. Avalokiteśvara is 'endowed with inconceivable virtues'. For aeons he has 'purified his Vow (*praṇidhāna*)'. Great 'might' (*prabhāva*) is attributed to him, and much is made of his miraculous, psychic and magical powers (*maha-rddhika*, *vikurvaṇa-prātihārya*, *māyopama-samādhi*). 'He has reached perfection in wonderworking power (*ṛddhī-bala*), / He is trained in abundant (*vipula*) cognition and skill in means.' He 'gives fearlessness to frightened beings', he is their 'saviour' (*trātaru*) and 'destroys all sorrow, fear and ill'.

There is, however, nothing unique about Avalokiteśvara, and he does no more than all Bodhisattvas are bidden to do. In the *Prajñāparamitā*, for instance, we read:

Desirous of the welfare of the world with its gods, men and asuras, desirous to benefit it, to make it happy, to make it secure, the Bodhisattva, when he has seen those ills which afflict beings on the plane of Samsāra, produces an attitude of mind (*cittotpāda*) in which he reflects: 'Having crossed over (*tīrṇa*), we shall help across (*tārayema*) those beings who have not yet crossed! Freed we shall free those beings who are not yet free! Comforted we shall comfort those beings who are as yet without comfort! Gone to Nirvana we shall lead to Nirvana those beings who have not yet got there!'[2]

More specifically the Bodhisattvas promise that, on having won full enlightenment, 'we will become a shelter (*trāṇam*) for the world, a refuge, the place of rest (*layanam*), the final resort (*parāyaṇam*), islands, lights and leaders of the world!'[3]

(2) From the earliest times onwards the Buddhists have described salvation as a process of crossing over.[4] In later times *Tārā*, the deity who ferries across (*tārayati*), became the 'Saviouress' *par exellence*. At one stage of her development she is closely connected with Avalokiteśvara,[5] and conceived analogously to him, as a kind of female counterpart who in China then evolved into the female Kwan Yin. She is said to have emerged from a tear he shed when beholding the misery of the world, or from a blue ray emanating from his eyes, or, alternatively, she 'arose from the countless filaments of the lotus-face of the Saviour of the triple world',[6] i.e. of Avalokiteśvara. Or, again, the Tārās are 'the mothers of the world, born of the power of Amitābha's vow and understanding, endowed with great compassion, created for the world's saving.'[7] And so, intent on freeing all beings from birth-and-death, the Tārā can say:

It is for the protection of the world that I have been produced by the Jinas. In places of terror, which bristle with swords, and where dangers abound, / When only my (108) names are recollected, I always protect all beings, I will ferry them across (*tārayishyāmi*) the great flood of their manifold fears. / Therefore the great Seers sing of me in the world under the name of Tārā.

What is needed is to 'correctly repeat her names' and Tārā will 'fulfil all hopes.' 'These 108 names have been proclaimed for your welfare; / They are mysterious, wonderful, secret, hard to get even by Gods; / They bring luck and good fortune, destroy all evil, / Heal all sickness and bring ease to all beings.' Then follows a catalogue of the benefits derived from their recital, and they include everything that worldly or unworldly men may desire, from wealth, health, cleverness and success in litigation to spiritual virtues and the promotion of enlightenment. 'Whoever meditates on our Blessed Lady in a lonely mountain cave, he will behold her face to face with his own eyes. And the Blessed Lady herself bestows upon him his very respiration, and all else. Not to say any more, she puts the very Buddhahood, so hard to win, in the very palm of his hand.'[8] She 'alone by herself, effectively removes all evil by the fact of her name being heard or recollected (*smṛtyā*),'[9] for 'her mercy flows out to all creatures without distinction.'[10]

(3) In Buddhist mythology Avalokiteśvara and Tārā, two Bodhisattvas, are held to be dependent on a perfectly enlightened Buddha—the Buddha *Amitābha*. The texts contain some information about Amitābha's antecedent 'Vow'[11]. Aeons ago, when he was the monk Darmākara he pronounced 48 Vows in front of the Buddha Lokeśvararāja. The 18th Vow is generally held to be the most important, and its essence is the promise that 'when the time comes for me to become a Buddha, I will not enter into full enlightenment unless all beings who believe in me and love me with all their hearts are able to win rebirth in my kingdom if they should wish to do so'. Once reborn in this Buddha-realm, they can be trained for enlightenment, 'because no being can be turned back from the supreme enlightenment if he has heard the name of the Lord Amitābha, and, on hearing it, with one single thought raises his heart to Him with a resolve connected with serene faith'. As a result of this Vow those who rely on Amitābha's 'promise' and 'solemn oath' will be reborn in the 'Happy Land' where they

will receive further training from Him. The faithful express their belief by invoking the Buddha's name ('Homage to the Buddha Amitābha!', 'Nembutsu' in Japanese). Shinran has formulated the doctrine in a somewhat extreme form:[12]

At the very moment the desire to call the Nembutsu is awakened in us in the firm faith that we can attain rebirth in the Pure Land through the saving grace of the Inconceivable Grand Vow, the all-embracing, none-forsaking virtue of Amida is conferred on us. Once belief in Amida's Vow is established, no other virtue is necessary, for there is no goodness that surpasses Nembutsu. . . . One who strives to accumulate merits through his own efforts is not in accord with Amida's Grand Will, since he lacks absolute, pure faith in its power. But if he re-orients his ego-centred mind and acquiesces in Amida's Grand Will, he will attain rebirth in the True Land of Fulfilment. . . . To be egoless means leaving good and evil to the natural working of karmic law and surrendering wholeheartedly to the Grand Vow. . . . For rebirth in the Pure Land cleverness is not necessary,—just complete and unceasing absorption in gratitude to Amida.

(4.) Avalokiteśvara, Tārā and Amitābha are three Saviours who belong to one 'family' (*kula*). They are connected with the world-system of Sukhāvatī, the Paradise or 'Buddha-field', which is situated far in the West. This Western Paradise has made an exceptionally strong impact on the imagination of the Buddhists, in accordance with a so far unexplained propensity of the archaic mythological imagination which in many cultures has placed the 'Islands of the Blessed' into the West.[13] But there are many, many more. The Scriptures mention thousands of Buddhas and Bodhisattvas, and dozens have become objects of cults in various parts of Asia. Though they may differ in minor details from the Amitābha family, they are all variations on the same theme of which the main outlines have been given, and there is no point in describing them any further.

II

What is common to all these 'saviours', however, is that they were unknown to original Buddhism and that the 'Hīnayāna' continued to ignore them, with the solitary exception of Maitreya, the coming Buddha. In fact, Amidism and similar cults may well be considered as almost a new religion, which arose five hundred years after the founder's death and owed much to contact with the non-Indian world. According to some it has completely departed from the original doctrine, turning it into the exact opposite of itself. The protagonists of the older Buddhism often claim that the 'historical Buddha' was not a 'saviour', that, as distinct from Christianity, Buddhism knows no external saviours, and that everyone must save himself and no one can save another. With the somewhat extreme views of Shinran we may contrast the equally extreme views of the present Theravāda orthodoxy in Ceylon. It will suffice to quote just one representative, the Ven. Walpola Rahula,[14] who, in the words of Professor Demiéville, presents an 'aspect of Buddhism'—'humanist, rational, Socratic in some respects, Evangelic in others, or again almost scientific'—which 'has for its support a great deal of authentic scriptural evidence' (see below, p. 77). Now let us listen to the Ven. *bhikkhu*:

A man has the power to liberate himself from all bondage through his own personal effort and intelligence. . . . If the Buddha is to be called a 'saviour' at all, it is only in the sense that he discovered and showed the Path to Liberation, Nirvana. But we must tread the Path ourselves. . . . According to the Buddha, man's emancipation depends on his own realization of the Truth, and not on the benevolent grace of a god or any external power as a reward for his obedient good behaviour. . . . Almost all religions are built on faith,—rather 'blind' faith it must seem. But in Buddhism emphasis is laid on 'seeing', knowing, understanding, and not on faith or belief.[15]

Though we must, of course, bear in mind that the extreme positions of Shinran and Rahula are rare and untypical. Far from sharing Shinran's exclusive reliance on Amida's Vow, the bulk of the Mahāyānists advocated innumerable additional practices as aids to salvation. Far from sharing Rahula's excessive rationalism, even the non-Mahāyānists have at all times and to a varying extent made provision for attitudes which can be properly called 'religious'. Rahula assures us that 'among the founders of religions the Buddha was the only teacher who did not claim to be other than a human being, pure and simple'. It is true that to win enlightenment the Buddha used only resources which are open to all humans and not beyond the capacity of human nature as such, and that his powers are supernormal merely because they are based on highly developed moral purification and mental concentration.[16] But though the Buddha was a human being, he was certainly a most extraordinary one. Like Jesus and Mohammed he had supernormal powers and could work miracles; his body had thirty-two special marks and much of it refused to burn up on his funeral pyre; and, though essentially a teacher who exhorts and instructs, he was more than an ordinary human teacher because omniscient, infallible and completely dependable. At least that is the tradition of all the schools. In addition he is often called *Bhagavad* and *Tathāgata*, and both these words have distinctly numinous connotations.[17] His followers appreciated not only his teaching, but also his mere presence, they craved for the very sight of HIM and expected protection from being 'brought to mind' by the Buddhas and Lords. They habitually venerated relics, Stūpas, Caityas and the Bodhi-tree, which were the visible signs of his presence on earth. Though, of course, a Buddhist's devotions are not so much petitions to a God, but a means by which he renews his own courage and confidence. The rationalist orthodoxy of Ceylon has a vision of Buddhism which is as truncated and impoverished as the fideism of Shinran, and it is no accident that they are both geographically located at the outer periphery of the Buddhist world.

III

Even the basic act of 'taking refuge' with the Buddha, Dharma and Samgha, which is common to all followers of the Dharma, involves a certain amount of faith, and may call forth devotion on the part of those who are thus inclined.[18] Essentially, however, it implies trust in the Buddha as a 'saviour' in the strictly limited sense that he had discovered the doctrine (*dharma*) which, if properly applied, must without any doubt lead to salvation. More than this is implied when we speak of Avalokiteśvara, etc., as 'saviours'. They effect the salvation of beings by more than the enunciation of a transcendental doctrine.[19] But all that is said about them respects in every way the framework of the original teaching from which the later developments have not radically departed and from which they can be derived without a break. Though the activities of these Bodhisattvas must seem quite miraculous and extraordinary, they operate strictly within the law of *karma*, and their power to do good is based on the enormous amount of 'merit' (*puṇya*) which they have accumulated, on the vast extent of the 'roots of good' (*kuśalamūla*) which they have 'matured'. 'Merit' is that quality of an action which leads to future happiness, either worldly or supramundane. As long as we stay within the strictly *moral* sphere, there is some correspondence and proportion between virtue and reward, between crime and punishment. So we are told in *Majjhima Nikāya* no. 135[20] of the karmic effects of seven wholesome and seven unwholesome modes of action. The first normally lead to rebirth in the hells, the second to rebirth in the heavens. But in case the offender is reborn as a human being, then the punishment fits the crime. Killers will be short-lived, the jealous will be people of little account, the stingy will be poor, and so on. And likewise, those who have abstained from killing will be long-lived, etc. From other sources we learn that a gluttonous person becomes a hog, a rapacious one a tiger, etc.

But this correspondence no longer holds good when we move into the *spiritual* sphere. An action is 'spiritual' when it is (1) directed to a transcendental object, or (2) completely disinterested. Whereas the reward of moral actions is limited, that of spiritual acts has no limit, and 'bears no comparison' to the merit of moral actions. This has two consequences:

(1) A simple act of faith, when turned on the Buddha or on a proclamation of his Dharma, produces an inconceivable amount of merit which may outweigh countless moral defaults. A well-known stanza which must be fairly old, because common to many traditions,[21] tells us that the Buddha is inconceivable, and so is his

Dharma, and in consequence faith in the conconceivable also produces an inconceivable reward. The commentary explains 'inconceivable' (*acintiya*) as 'that which seems incredible to unbelievers,'[22] and alludes to what is said in a Sūtra about the enormous consequences of 'one single thought of faith'.[23] In consequence a faithful and devout longing for the Transcendental purifies the believer to quite an extraordinary extent, and through faith he jumps ahead by leaps and bounds, whereas morality, meditation and wisdom can advance him only at a comparative snail's pace.

(2) A Bodhisattva reaches on the seventh stage a condition where, now a 'celestial Bodhisattva',[24] he is quite disinterested in what he does, and acts exclusively out of consideration for others. He has solved all his own personal problems, he could enter Nirvana, but during the 7th, 8th and 9th stages of his career he chooses to stay in the world. The fact that he could enter Nirvana shows that he has enough merit for himself, and that all the further merit generated by his good deeds has no karmic effects on him and cannot benefit him personally. So he bestows it on others through what is called the 'dedication of merit,'[25] drawing on what is known to Catholics as the *thesaurus ecclesiae*, or the *thesaurus meritorum Christi et Sanctorum*.[26]

In this way the believer's progress is immensely accelerated, partly because he generates extra merit by his acts of faith, and partly because he benefits from the merits generated by the celestial Bodhisattvas. For the Mahāyāna salvation does not depend on the teaching alone, but on manipulating 'merit' in such a way that conditions are produced in which it can be appreciated and understood. What is the use of preaching the holy doctrine to the mill hands of Manchester?

So far about the karmic side. A few words must still be said about three other aspects of the Bodhisattva's activity. (1) His *motive* is compassion, pure and simple. (2) One important step in *carrying out* his compassionate intentions is the Vow (*praṇidhāna*), which occurs twice in his career. First at the beginning, when he resolves to win enlightenment and to save all beings,[27] and then again on the ninth stage of his career, when the Vow has become a completely disinterested intention (*anābhoga-praṇidhāna*)[28] which, as a purely spiritual act, can have the most marvellous effects. And then (3), most difficult to understand for modern Europeans, there are his *wonderworking powers*. They are the normal concomitants of the fourth stage of trance[29] and the celestial Bodhisattva has completely mastered them. In consequence, subjectively his body is no longer the gross material body of earthlings, but the 'dharmic' body of the sages, an 'adamantine' body far surpassing all terrestrial circumstances; objectively, the world he deals with is not the world of brutish, given facts which hem in the average worldling, but a world of artefacts, conjured up by his magical power, a magic show generated by his unwavering concentration (*māyopama-samādhi*). The good which he does to others lies not only in his teaching, but in his magical transformations which open the minds of people to its message. This is hard to believe, but essential to Mahāyāna doctrine.

IV

We can now return to the problem of the apparent antithesis between the Buddhism of Faith and that of Self-exertion. In Japan it is known as the contrast between *Tariki* (Other-Power) and *Jiriki* (Self-Power),[30] the first being represented by the Pure Land schools which thereby seem to side with the theistic religions, and the second by Zen which has Taoism for one of its principal antecedents. It is, however, arbitrary and misleading to postulate a real opposition between those who just passively sit about waiting for somebody else to release them from their troubles, and those who nobly and strenuously exert themselves. The fact is that those who exert themselves must have plenty of faith to induce them to turn their energies in that particular direction,[31] and that those who wait for Amitābha to take them to his Paradise will have plenty of opportunity to exert themselves when they get there. 'Self-power' and 'Other-power' constitute a duality, and all duality is *per se* falsely imagined and cannot possibly be ultimately valid.

Moreover, in a system of thought in which there is no 'self', the distinction between 'self' and 'other' is at best provisional only.

Likewise, from a system which declares all dharmas to be 'inactive' (*nirīhaka*), no dogmatic statement about the agent of salvation can be expected. The situation differs greatly from that prevailing within Christianity. As conceived by both Christians and Buddhists, salvation, or emancipation, must obviously involve the co-operation of the individual with some spiritual force. To Christians it has seemed a meaningful undertaking to find some overall dogmatic formulation which would define the relative strength of the two factors for all cases. In consequence innumerable discussions of incredible subtlety have tried to determine the relative weight of divine grace and the power of man's own good works, as well as the relation of the Divine Will to the freedom of the human will. Dogmatic formulations of this kind have not been attempted by Buddhists, who believe that circumstances alter cases.

For instance, we may read that it is the Tathāgata who 'gives' (*dạsyāmi*) to suffering beings 'both pleasures and the Final Rest.'[32] On the other hand we have, 'you yourself must make the effort (*kiccam ātappam*), the Tathāgatas do but point the way (*akkhātāro*)'.[33] 'Everyone is his own protector (*nātha*); what other protector could there be?'[34] 'Dwell in such a way that you are an island and a refuge to yourselves, and do not seek any other refuge!'[35] Buddhists offer two distinct explanations for the discrepancy between such *ad hoc* pronouncements. The Theravādins believe that that those which stress 'self-striving' belong to an earlier and more authentic tradition, whereas the stress on faith and the power of the Buddhas represents later concessions to human weakness. Their assertions are incapable of proof, and I personally prefer the Mahāyāna explanation according to which all statements for or against 'self-activity' are pedagogic devices, not propositions aiming at universal theoretical validity. They are advice given to people of different temperament and situated on varying levels of spiritual maturity and endowment, suitable to some and unsuitable to others, and there is no antagonism between the higher and the lower.

In its true reality salvation (*moksha*) is the fading away of the bonds which imprison men in the conditioned and defiled world of Samsāra, and the restoration of the absolute freedom of the unconditioned and undefiled reality of Nirvana. What or who then is saved? Nothing and nobody. None of what is here can be carried over there, for Nirvana is *das ganz Andere*. Nor is anyone ever saved, for 'anyone who distinguishes between self and other is still under the influence of karma',[36] and therefore unsaved.

Ineffable in its true reality, the process of salvation can nevertheless be viewed from three points of view: (1) as the result of an external personified agent accepted in faith; (2) as the result of self-striving guided by an infallible teacher; (3) as the doing of the Absolute, or the *dharmadhātu*, with which Amitābha is readily identified. Of the three viewpoints the third would be the most valid because, as against the first it is based on wisdom, so much superior to faith, and as against the second it realizes that no one can really rely on a 'self' which is a mere fiction, and that, in any case, a puny individual is unlikely to have the strength to direct his own spiritual destiny. And as to the division between viewpoints (1) and (2), mystics generally tend to blur the dividing lines between the external and the internal. 'Look within, thou *art* Buddha.' 'I and my father are one.' 'I am not the doer, mine is not the doer.' 'It is not I that speak but my Father who is speaking in me.' And so on. ' "Not my will but thine be done", he says to the universe, and begins to feel that the Power which he seeks within, by which he heals and teaches and makes one, is not *his* power within or without, but a force which works in its own sweet way.'[37]

V

These doctrines obviously cry out to be compared with Christianity. From a Christian point of view this comparison has been ably carried out by the Père de Lubac S.J.[38] for the Roman Catholics, and by H. Butschkus[39] for the Lutherans. My own comparison, made from a Buddhist point of view, is here constrained by the need for brevity which must excuse a certain bluntness which, in any case, should not offend those who were told to turn the other cheek.

(1) While Buddhists would be willing to accept Jesus as one Bodhisattva among many, the idea that he is unique, as the one son of God, and so on, is anathema to them, as likely to lead to intolerance, persecution and bloodshed. Buddhists desire to multiply saviours, not to restrict them. (2) The great stress laid on 'the blood of Jesus Christ' and on the Crucifixion[40] is distinctly distasteful to Buddhists. (3) Salvation consists in the removal of ignorance. It cannot be effected by the extirpation of a sin which is seen as a rebellion against God. A man may be morally without blemish, and yet for aeons to come he may have to remove the vestiges of his ignorance before he can become fully enlightened. (4) There is no 'forgiveness of sin'. Karma takes its course, and the consequences of acts can never be annulled, though in time they may wear off and though spiritual practices may to some extent whittle them away.

(5) Buddhists have no historical sense, and no one wants to know exactly when Amitābha made his Vow, or when the Bodhisattva sacrificed himself for the tigress.[41] Nor is this regarded as a weakness. The 'historical basis' of Christianity is not always an aid to faith, and the dissection of the Resurrection accounts has often appeared to leave them without much solid foundation in fact. (6) Centuries of theological controversy have habituated Christians so much to the opposition between 'good works' and 'grace' that they find it not easy to see how 'grace' can be based on good works, or 'merit', as explained in III. (7) It comes natural to Buddhists to subordinate the personal to the suprapersonal, i.e. the Buddha to the Dharma, Amitābha to the *dharmadhātu*. This goes very much against the grain of Christian thought. (8) The higher stages of a 'celestial' Bodhisattva's life show close analogies to the doctrine of the *communicatio idiomatum*. (9) The Mahāyāna assertion that all saviours, Buddhas and Bodhisattvas alike, are mere fictions and images in a dream, that they have issued from the Void and are projections of man's inner consciousness, is well nigh incomprehensible to Christians, who find it hard to believe that anyone can maintain such a thesis in good faith.

This is a rather fumbling way of dealing with a great problem. When we compare the doctrinal formulations of two such religions as Buddhism and Christianity we often feel that they converge so closely that they seem bound to meet at some point. But in fact they never actually do meet, and when we remember the roots and aspirations behind those formulations, a gulf yawns at once. Leaving behind the doctrinal formulations, we may turn to the ideal type of person whom these religions tend to produce. The gulf then widens still more. I once read through a collection of the lives of Roman Catholic saints, and there was not one of whom a Buddhist could fully approve. This does not mean that they were unworthy people, but that they were bad Buddhists, though good Christians. Ultimately, when viewed as pure germinal intuitions, all religions are probably inspired by the same vision of man's true and original nature. In their doctrinal formulations no such unity can be discerned, they seem to be mutually incommensurable, and constant misapprehensions are unavoidable.

NOTES

1 *Saddharmapuṇḍarīka-sūtram*, ed. U. Wogihara and C. Tsuchida (1958), 362–74.

2 E. Conze, *The Gilgit Manuscript of the Ashṭādaśasāhasrikāprajñāpāramitā* (1962), 248.

3 *Ashṭasāhasrikā Prajñāpāramitā*, ed. R. Mitra (1888), 293. These terms are then explained in pp. 294–9.

4 For the details see I. B. Horner, *The Early Buddhist Theory of Man Perfected* (1936).

5 But after A.D. 750, under the influence of the theory of the *Five Jinas*, the green Tārā was assigned to Amoghasiddhi (as in the *Sādhanamālā*, trans. E. Conze, *Buddhist Meditation* (1956), 137) and the Vajratārā to Vajrapāṇi, of the Akshobhya family. At about the same time 'Tārā' became a general term for 'saviouress', or 'helpful goddess', or 'beneficent deity', and this resulted in great indefiniteness and gave her a truly Protean character. Long lists of Tārās were elaborated, some due to separating the services which she may render, while others refer to the localities in which she had a shrine. One of these lists is *The book of praises of the 21 forms of Tārā*, ed. and trans. into German by S. Hummel, *Lamaistische Studien* (1950), 97–109.

6 Hummel 97, of the *rab-tu dpa'-ba'i sgrol-ma.*

7 *The 108 Names of the Holy Tārā*, trans. E. Conze, ed. *Buddhist Texts* (1954), no. 176, p. 197. Also the following quotations are from this source.

8 *Sādhanamālā* in E. Conze, *Buddhist Meditation* (1956), 138–9.

9 Sarvajñamitra, *Sragdharāstotram*, ed. S. Ch. Vidyabhushana (1908), v. 8.

10 *Ibid.* v. 3.

[11] See *Hobogirin*, ed. P. Demiéville (1929), 26; H. de Lubac, *Amida* (1955), 65–7; *Buddhist Texts*, 206. I have glossed over the considerable divergences between the different sources, which would be of interest only in a specialized study.

[12] *Tannisho*, trans. Higashi Honganji (1961), 2, 6, 33, 45.

[13] E. Conze, *Buddhism* (1951), 205; H. de Lubac, *Amida* (1955), 63.

[14] *What the Buddha Taught* (1959), 1–15.

[15] As Winston L. King well expresses the Theravāda theory in a book soon to be published: 'The Buddha is not a saviour in the religious sense. For one cannot address a prayer to him, saying "save me!" Nor make an offering to him to "please" him. Nor expect acts of grace to emanate from him nor experience his love. One reveres the memory of the Buddha as a supreme teacher and example.' For a more extensive explanation of the Theravāda position see *Devotion in Buddhism*, Buddhist Publication Society (1960), Kandy, Ceylon.

[16] Though if we go more deeply into these things, they become also more complicated. The Son of God was also called the Son of Man, and Buddha, the man, was also known as 'the god above the gods'.

[17] See my *Buddhist Thought in India* (1962), 27.

[18] E.g. sGampopa, *The Jewel Ornament of Liberation*, trans. H. V. Guenther (1959), 103 sq.

[19] In fact they rather exert the three functions of the Blessed Lord which are enumerated in *Bhagavadgīta*, IV, 8.

[20] A more elaborate account on the same lines is the *Mahā-Karmavibhanga*, ed. and trad. S. Lévi (1932).

[21] S. Lévi, 153–5, 169–70, 176.

[22] *Ibid.*, 154–5.

[23] See also *Apadāna*, 336, for the miraculous results (*acchariyam*) of one single act of devotion.

[24] *Buddhist Thought in India* (1962), 236–7.

[25] Har Dayal, *The Bodhisattva doctrine in Buddhist Sanskrit Literature* (1932), 188–93; *Buddhist Texts* no. 128.

[26] For the fascinating details see H. Denzinger, *Enchiridion Symbolorum*. Also H. Bechert, *Bruchstücke buddhistischer Versammlungen 1* (1961), 38–9.

[27] A very beautiful poetical description of the Vow is *Samantabhadracaryā-praṇidhānarāja*, now critically edited by S. Devi (1958).

[28] *Daśabhūmikasūtra*, ed. J. Rahder (1926), 73–81.

[29] *Buddhist Scriptures*, trans. E. Conze (1959), 121–33.

[30] The advantages and disadvantages of the two have been well discussed by Chr. Humphreys in *Young East* (1961), 2–4. Of outstanding importance in this context are the studies of D. T. Suzuki, especially *A Miscellany on the Shin Teaching of Buddhism* (1949); *Mysticism, Christian and Buddhist* (1957), 161–214; *The Eastern Buddhist*, III (1925), 285–326, and VII, 1–58 (offprint).

[31] *Buddhist Thought in India*, 47–51.

[32] *Saddharma-puṇḍarīka*, V, v. 18.

[33] See *Dhammapada*, 276. Also M. N., iii, 6, 'A shower of the Way is the Tathagāta'; so also *Saddharmapuṇḍarīka*, V, 115, 20–1.

[34] *Dhammapada*, 160. My translation takes *attā*, etc., as reflexive pronouns; others take them as substantive nouns.

[35] *Dīghanikāya*, in E. Waldschmidt, *Das Mahāparinirvāṇasūtra* (1951), 200. Though this is much less convincing when the context and sequel are considered. Miss I. B. Horner tells me that also the following passages are relevant: A, i, 189, 11, 191; S, iii, 108–9, iv, 179–81, A, ii, 5–6, Iti., 113–15, Sn. 1053, 1064, Dhp. 168–9.

[36] Candrakīrti, *Prasannapadā*, XVI v. 9.

[37] Chr. Humphreys, *Young East* (1961), 4.

[38] *Amida* (1955).

[39] *Luthers Religion und ihre Entsprechung im japanischen Amida-Buddhismus*, n.d. (*c.* 1950?).

[40] The mild Suzuki says in *Mysticism, Christian and Buddhist* (1957), 136: 'The crucified Christ is a terrible sight and I cannot help associating it with the sadistic impulse of a psychically affected brain.'

[41] E. Conze, *Buddhist Scriptures* (1959), 24–6.

VI

SOME ASPECTS OF ANTHROPOMORPHISM

by

J. DUCHESNE-GUILLEMIN

THE microcosm idea, perhaps because it makes everybody feel personally concerned and nicely placed at the centre of all things, has a strong, universal appeal. It is present in many religions and speculations, Zoroastrianism amongst them.

The most explicit passage in Pahlavi literature, *Great Bundahišn*, 189, 3 sq., was studied by Götze who in his famous article 'Persische Weisheit in griechischem Gewande', *Zeitschr. f. Indologie u. Iranistik*, 2, 1923, 60 sq., compared it with a Hippocratic text, the *Περὶ Ἑβδομάδων*. Now, there is a word in the very first sentence of the Pahlavi text, 'the body of man is a *handācak* of the world', which does not seem to have received the attention it deserved. It had come to signify 'manner, analogy' (see Zaehner, *Zurvan*, 1955, 469), but it meant literally 'measure', a meaning still alive in the Modern Persian *ändāzä*. Translated into Greek this would give *μέτρον*, and we would, therefore, be reminded of Protagoras' celebrated sentence, preserved in Plato's *Theaetetus*, 170 d, *πάντων χρημάτων μέτρον ἄνθρωπον*. Since this sentence, diversely interpreted, was often quoted throughout Antiquity, from Plato through Xenophon and Aristotle to Plutarch, it may very well have been known to the Iranians.[1]

But the question of historical influences will not be our chief concern here, as it will be more interesting to place the microcosm idea in a more general, phenomenological perspective. To begin with—without even, for the moment, leaving Iran—the microcosm idea can be combined with that of man as an image of God.

According to the *Dēnkart*, 321, 34, 'all creatures are mirrored in man, who is the symbol (*daxšak*) of Ohrmazd'.

This double connection of man with God and the world might be graphically represented in the following manner:

God
/
Man---------World

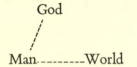

This being so, we may expect to find similar expressions of the other side of the relationship, namely, that between God and the world. This is what we do in fact observe. According to *Great Bundahišn*, 16, 10–11, Ohrmazd carries in himself, like a mother her child, the *mēnōk* (spiritual) form of the world. In a passage preserved by Jayhānī (see Menasce, *Donum . . . Nyberg*, 1954, 52), Ohrmazd says, 'I have created the whole world from myself: the souls of the just from the hair of my head, the skies from my brains, . . ., the sun from my eyes, etc.'

In a more elaborate fashion, the creation of the world is said to have proceeded in successive stages, one of which is a cosmic man. This doctrine has long been somewhat obscured by the difficulty of interpreting a certain term, *asrōk karp*, designating the intermediate stage between 'Infinite light' and 'all the creatures'. But I think it may be shown (as I have tried to do in *East and West*, 1962, and *Unvala Memorial Volume*, 1963) that *asrōk karp* meant 'a form of fire', elsewhere designated as *ātaxš karp*.

From this form of fire, which was 'bright, white, round and manifest afar', all creatures were made. Now, we learn more about this form from Manuščihr who tells us in his *Dātastān i Dēnīk*, Quest. 63, K 35, 177 v. 3, that its name was Ohrmazd: *'kē-š 'nām*[2] *'ān i Ohrmazd . . . būt*. This name may cause surprise, for what could the meaning be of Ohrmazd creating a form called Ohrmazd? All becomes clear, however, if we remember that in Manichaeanism (in which Zurvanite theology was reflected and God was called Zurvan) Ohrmazd was the name of cosmic Man. The original myth seems, therefore, to have told how Zurvan created a spherical body of fire called Ohrmazd.

Be it as it may, Manuščihr goes on to say that within this fo of fire God 'created the entity called Man': *'andar 'ān asrōn ka dāt martōm 'xvānēhīt stig*. And this was Gayōmart, the Primeval Man.

The notions here illustrated will become clearer, I think, when we adduce parallels from other religions. We can for the moment be content with adding three more references to Pahlavi writings. In the *Pahlavi Rivāyat* (Dhabhar, 127–37) the world is created from the body of a giant. It is probable, as Zaehner has shown (*Zurvan*, 136 sq.), that this doctrine was borrowed from the famous Indian Puruṣa-myth. This is evidently the case, as Zaehner has seen (*Zurvan*, 143 sq.), with the slightly different doctrine which divides the body of man 'between the four castes on earth: priesthood (corresponded) to the head, warriorhood to the hands, husbandry to the belly, and artisanship to the feet'. This text occurs, in two slightly different versions, in the *Dēnkart*, 429, 5–10, and in the *Škand Gumānīk Vicār*, I, 20–5. In the first one explicit reference is made to foreign sources, Indian and Greek. The Indian origin is borne out by the passage in the Puruṣasūkta, *RV*, X, 90, 12: 'His mouth was the Brahman; his two arms were made the warrior; his two thighs the vaiśya; from his two feet the śūdra was born.' The length of time between the Vedic hymn and the Pahlavi treatises has unnecessarily embarrassed Zaehner (*Zurvan*, 138), for the doctrine was current in India (cf. Lamotte, *Notes sur la Bhagavad-gītā*, 1924, 94, cited by Menasce, *Une Apologétique mazdéenne*, 1945, 31).

However, a term occurring in the other Pahlavi version (*ŠGV*, I, 10) to describe man as *gēhān i kōtak* 'microcosm' seems to point to Greece.[3] It is not at all excluded that borrowings from both quarters should have concurred in enriching the Iranian doctrine of the Man-World relationship. Glancing back at the other Iranian texts it may be said that they appear to reflect two different views, a rather crude one on the gestation of the world by Ohrmazd, and a more elaborate one on creation by stages. The first stage, Infinite light, is said (*Great Bundahišn*, 11, 2), to have been created by God from his own substance, which is that of material light. That is all, whereas in the *Gathas* we are told of an Entity involved in the creation of light. The passage, in Humbach's translation, slightly revised, ran as follows (*Yasna*, 31, 7): 'He who first created through thought, through intelligence, Truth penetrating the free spaces with lights . . .' It may be that this particular tenet had fallen into oblivion; but it is necessary to recall it, because of the possible parallels which will suggest themselves later on with this role of an entity, which is, as I have tried to show elsewhere,[4] comparable with the Logos.

Before we turn to Israël, and the religions derived therefrom, preparatory to considering Iranian soteriology, it seems advisable to clear the ground by dealing with more aberrant traditions, namely those of the Primitives, China, India, and Greece.

On the Primitives, we may refer to what F. Herrmann says in his *Symbolik in der Religion der Naturvölker*, 1961, 48 sq., on the microcosm idea. He first quotes Baumann to the effect that in the African dual systems 'above' and 'below' clearly refer to the sky-earth couple, and that the carriers of the myth came as invaders with their microcosm-macrocosm idea—an idea characteristic of higher cultures—namely, with an arrangement of the world into sky (sun)–man–right and earth (moon)–woman–left.

Further, on p. 127, the representation of the earth as mother and of the masculine sky is said to have originated in the so-called archaic high-cultures, in the context of the microcosm-macrocosm correspondence in which the king is compared to the sky (or sun) and the queen to the earth (or moon).

The 'supreme being' or 'high god' also belongs here. He is thought of as a goodly old man, and addressed as Father or Grandfather (p. 67). It may also be a woman. 'She gave birth to us in the beginning', the Kagaba say (p. 68). Or it may be both man and woman in one.

In the general frame of primitive thinking both the idea of a supreme god and that of man as a microcosm appear to result from a process of generalization. Taking into account Levi-Strauss' considerations in *La Pensée Sauvage*, 1962,[5] the microcosm idea may be said to be a particular case of man's projection on to his surroundings, namely, the extreme case in which these surroundings are embraced as a whole, as 'the world'. As for the supreme being, it also occupies an extreme position, namely, as the last link in the series of all the imaginable beings into which man could project himself.

Turning now to China and leaving aside the more popular beliefs, we come across the remarkable fact that in China's most typical conception our God-Man-World triangle collapses, is reduced to a Man-World relationship. This is Chinese 'Universism', especially represented in Taoism. We may refer to H. Köster, *Symbolik des chinesischen Universismus*, 1958, 39–40, and to Brandon, *Man and his Destiny*, 1962, 366 (with the footnote): man was regarded as a microcosm. Then, we may recall the myth of the primeval giant P'an-ku: from his breath the wind was born, from his voice thunder, from his right eye the sun, from his left eye the moon, from his hair the plants, etc. Since the myth is found also in Cochin-china, Central Asia, India (the Puruṣa-myth mentioned above), in the Scandinavian sagas, and even in ancient Babylonia, it seems probable that the Indo-Europeans would have known it.[6]

In India, apart from the Puruṣa-myth and its sequels in the *Atharvaveda* and the *Upanishads* (see Filliozat in *Anthropologie religieuse*, 1955, 110 sq., and Brandon, *Man and his Destiny*, 322), there is the remarkable simplification or 'flattening' of the God-Man-World triangle: here it is the world that tends to be ignored, so that there remains simply a God-Man relationship. This is already apparent in the *Upanishads* with their doctrine of the *brahman-ātman* equivalence and of the world as a passing illusion; also in Buddhism, where, despite the denial of both the existence of God and the reality of the world, Buddha himself has taken the place of God, thus uniting in a most thorough fashion humanity and divinity.

An analogy to this Indian attitude is to be found in Gnosticism, as we shall see after dealing with ancient Greece first.

In Greece we come across yet another reduction of the theoretical God-Man-World triangle, this time through suppression of man. I am alluding, of course, to the war declared by Xenophanes, Heraclitus, etc., on anthropomorphism. As a result of this condemnation, we may expect to find expressions of a purely God-World relationship. In fact, with Heraclitus the unity between

God and the world becomes 'a coherent pantheism' (Nestle, cited in Zeller-Mondolfo, *La Filosofia dei Greci*, I, IV, 1961, 407). Thus fragment 67 (Diels) describes God in terms of cosmic oppositions: day-night, winter-summer, war-peace, etc.; according to fragment 30 this Cosmos was not created but is fire ever-living, which should mean (Z.-M., 258) that it is identical with its own generating principle.

What, then, becomes of man? Is he completely left out of this God-World identity? Not at all; but he is subordinate to it, being only intelligible as part of the world, and, on the other hand, having laws which are nourished by the divine law (114). Moreover, thanks to the *logos* idea, man is re-introduced into the picture as in a way co-extensive with the cosmos: for the logos of the soul is so rooted in the eternal logos that it penetrates the whole universe and reaches to the limits of the All (71). This seems to prefigurate the monism of the Stoics; but of this we shall speak further.

On the whole, it is characteristic of the view of Heraclitus, as defined by Jaeger (*Paideia*, 1934) that his philosophy of man was the innermost of three concentric rings: his anthropology is commanded by his cosmology, which in turn depends on his theology. This might be represented in the following diagram:

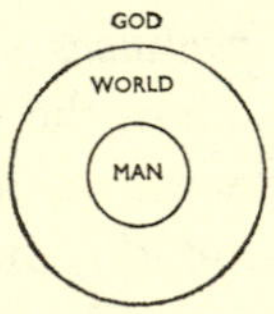

Now, it will be interesting to note that this picture, although purely symbolic, closely resembles that illustrated in the myth. According to Aristophanes, in Plato's *Symposium* primeval man was spherical. This was not a poet's fantasy but, as Ziegler has shown ('Menschen- und Weltenwerden', *Neue Jahrbücher f. d. Klass. Altertum*, 1913, 529), it is an application to man of the Orphic theory of the origin of the world. Since the world was originally spherical—the cosmic egg—so must have been man. The picture would then be:

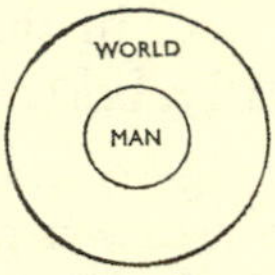

The similitude of this picture with the preceding one is probably not fortuitous. For they both express a tendency characteristic of Greek thinking in the middle of the fifth century, namely, that of explaining man in terms of physics—a sort of anthropomorphism in reverse. For instance, Empedocles not only equates—in a rather banal way—man's hair with leaves and birds' feathers (82, Diels), but says (109) that 'we see Earth by means of Earth, Water by means of Water, divine Air by means of air, etc.' And the same principle, witness Plato in *Phaedrus* 270c, is the very base of Hippocratic medicine: it is not possible, Plato thinks, to comprehend the nature of the soul without that of the universe, nor can we even, if we are to believe Hippocrates, speak of the body without this method.

In the Hippocratic Corpus the man-world correspondence is illustrated several times: not only in the *Περὶ Ἑβδομάδων* alluded to above, p. 83, but in the *Περὶ διαίτης* and other similar texts.[7] This conception was to lead directly to Stoic monism, in which God is identical with the world, which in turn is conceived of as a great human being, whose soul is the Logos.

One is, on the other hand, reminded of the Iranian myth. We can refer to the passage already quoted above, Manušcihr's *Dātastān i Dēnīk*: 'within the "form of fire" (which God had created from infinite light) he now created the entity called man', i.e. Gayōmart, Primeval Man. And according to *Great Bundahišn*, 21, 6, Gayōmart was as broad as he was high, which can hardly mean anything else but that he was spherical.[8] In this he imitated, so to speak, the sphericity of the 'form of fire'.

Here we may be allowed a short historical parenthesis, for an inference suggests itself as to the connection between the Greek and the Iranian myth. Since the idea of a spherical universe probably originated with Anaximander[8a] and passed from Greece to Iran it may be that the myth of a spherical Primeval Man, which justifies itself, as we have seen, in the context of fifth-century Greek thinking, was similarly borrowed from the Greeks by Zoroastrianism.

To return to Greece. Orphism was pregnant with a more radical tendency, in that it considered above all man's fall and his salvation, thus tending to leave the world out—as was the case in the *Upanishads* and Buddhism. This tendency came to a head in Gnosticism, Christian or pagan. But Gnosticism cannot be understood apart from the heritage of Israël.

Israël presents its own version, sharply characterized, of the God-Man-World relationship in that, while stressing the affinity between God and man, the latter being made 'in the image, after the likeness' of the former, it tends on the contrary—in reaction against the nature-cults of the Gentiles—to sever the connection between God and the world. There is no common measure between the two: the world does not spring from God's substance. It is created 'ex nihilo'. It would be possible to represent this in the following pattern:

God
/
Man World

However, this is not, of course, the whole story. For God's creative word, the 'Fiat Lux' of Genesis, came to be hypostatized, personified in the manner in which it was represented in Egypt, Sumer and Babylonia, as a distinct being. Egypt used to figure it concretely as a little man issuing forth from the mouth of the god whose will he expressed, whose orders he carried. The Second Isaiah (55:11) saw this word quite concretely: 'So shall my word (*dabhar*) be that goeth forth out of my mouth: it shall not return unto me void, but it shall accomplish that which I please.' Similarly Psalm 147:15: 'He sendeth forth his commandment upon earth: his word runneth very swiftly.'

In order now to translate this 'word', the Septuagint used the best term available in Greek, namely *logos*, although its background and connotation were rather different. It was then used in the Greek Book of Wisdom (18:14–16), in which the word of God is personified as a warrior. This concretization was probably helped along by that of Wisdom herself (*Hoxma-Sophia*), a process which had in turn already been stimulated by Hellenistic Stoicism.

This logos-notion was further elaborated by Philo, with whom we shall briefly deal later. As for the image of the war-like logos, it was to be taken up and developed in St John's Book of Revelation (19:13 sq.). But the most important text—overshadowing the Christian and Jewish Apocalypses, Jubilees (12:5), IV Esra (9:5), the Syriac Baruch (14:17)—is certainly the Prologue to the fourth gospel, thanks to which the Logos notion became the very centre of the Christian theology.

Jesus was there identified with the Logos, who consequently tended to be primarily regarded as Saviour, rather than Creator. However, his creative character of the Logos—inherent in its very definition—could not be entirely forgotten; and since, on the other hand, the Incarnation was an extra-temporal process, making the Logos 'true man form all eternity' (cf. Joh. 3:13 and 6:22, and 1 Cor. 15:47),[9] it follows that in this theology creation can be represented as follows:

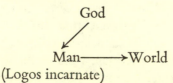

God
↙
Man ⟶ World
(Logos incarnate)

But this gives, of course, only one side of the picture, leaving aside Eschatology. With the complete picture, Christianity achieved a new pattern, perfectly symmetrical, and this resulted from a projection of the Jesus figure both into the past and into the future. For Jesus, as Man-God, is first the Logos-Creator, then the historical Saviour who was crucified under Pontius Pilatus, and finally the eschatological Saviour and Judge.

This perfect symmetry and simplicity is unique, although the trend that it consummates was rather wide-spread, as we shall see presently when dealing with Gnosticism and with Mazdean soteriology. But first a word about Philo.

Philo's conception of the Logos, which was to play a decisive role in the formation of the Christian theology, was connected, as C. Colpe has shown,[10] with the idea, probably Stoic in origin, that the world is a gigantic man: 'According to *De Vita Mos.*, II, 34, the whole world takes the place of the Logos. In *De Ebr.* 30, the whole world is called "Son of God", thereby receiving a predicate which otherwise very often applied to the Logos. If "Son of God" was thus predicated of the universe, it is certainly because the universe was thought of as a great man. The universe as macro-anthropos and the Logos are thus conceptually contiguous (gehen begrifflich ineinander über).' This is the kind of speculation that provided the background for the Corpus-Christi ecclesiology in the *Epistle to Ephesians.* But this is not yet Gnosticism.

All Gnostic systems—Hermetism, Gnosticism, Mandeism, Manichaeism—are characterized on the one hand by the prominence of a Cosmic Man,[11] and, on the other, by the dominance of Soteriology over Cosmology. In all these systems Primeval Man is said to have fallen into Matter—succumbed to the allurements of Nature, been vanquished by the forces of Darkness; to have risen again from this state of corruption; and to have recovered his former place in God. By thus saving himself, he has virtually saved us all: he is the saved saviour.

It is immediately apparent that in this conception, as in the Upanishadic doctrine and in Buddhism, the stress is on the affinity between God and man, whereas the world, being merely what tends to separate them, is something utterly different and inferior.

In Gnosticism a certain symmetry is achieved with the idea that the prophets are all reincarnations of the First Man: we have thus, in the *Clementine Recognitions*, the succession from Adam to Jesus; to which Manichaeism adds Mani, and Islam Muhammad, 'the seal of the Prophets'. But this symmetry is obviously very limited, since it includes neither creation nor eschatology.

The complete symmetry, which we find in Christianity, is also lacking in Mazdeism: the Saošyant, the final Saviour, is *not* identical with Gayōmart, the Primeval Man. But a tendency manifested itself in various ways towards presenting the eschatology as a return to the origins.[12] First, Gayōmart, who had been the first man at Creation, was also to be the first at Resurrection.

Second, Gayōmart and the Saošyant were described in similar terms. Not less than five traits common to both have been pointed out by E. Abegg in his recent, posthumous paper, 'Urmensch und Messias bei den Iranern', in *Asiatische Studien*, 1961, i sq.:

1. Gayōmart was as bright as the sun (*Gr. Bund.*, 21, 4–5, etc.), and so will be the Saošyant (*Dēnkart*, 675, 5–6);[13]

2. Both Gayōmart and the Saošyant possessed x^varənah, the heavenly vital force (on which see J. Duchesne-Guillemin in *AION*, 1963);

3. The Saošyant is victorious (*vərəθrayna*, *Yašt*, 13, 129, 145), and so was Gayōmart, who according to the *Mēnōk i Xrat* (27, 15) killed Arzūr, son of Ahriman;

4. Gayōmart is the first righteous one, and the Saošyant will be the eschatological judge;

5. The Saošyant will confer immortality on the resurrected, and Gayōmart was for 3000 years immortal.

However, none of these resemblances is close enough or characteristic enough to constitute a real identity, and Abegg is right in concluding that the widespread conception of a primeval saviour returning at the end of time is lacking in Mazdeism. In other words, we are still a far cry from the Gnostic dogma of the identity of Primeval Man and Final Saviour. It is, therefore, not permissible to project this conception into ancient Iran, as do Ringgren, *Word and Wisdom*, 1947, 90, and Widengren, *Religionens Värld*,[2] 1952, 363, and to see in it the model of the fusion of the Primal Man of Job 15:7 and Ezekiel 21:12 with the Son of Man—a purely eschatological figure—of Enoch, etc.—an identification which was itself the prelude to the Christian symmetrical pattern analysed above.

There is yet another correspondence between beginning and end in Mazdean speculation. Arta or Aša, Truth and Justice, participated, as we have seen, in the very first act of creation, when God, through her, filled the free spaces with lights. Now this primeval Entity will have a role to play at the end. We read in *Zātspram*, 34, 38 (and also in the *Pahlavi Rivāyat*, 48, 20 and

Dēnkart, 669, 16 sq.[14]) that in the last millennium before the advent of the final Saošyant, Artavahišt 'will come to earth with the powerful help of Airyaman' to find a means of overcoming Āz ('Concupiscence') and that from then on those who obey Artavahišt will turn from the slaughter of cattle and the eating of flesh, so that one quarter of the power of Āz will dwindle.

But Arta will also be present in another way. The last Saviour is often simply called Saošyant 'Saviour', since he will be the Saviour *par excellence*. But he has also a proper name and this, *Astvaṱ.ərəta*, means in Avestan 'Arta incarnate'. It seems to be based on a Gāthic passage, 43, 16, in which Zarathuštra speaks of the future blessings when Arta will be corporeal. It is this materialization of Truth and Justice, then, which was made the very essence of the last saviour.

If we remember that Arta can be compared with the Greek Logos, we might say that the last saviour in Zoroastrianism is called, in free paraphrase, 'Logos incarnate'. But the resemblance with the Christian dogma should not be overstressed: it may be fortuitous, and, in any case, neither the Mazdeans nor the Christians appear ever to have been conscious of it. However, the fact remains that another trait is added to the symmetry between beginning and end in the Mazdean world-drama.

It may well be that Mazdeism influenced the Muslim theory of the Perfect Man. The latter, however, seems to have originated chiefly in Gnosticism and Neo-platonism, while, on the other hand, it could claim merely to interpret a Coranic passage which said—in patent imitation of Genesis—that God made Adam 'on his image'. This was the corner-stone—the orthodox foundation—on which the theologians have built. According to Ghazzālī, as summarized by Annemarie Schimmel (after Wensinck) in *Anthropologie religieuse*, 146,

> the image of God refers itself to the essence as well as to the attributes and actions: so is the spirit a being *per se*, neither accident nor substance nor body, which can also be said of God; and the attributes of knowledge, sight, will, etc. suit it as they suit God. The human forces are arranged parallel to the heavenly spheres: the heart corresponds, as centre of the

lordship of God, to the divine throne, the brain to God's pedestal, the senses to the angels, the nerves and limbs to the different heavens, etc.

The doctrine of the Perfect Man does not appear until Ibn 'Arabī, although the Brothers of Purity, in the ninth century—therefore at the time of the Pahlavi treatises—professed the microcosmic function of man. And this is how a *hadīth qudsī* (quoted by A. Schimmel, 151) expressed the God-Man-World relationship: 'O Man, I created thee for my sake, and I created all things for thy sake.'

It is from Abd al-rahīm al-Gīlī that the doctrine of the Perfect Man received its classical form. 'Only the Perfect Man', A. Schimmel writes p. 152, 'displays the sum of the divine attributes and carries in himself the prototypes of all things material and spiritual. . . . So are God and the world but aspects of one reality, which unite in the Perfect Man.'

This theory might be represented as follows:

God ⟶ Man ⟵ World,

or rather in this way:

God ⟵ Man ⟶ World,

so as to show it for what it really is: a truly extreme form of anthropomorphism.

NOTES

[1] On Iranian borrowings from Greece see Bailey, *Zoroastrian Problems in the IXth Century Books*, 1943, and J. Duchesne-Guillemin, 'Quaestiones graeco-iranicae', *Klio*, 38, 1960, 122–7.—On the Hippocratic text, see below.

[2] Zaehner's reading, *BSOAS*, 1959, 367, *dām* 'creature' instead of *šem* 'name' gives a less satisfactory sense.

[3] It is quite evident with the other occurrence of the term, *SGV* 16, 24, where it is used in correlation with *gehān i guzurg* 'macrocosm', though with the slightly different meaning of 'man, cattle and the other animals'. The passage deals with the Manichaean doctrines. Cf Cumont, *Recherches sur le Manichéisme*, p. 44, n. 4.

[4] *Filologia* (Torino), 1962.

[5] And perhaps my own reflections on the idea of Totality, *Hymns of Zarathustra*, 1952, Introduction, as well.

[6] J. Duchesne-Guillemin, *Harvard Theol. Rev.*, 1956, 120 sq., with reference to Olerud's fundamental work on *L'idée de microcosme*, Upsala, 1951.

[7] W. Kranz, 'Kosmos und Mensch in der Vorstellung frühen Griechentums', *Nachr. der Gesellsch. der Wissensch. z. Göttingen*, Pilol.-histor. Kl., Fachgr. I, 1938, 121–61.

[8] Cf. the same phrase applied to the sky, *Pahlavi Rivāyat* (Dhabhar) 128.

[8a] See Charles Kahn, *Anaximander*, New York, 1960.

[9] The quotation is from T. H. Green, cited in Inge, *E.R.E.*, 8, 136b.

[10] 'Zur Leib-Christi Vorstellung in Ephesierbrief', *ZNTW* Beih., 26, 172 sq.

[11] The microcosm doctrine was in great vogue 'aux premiers siècles de notre ère parmi les juifs, les chrétiens, les gnostiques de toute espèce', Menasce, *Une Apologétique Mazdéenne*, 1945, 31–2, with bibliography.

[12] J. Duchesne-Guillemin, *La Religion de l'Iran ancien*, 1962, 349 sq.

[13] The reference in Abegg is inexact.

[14] See Zaehner, *BSOAS*, X, 625, and *Zurvan*, 346 and 350.

VII

THE IDEA OF CREATION AND CONCEPTIONS OF SALVATION

by

H. D. LEWIS

IT may appear strange that the idea of creation should be thought to have anything to do with doctrines of salvation. Admittedly, in order to be saved we must exist, and for those who believe that we could not exist except as objects of God's creative activity the idea of salvation presupposes the idea of creation in this way. But this is a very formal and general relationship. It seems to throw little light directly on the need for salvation or the way it is provided. All finite beings are created but they do not all stand in need of salvation.

It might be urged, however, that the way we have come to be in our present state will have had a large share in determining the needs that arise out of it. This is undoubtedly true, and it would certainly be inadequate to consider the present need of salvation or the mode of it without proper heed of the antecedents of the state in which we find ourselves at present. Many religions, the Christian one for example, give particular prominence to the past in their account of the conditions which place us in need of salvation.

But the past is one thing, even when extended to dimensions other than strictly historical ones—as in the assertion repeated recently by Reinhold Niehuhr that the 'Fall of Man' is involved in the 'Fall of the Devil'. The doctrine of creation does not refer strictly to the past. We may say 'In the beginning' and so on. But this is a very peculiar beginning. It refers to the dependence of temporal things in some non-temporal way, and beyond normal comprehension, on some Reality altogether beyond the flow of events in time. It takes us outside the finite sphere of things altogether.

As such the status of creature, or created being, seems so universal as to prescribe nothing about the lot or destiny of any particular beings. It seems to tell us nothing about this life.

In the case of self-conscious or rational beings, however, the status of created being can become the subject of reflection, and almost invariably does so in some way or another. But in becoming aware of ourselves as finite created beings we *ipso facto* become aware of our Creator. This is the obverse of the sense of creaturehood. It may not follow from the awareness of finite limitations as such but it is clearly involved in the apprehension of the finite state as essentially a state of createdness. But the sense of our own creatureliness and of the starkness of the opposition of this to the status of absolute Creator is an indispensable feature of the attitude of worship, as has been much stressed of late, not only by followers of Otto but also as one of the outstanding factors in recent philosophical controversy about religion. In coming to think in these terms of ourselves as worshipping beings we get closer to the situation in which we may seem also to stand in need of salvation.

The formulation of these ideas in abstract terms is only possible when a high state of sophistication is reached. Indeed the philosophical presentation of them, and detached reflection about them, may be almost wholly absent in very high cultures where the sense of God's holiness as involving His being absolute Lord and Creator of the Universe is particularly marked. The Hebrews are the obvious example. The majesty and transcendence of God found classic expression in the Old Testament. It is not for us to consider here why the Hebrews were not also more philosophically minded. The point is that the sense of God as Creator is not primarily or initially the result of detached formal reflection.

The widespread character of the sense of God as supreme and absolute being, not only in high and sophisticated cultures but among all sorts of peoples, including some very backward ones, has been a recurrent theme in recent anthropology and the study of religions. Nor have there been many who have illumined this subject more, or shown us with more skill and precision how the relevant evidence should be assessed over a wide area, than the distinguished scholar in whose honour this volume has been prepared. Those of us in London who had the privilege of hearing Professor James's Jordan Lectures on the theme of the High God, will be looking forward with particular keenness to the appearance in print of his examination of the persistence of the idea of the High God and the ranging degrees of distinctness with which it appeared in its association with other religious beliefs and attitudes. But this is not the only quarter from which the same testimony has come of late.

This represents a very sharp difference in our approach to the study of religions today from the time when the subject began to be a serious systematic one towards the middle of the last century. The naturalism which presided over the inception of the subject then known as comparative religion and which had received at an earlier date a classic expression in Hume's *The Natural History of Religion*, has been gradually giving place to an approach which does more justice to the complexities of religious phenomena and the persistence within them from very early times of some sense of the supra-rational, the mysterious and 'wholly other' so impressively analysed by Otto in work which the student of religion should never leave far from his thought, however familiar it has now become.[1]

It is not true, however, that the sense of a supreme or ultimate reality on which we are all, as finite beings, dependent has always been understood in terms of the absolute contrast between ourselves and the ultimate which the idea of God as Creator properly implies. In many religions, as in many philosophical systems, the status of the finite individual tends to be very uncertain. Our ultimate destiny, indeed our true reality at all times, appears to lie in some identification with the whole of being. We are 'modes of the being of God', 'appearances of the absolute', 'limitations of the infinite', 'manifestations of the One Universal Mind', 'reproductions of the Eternal Spiritual Principle', to instance some of the terms in which monistic theories have been presented by philosophers from time to time. The idea of emanation occupies a somewhat ambiguous position between the belief in absolute creation and expressly monistic systems. These have their parallels in more explicitly religious settings, being themselves in large measure reflections of religious moods and attitudes. In much oriental religion the lot from which the individual requires to be saved is that of his apparent dissociation from the One Being in which he has his home. To realize the illusory or unreal character of the independent status we are apt to accord ourselves is a very important feature of our release and our salvation from the ills that afflict us at present. We rise above the perils and contingencies of our present existence by realizing that, in the way it presents itself to us at least, this is unreal and must give way to the true reality and significance of our lives in identification with the Supreme Reality, the true Self in all selves, the one Life in all lives.

The way this is achieved, and the clarity and consistency with which the ultimate aim is conceived, varies a great deal from one religion to another and in different forms and levels of the same religion. The absorption into the ultimate is much more complete in some cases than in others. There are corresponding differences in the significance accorded to the efforts and interests of men in their limited or temporal state 'in the world', and there are many degrees of subtlety in the considerations by which it is sought to bring monistic systems into accord with the facts of our normal experience. One of the advances in recent study of religions has been greater sensitivity to variations of this sort.

In some forms of mysticism, in the West especially, the 'union with God', while exceptionally close, is intended in a metaphorical sense which does not jeopardize the distinctness of the finite person. 'Soul is soul and God is God'. Others, or the same person in different moods, take the mystical claim with such seriousness as to deify themselves even in the present existence. This was the offence of Hallāj and the cause of his death at the hands of more orthodox Muslims. Professor W. T. Stace, in a recent work,[2] has tried, somewhat desperately it seems to me, to uphold both these attitudes. He believes that it can be held that the One 'is not differentiated' and that there is also a 'differentiated world',[3] 'that the world, which is the multiplicity, is both identical with God and distinct from him',[4] we can affirm that 'in the One there are no separate items to be kept distinct'[5] and that we have also to deal with 'a *multiplicity* of separate items', we can proclaim 'the dissolution of individuality'[6] and also 'the otherness of God to man and the world',[7] making the gulf, in the common metaphor 'as wide as we like'.[8] Nor is this attained by diminishing the force of one side of the paradox or taking it in some ambiguous or not very rigorous sense or as having a different location from its opposite. We are expressly urged to avoid solutions of that sort and to take the full force of the paradox without prevarication. This can be achieved, it is argued, by keeping strictly apart the 'different territories' which are occupied by logic and illogic, 'the many is the sphere of logic, the One the sphere of paradox'.[9]

I cannot, in the space now available, follow the subtle arguments by which Professor Stace tries to support this position. One admires the boldness and the uncompromising character of his stance, but I have not been persuaded that we can let consistency and logic go, in the final reckoning, in quite this way. To relegate logic to a particular sphere is always dangerous, and one cannot but be concerned to find Professor Stace inveighing against the conventional view and the dogma 'that no experience could ever conceivably contravene the laws of logic'.[10] Admittedly, anyone who takes the idea of transcendence seriously has a problem of the supra-rational on his hands. This is indeed the very core of our problems in the philosophy of religion. But to say that we are confronted in religion with a mystery which goes beyond all rational explanation, that the universe is ultimately supra-rational, is one thing. It is quite another to claim to understand the supra-rational sufficiently to proclaim the dissolution of the individual in it. Professor Stace presumes too much, and it might almost be said that he disregards his own counsel by seeking to rationalize religion in that aspect of it which, on his own showing, goes beyond reason. It is not for us to make demarcations between the sphere of logic and the sphere of illogic and assume that we can say what we like about the latter in defiance of reason. Our problem must be handled much more subtly. We can acknowledge the supra-rational and consider cautiously how it comes also to be characterized from within present experience. But we go beyond the limit when we legislate for the supra-rational as such or prescribe its relation to the world as we find and understand it. The universe is certainly a unity in some way which goes altogether beyond the sort of unity or relatedness by which we make sense of our experience, but these are not thereby annulled; nor is there justification, in the limited nature of finite experience, for discrediting the characteristics of 'the world around us', including ourselves, as in fact we find them to be. We cannot both trust the facts of experience and go against them. But we can proclaim that the world, as we find and understand it, has a character which takes us beyond the world and of which further rational account is not possible.

This certainly leaves us with a nest of problems. And I shall make no attempt to deal with them here. All that I wish to insist upon is that, in acknowledging the transcendent and proclaiming that reality in some way goes beyond reason, we are not forced to repudiate the ordinary terms of experience. On the contrary, it is in affirming these to be as we find them, and having full confidence in reason in all the ways in which we exercise it, that we apprehend best the true character of the transcendent and the completeness of the contrast between it and all finite reality.

This is the insight which the idea of creation is especially designed to preserve. It is not the idea of making in any ordinary sense. Nor is there any proper analogy to it in the way we speak of artistic creation. There is indeed a very special newness and spontaneity in the latter case, but it is still the exercise of certain aptitudes we find we do have and the attainment of insights which, in the last resort, 'come' or are 'given' to us. We can seek inspiration but we cannot absolutely command it. But creation is absolute, it depends on nothing beyond itself, it is an origination which is total and self-contained as nothing in the world of finite things can be, and this is why the Bible, as many scholars have pointed out of late, makes little attempt to describe the process of creation; it does not offer us cosmologies or speculations about form and matter, but speaks rather of 'the word' or *fiat* of God, ascribing all existence to the transcendent and incomprehensible power of God.

A further view, and one more familiar to us in the West today, which also fails to do justice to the idea of God's transcendence and its corollary of our own created status, is that of Hegelian idealism, especially in that aspect of it which was developed by the more rationalist followers of Hegel in the nineteenth century and sharply corrected in the supra-rational idealism of Bradley. According to rational idealism the universe is one whole such that everything within it follows by rational necessity from the nature of the whole. Everything is an element in or 'a phase of' the absolute, and the more our own personalities develop the more is their identity with the whole, and their true reality, disclosed. Our destiny is thus to be more completely identified with one another and with the whole of being. In the last analysis there is only one Person and all other persons are phases or limitations of His being.

The obvious difficulty which this view encounters is that of 'saving the appearances' and doing justice to the seeming distinctness, the freedom and responsibility of finite beings. Many writers, especially in the heyday of British and American idealism, were deeply concerned about this issue and extremely sensitive over the threat to our normal evaluations and attitudes and to common sense which their theories seemed to involve. They qualified substantially the more ruthlessly monistic claims of some of their contemporaries, and much of the work of leading idealists like Pringle Pattison, G. F. Stout and A. E. Taylor centred on this aim, most of all in major works which were at one time widely read and admired.[11] I do not think many would consider these writers successful in their enterprise, although their candour and determination to preserve the normal distinctions of worth and responsibility earn our esteem and gratitude. But the palm, in respect of consistency, seems to go to more severe idealists who were prepared to jettison more of our ordinary assumptions and expectations.

Along with the failure of monistic idealism to do justice to the facts of finite experience and the significance of the individual is the complementary failure to recognize the absolute character of God's transcendence. For Hegelian idealism there is a continuity of human and divine natures, the difference between the two, however great, being ultimately a matter of degree. The divine is thus the human with all its potentialities fulfilled, and in our exercise of reason we have our main clue to the nature of divine being. There are obvious advantages in this view, especially when account must be given of our knowledge of God and His specific dealings with us. But these advantages are bought at the price of surrendering just that feature of the being of God by which we are most compelled to believe in His existence, namely His having to be as the completion of what is radically incomplete about our rational account of things. To develop this thesis here is hardly possible,[12] but if it is sound it will be seen to give us a much more radical and complete sense of God's transcendence and the gulf, as it is sometimes put, between God and man than normal idealism allows. This, in spite of its dangers and the difficulty of accounting, in consistency with it, for the commerce of God with man, seems to do more justice to the religious sense of the majesty and holiness of God. The latter are accommodated better in a monism like that of Professor Stace than in rational idealism.

The monism of Hegelian and post-Hegelian thought found much community of interest with oriental cultures and religions. This was due in part to misunderstanding and to excessive confidence about the essential and exhaustive rationality of cultures and religions. That attitude was endorsed by Eastern scholars educated in the West. But we understand better now that, while some forms of Eastern religion, parts of the Upanishads for example and kindred forms of later Hinduism, come very close to Western idealism, there are other aspects of Eastern religion which resemble more the sort of mysticism which Professor Stace described and which he calls, not altogether suitably in my view, pantheism. The study of these and other variations on religious monism is one for which the time seems particularly opportune today in the study of religions.

There is however much that is common to all forms of religious monism and to these and some beliefs which are not monistic at all. They all tend to extol some supreme or ultimate being and to find the destiny of the individual in some union with it. None of the monistic views, in my opinion, do justice to the majesty and holiness of God in the same way as those religions of transcendence which emphasize the contrast between God as absolute Creator and ourselves as distinct and essentially dependent beings. But in most at least there is some sense in which it may be said that the proper end of man is 'to glorify God and enjoy Him for ever'.

It is when we turn to the more distinctly human side of the need for salvation that the sharper differences present themselves in these contexts. For monistic views, especially the more rigorous and those described by Professor Stace as pantheistic, the main concern tends to be to draw away from the troubles and painful limitations of our present existence and realize more fully our union with the whole. This is an aim which, in some fashion, is shared also by pluralistic religions of a Creator God such as Judaism, Christianity and Islam. They also have a 'world beyond' in which 'the tears are wiped from our eyes', where the wicked cease from troubling and in terms of which 'our light affliction which is but for a moment, worketh for us a far more exceeding and eternal weight of glory'. In one sense most, if not all, religions offer some escape from the ills and frustrations of the present life and some kind of eternal rest, and in most again the glory and perfection of a supreme reality is the source of this. But there are further elements which become prominent in the individual's need for salvation as it appears in the non-monistic religions and which seem altogether absent in some monistic ones. These become more sharply defined when the transcendence of a Creator God and the distinctness of our own created status are properly heeded, as they seem to be especially in Judaism and Christianity; and it is to these features of the notion of salvation that I most wish to draw attention, albeit very briefly, in this paper.

Self-conscious beings, and I think we may add all sentient beings, are in one very important sense a world to themselves. They know their own experience directly in having it, although 'know' may be a rather ambitious term here for some levels of experience. The experience of others they know indirectly, usually by inference of some kind from observable evidence. This view is much out of favour today, the notion of a private access to one's own thoughts and sensations having been exposed to particularly forceful attacks the best known of which is found in Professor Gilbert Ryle's *The Concept of Mind*. There are not many philosophers who would endorse Professor Ryle's total rejection of private access now, and his own arguments in support of that position have been widely thought to be discredited.[13] This does not mean that philosophers are reverting to a position like the dualism of Descartes. They are very loth to do that even when anxious also to affirm some kind of private access to our own experience. In my opinion there is no halfway house between the behaviourism of Professor Ryle and a dualism not in essentials different from that of Descartes. Some of my reasons for maintaining this have been advanced in other papers,[14] and here I can only reaffirm my view that we know our own experience directly in having it and thus in a way radically different from our mediated knowledge of others. The conversion of this heresy, as it seems to be at the moment, into orthodoxy seems to me essential for a sound understanding of ourselves and of our relations to others. It does not follow that we have in all ways infallible knowledge of ourselves. We may forget what past experiences were like and be much mistaken about future thoughts and attitudes. We may be in error about our dispositions, about what we would do in certain contingencies and so forth, and this may extend to cognitive dispositions as well. We may be wrong about the implications of what we think or feel or intend at some particular time, but it is hard to see how we can fail to know what it is that we do in these various ways at the time of doing it. The objective reference is another matter with problems of its own.

This knowledge of having a certain kind of experience is not, in the first place, the result of deliberate introspection although that is one means of refinement and sophistication in our knowledge of ourselves. It is a constant inescapable feature of experience; if metaphors were not so apt to mislead we might describe it as the inner side of all knowledge and belief concerning other things. It is that for which Samuel Alexander found such helpful designations in the terms 'living through' or 'enjoyment'.

It is sometimes thought that there is a further sense in which experience is private, namely that whereby the 'real' or genuinely physical world is mediated for us by sensations or impressions private to each. The truth here seems to me rather complicated. I believe we are confined, in the first instance, to impressions of our senses, although these are not, as has been thought, modifications of our minds; and I have maintained elsewhere that the modes in which we have such impressions, even their initial extendedness,[15] may vary radically from one case to another. But I much doubt whether this mediates for us an objective world that is not to be understood in terms of correlations within our own experiences and as between those and the experiences of others. But this alternative to Representative Perception, and the account of the communication with others to be given in terms of it, is too large a subject to be embarked upon here. At the moment my concern is to distinguish between the senses of private world involved in the present contexts and the more complete and immediate privacy by which each of us is aware of his own experience in having it but can have no such direct access, not even in paranormal cognition, to the experiences of other persons.

The latter privacy is not without kinship with the initial privacy of our sense impressions, important though it may be to distinguish the two. But the main point at the moment is that, in both these respects and in the first in particular, man is essentially a solitary being. He is also of course an essentially social being. The life that we know could not be conceived without relations with others, mediated though they must be. The mediation is so unobtrusive that we are not usually aware of it and only sophisticated people reflect upon it. We can therefore have extremely close and intimate relationships, and the solitary aspect of human experience is thus not always obtrusive. But it is never absent. Nothing can eliminate it, for it is an essential characteristic of finite experience as such. This is what ultimately lies behind such expressions as 'the flight of the alone to the Alone' or the oft-quoted, and rarely understood, definition of religion as 'what a man does with his solitude'.

Aloneness in this sense is apt to be made obtrusive by loneliness in the ordinary sense. When relations with others are slight or have been cut off, a person is thrown much on his own resources and apt to be driven in on himself. He becomes in this way more conscious also of the special inwardness which characterizes all finite experience as such and which is made more explicit for us in some situations, very often the situations which impress on us also the irrevocable character of external events and those features of our environment which most resist moulding to our own desires. Realism and proper subjectivity go together more often, and more naturally, than is usually appreciated.

These are matters for which much evidence may be found in recent and contemporary literature. As has often been observed, there is much in the life of today to induce loneliness and to sharpen the sting of it. The organization which improves our amenities and makes for greater mobility is apt also to make our relationships more impersonal and remote even in the very process of throwing people more closely together. The social surroundings, often very homely ones, in which we grow easily and naturally into ripe relationships with one another are disrupted and give place to more contrived and unstable situations in which the individual finds it harder to feel that he is at home and belongs. The paradoxes of this situation, the manifest distress of many whose life seems also to be the gayest, the outright complaints of loneliness where life appears also to be most gregarious, the herding of peoples in impersonal artificial communities where outward prosperity leaves them more and more frustrated—all this has been told often enough in literature and public pronouncements which also show how much these conditions have been accentuated in our time. It is not surprising therefore that loneliness and its problems have become at various levels, from the simplest to the most sophisticated, a subject for much discussion and concern. Nor is it surprising that in the probings of more shrewd and sensitive writers there should be intimations not merely of the isolation and aloofness specifically induced by certain social situations and modifiable in various ways, but also of the deeper and inescapable sense in which an individual is bound to be a world to himself.

It is not expected that fiction and general literature should discriminate neatly between these different sorts of solitude and their ramifications in the complicated web of human affairs, least of all when they affect one another so much. But it is not an accident that those writers of creative literature who are also given to general reflection and philosophical thinking, for example existentialists, should give so much prominence to the sense of isolation and destitution in a very profound and disturbing form as a feature of human experience as such and, as many suppose, beyond remedy. These writers may often be muddled philosophers but that would not preclude them from stumbling, in ways which amateur and uncertain philosophizing may have helped, on profound truths of great importance for their time.

I was much impressed recently to read the closing words of a collection of stories[16] which have deservedly been widely praised for their literary excellence and penetration. They belong to the tough-minded variety of modern fiction, but their realism is the genuine one of a skilled and sensitive artist. The last story ends with the words: 'What really, can any of us know about any of us, and why must we make such a thing of loneliness when it is the final condition of us all. And where would love be without it?'

The secularist copes with this situation by acceptance and as much charity as one can muster. Religions offer more positive remedies. In monistic religions the aim is to eliminate the isolation of the individual by absorbing him entirely into the whole. He is no longer a world to himself but as completely at one with others and with God as it is possible to be. There are no barriers but the total flow of one life into another. This seems however to release the individual by totally destroying him as such, and there are in fact many other difficulties, on which I cannot dwell now, in the notion of our total absorption into the life of the whole. In the non-monistic religions the ultimacy of our finite status is accepted and the ills attendant upon this, in the various ways in which these are felt and understood, present a situation for which a remedy is sought. There is no attempt to supersede or eliminate our finite state. Nor is there mere stoical acceptance of the inevitable. But acceptance has none the less an important part to play in the solutions that have most understanding of the situation to be met.

This will be acceptance of the essential conditions under which we find that we exist, but acceptance based on the recognition of our status as a dependent one and involving an acknowledgement of the Unconditioned or Supreme Reality in relation to which all else has its place and significance. Acceptance, in humility and gratitude, is part of the worship we give to God, and in recognizing His glory and transcendent claims we submit ourselves to the fulfilment of ourselves appropriate to our place in relation to God and in this way find rest in Him.

This is especially prominent in the religions where the idea of creation sets its seal most explicitly on the distinctness of the finite individual. There is here no inducement for the individual to seek to transcend himself. He is not in rebellion against being the sort of creature he is or having the mode of experience which he finds that he does have. And if we find, as I maintain we do, that a certain inwardness is an incident of all finite experience and that fellowship with others, both man and God, has for this reason an essential element of mediation, we do not set ourselves in hopeless rebellion against these conditions or attempt the futile and inhibiting task of bursting the bonds of our finite nature and raising ourselves to the level of God. We acknowledge the mystery of God and find in this acknowledgement an enhancement of the mediated knowledge of God which is possible for us within the modes of the experience we do have.

In the same way we accommodate ourselves to the sort of knowledge we have of one another. We do not seek to know as God knows and we recognize that we can never have direct or immediate knowledge of other persons similar to that which we have of ourselves. In duly acknowledging God as our Creator we are helped also to appreciate that aspect of the sanctity of persons by which they too are, in a more limited way, mysteries we must not seek to reduce; the mystery of their creation is written into the distinctness of persons and is not suspended even in the most intimate fellowship we may have with one another. On the contrary, fellowship is deepened and enriched when we come into it with due understanding of what it means for us all to be, in Biblical language, the children of God and severally the objects of the loving concern which begins with our creation.

The more we appreciate this the better equipped we shall be to cope with ills which seem to have been much aggravated in recent times. We read much, in fiction as in social studies, of unnatural passions and perversions, of violence and sex in most unruly forms. One reason for this, I submit, is that, with our growing sophistication, we have a great urge to break into the inner recesses of the lives of others, to find them off their guard and without disguise in extremes of fear or passion, and this is one form of the desire to know others wholly from within, to know as we know ourselves and as God knows us, to pass beyond irremovable barriers of our finitude which religious humility teaches us to understand and accept. Sartre and other existentialists, in their strange way, have taught us much of this.

But it is not merely in these general ways that the recognition of our created status, and of the inwardness, ultimacy and sanctity of personal experience which this involves, affects our conception of salvation and the needs from which it springs. There are further, more specific, applications of the same principle apprehended in varying degrees of adequacy in different religions and their theologies.

We find, for example, that in virtue of being confined, in one way which I maintain is a very fundamental one, to a world of our own, we are very prone to allow this to impose itself unduly on our conspectus of the public world as each one apprehends it. This is one of the main reasons for the distorted pictures we often present to ourselves of our environment, the lack of realism or the superficial romanticism for which artists and prophets have often to supply the corrective. But the more we appreciate that all things do not in this way revolve around ourselves and that the whole of the reality encountered in experience is God's creation, the more, that is, that we think of ourselves and of all things in relation to God, the less shall we be tempted to view them through artificial and misleading perspectives of our own. The ultimate cure for romanticism, and the false moral impressions which this involves, is in understanding the basic source of it and the essentially religious character of its ultimate corrective.

But it is when we consider the specifically ethical aspects of experience that the main importance of our recognition of the distinctness of persons appears. On monistic views there can be no proper place for the final moral responsibility of persons. Nor has the sense of sin and guilt been very prominent in the cultures most affected by monistic views of the world. It is not that ethical ideas are absent in these cultures and the religions which inspire them. No one conversant at all with Hinduism and Buddhism could maintain that. The compassion we find, for example, in the thought and practice of the highest forms of Buddhism is extremely impressive. So are ethical features of the Gitā and of parts of the Upanishads. All the same, the moral life presents itself here in the main as a discipline, not as a categorical demand which the agent is totally free to accept or reject and which leaves him, in the event of failure, with a burden of guilt. Even where the ideas of guilt and accountability appear in their proper form, and not in the travesties of mere pollution or spiritual disease, this is not easily accommodated to a view of the individual which regards him as an element in one Whole of Being where everything takes its place inevitably by the necessity of the Whole. If man is really a part of God what room is there for sin?

This is not the place in which to discuss closely the nature of freedom and responsibility. I have attempted to do that elsewhere and must be content now with a statement of my own belief that the choice required by moral accountability is of an absolute kind, not determined by character or environment or even by God, and that the proper appreciation of this is of quite fundamental importance for our understanding of the main problems of human life and its worth. I cannot expand this principle here, but it will be evident that, if I am right in subscribing to this libertarian view, there is here a quite radical feature of human experience for which no place can be found in monistic conceptions of the world. It was this, as I have noted, which troubled many Hegelian idealists, and it is interesting that thinkers like Sri Aurobindo show the same concern today about Oriental monisms.

But wrongful choice is not only evil in itself, it is the cause of other evils. It tends to infect the whole of life and poison all our attitudes and relationships. We are moreover, in our closest social relationships especially, the heirs to the accumulated evil effects of wrongful deeds in the past. This is one element of truth, but one that is largely misrepresented, in the traditional doctrine of original sin.

The most grievous and lasting effect of sin is to slacken our hold on the world around us and distort our impressions of it. In more religious terms, it alienates us from our neighbour and from God. The state of the sinner has its analogue in that of sick persons in conditions of extreme debility. They have lost their hold on life and the world around them, and the sinner in the same way has not the concern for himself and others which he would normally have. In some religions a condition not very dissimilar to this is part of the goal of life or a feature of the final release; in others a sounder instinct presents the state of isolation, privation and debility as the appalling penalty of sin, the death which is the renunciation of life. In this living death, in the sense of unreality and the dissolution of the world around us, the individual is driven more and more into himself, and the inwardness inevitably attendant upon his experience and having a function in the economy of his relations with others, becomes the dominant feature of experience unrelieved by a properly objective grasp of the world and healthy relationships with other persons. His own world becomes the centre and discloses itself, in this isolation, as a bleak unsustaining one.

This is the deeper dimension of the loneliness which, as a pervasive malaise of present society, is presented in more general terms, and linked more exclusively to features of contemporary life, in fiction and other works of art today. The ultimate understanding of it is, I submit, religious; and this begins with due appreciation of the relation of created beings to their Creator. It is not insignificant that much of the literature to which I allude has profound religious undertones, however remote it may seem from conventional religion.

It is the sense of desolation and destitution engendered by sin and guilt which constitutes, in the non-monistic religions, the need to which salvation and redemption are specially addressed. The issue is no longer that of coping with limitations and ills inevitably attendant on a finite state, but of cleansing the individual and his society of the evil which individuals first bring on themselves and which imprisons the individual in a frightening world of his own unrelieved by a proper sense of God and our neighbour within it.

Of the ramifications of this in a social context and of the variety of ways in which religions claim to meet it, little can be added here. Nor can I go into the distortion of the truth in various doctrines and creeds in which these ideas of salvation and redemption are often enshrined. Space likewise precludes speculation about the appearance in cultures that are mainly monistic of ingredients, like certain notions of cleansing and redeeming, which only take their place properly in non-monistic cultures. We have at all times to remember the varieties and complexities of religion and the many deviations of live religion from its more sophisticated expression. But there seem to me to be few more valuable guides to the varieties of religious thought and practice, as the scholar makes these more fully and reliably available to us today, than that of considering them in terms of their appreciation of the significance of creaturely status and the implications of this for ideas of sin and salvation. Professor R. C. Zaehner, in a celebrated lecture,[17] has reminded us sharply of the considerable difference of substance there may be in religious notions, like the doctrines of release or incarnation in various religions, which may appear superficially very similar. If the thesis of the present paper is sound it offers one way in which the points of affinity and of differences in the leading notions of various religions may be discriminated better.

In the Christian religion the idea of salvation is directed especially to the alleged bondage of sin and the alienation of man from God. The Christian doctrines of Reconciliation and Atonement, and of the work of the Holy Spirit within this scheme, do not require us to suppose that the influence of the Holy Spirit is such as to deprive us of our own freedom and responsibility in moral choice, although this has often been supposed in Christian theology. Reconciliation is directed to the situation of estrangement consequent upon sin, and the operation of grace in this process does not remove all possibility of genuine temptation. We shall understand this and other main features of Christianity better when we link the Christian doctrine of the Incarnation, and especially its once for all character, closely to the Judeo-Christian understanding of the creaturely nature of man and the consequent imprisonment of each in a forlorn unsustaining world of his own by which the wages of sin are collected. This is the world into which God enters in Christ and whose bonds He breaks by the completeness of His penetration of it. The proper elaboration of this theme would require a closer scrutiny of Christian doctrines and traditions than can be attempted here. But we may do well to reflect how significant a feature of the work of Christ is disclosed to us when, at the climax of His passion, he uttered the cry of extreme destitution:—'My God, my God, why hast thou forsaken me?'

The significance of this cry is only properly plain to us when we have a sound conception of man as well as of God, and while this has ramifications too wide to be considered further now I cannot forbear to quote, for the point they give to this theme, the well-known and beautiful lines of one of the most percipient of our poets, Walter de la Mare,

> Though I should sit
> By some tarn in thy hills,
> Using its ink
> As the spirit wills
> To write Earth's wonders,
> Its live, willed things,
> Flit would the ages
> On soundless wings
> Ere unto Z
> My pen drew nigh;
> Leviathan told,
> And the honey-fly:
> And still would remain
> My wit to try—
> My worn reeds broken
> The dark tarn dry,
> All words forgotten—
> Thou, Lord, and I.

The limited mystery of man is bound up with the absolute mystery of God.

NOTES

[1] A brilliant recent defence of Otto and correction of misunderstandings of his work, together with an exhibition of its very close relevance to present controversy, will be found in C. A. Campbell's *Selfhood and Godhood*, chap. XVI.

[2] *Mysticism and Philosophy*.

[3] Op. cit., p. 273.

[4] Op. cit., p. 271.

[5] Op. cit., p. 271.

[6] Op. cit., p. 270.

[7] Op. cit., p. 250.

[8] Op. cit., p. 250.

[9] Op. cit., p. 272.

[10] Op. cit., p. 272.

[11] E.g. Pringle Pattison's *The Idea of God*, Stout's *God and Nature*, and Taylor's *The Faith of a Moralist*.

[12] I have attempted the task in my 'God and Mystery' in *Prospect for Metaphysics*. Edited by I. T. Ramsey.

[13] See in particular 'Ryle on the Intellect' by C. A. Campbell, *Philosophical Quarterly* 1953 and reproduced in *Clarity is not Enough*. Edited by H. D. Lewis.

[14] E.g. 'Mind and Body'. Presidential Address delivered to the Aristotelian Society and published in the *Proceedings of the Aristotelian Society*, 1962–3.

[15] See my 'Public and Private Space'. *Proceedings of the Aristotelian Society*, 1952.

[16] *Sermons and Soda-Water*, by John O'Hara.

[17] *Foolishness to the Greeks*. Inaugural Lecture at Oxford.

VIII

AN AFRICAN SAVIOUR GOD

by

E. G. PARRINDER

IT is sometimes thought that the ancient gods of tropical Africa are either vague, animistic rather than theistic, or mostly vengeful and needing propitiation. If this were so a kindly Saviour would be hard to find. But in fact the mythologies relate stories of many kinds about beings of diverse character. The myths differ from tribe to tribe, of course, and many of them are totally or only partially recorded. The Yoruba people of Western Nigeria are to be considered here, as one of the best known, possessing a clear pantheon, and having a number of myths on record though mostly uncollated and to be traced in old and new writers.

It is agreed by all authorities that the Yoruba believe in a Supreme Being, Ọlọruñ or Olodumarè, 'the owner' or 'lord of heaven' (*ọruñ*). This deity is creator of gods and men, kindly disposed, ruler of nature and destiny. But, like a great chief, he is distant and the intermediate gods through whom he is approached tend to oust him in worship and ritual. For the Supreme Being has no temples, priests or regular worship, whereas the lesser gods have these in abundance.

There are fierce gods of storm and disease in the Yoruba pantheon. But there are also gracious divinities, of heaven and earth. Outstanding among these is Ọruñmila, 'heaven knows salvation', or 'heaven effects deliverance'. As will be seen, Ọruñmila is the oracle divinity and he brings the messages of God to man and declares human destiny. His home is in the sacred town of Ifè, senior of all Yoruba towns for religious affairs. The form of divination known as Ifa is the means whereby Ọruñmila declares the heavenly salvation. Ifa is often identified with Ọruñmila, and stories told about the god may use either name, Ọruñmila or Ifa.

One version of a myth gives Ọruñmila a part in creation under the direction of Ọlọruñ. When the Supreme Being had prepared the elements of creation he sent a messenger, the morning star, to call the gods to receive the elements, but only Ọruñmila responded. The messenger told him to wait, since the materials were kept in the shell of a snail, kept in the Bag of Existence lying between the thighs of the Almighty. Ọruñmila took this Existence-bag and the snail shell and made his way towards the world. He found the other gods held up by water which covered the earth. Ọruñmila put his hand in the bag and took out a net which he threw on the surface of the water; then he took sand out of the snail shell and cast it on the net; finally he took out a cock which began scattering the sand and eventually land appeared. A pigeon and a chameleon were also taken out of the bag and figure in other stories, such as the one which tells of the coming of death. It is perhaps worth noting that the long conical snail shell is used as an offering to various celestial gods. Ọruñmila, the creator of the land, was the first being to step on the earth and so one title of his is 'owner of the land', like the old village chiefs who have rights over land that cannot be alienated. The place where he set foot was Ifè, or Ilé-Ifè, 'the house of Ifè', a word that may also be translated as 'earth-spreading'. This town is also sometimes called 'the town of the people who never died'.

This creation myth is sometimes credited to Orisha-nla, 'the great divinity', who is another intermediary between God and the creation. Ọruñmila also figures in a legendary deluge. After living some time in the world he returned to heaven. Men were unable to interpret the will of the gods in his absence, for he is a great diviner and interpreter, and Olokuñ, 'owner of the sea', destroyed most of the inhabitants of the world in a great flood. Once again the world was nothing but mud and unfit for habitation, till Ọruñmila came down from the sky again and made it habitable once more.[1]

Most African myths have a number of variants, for in the absence of writing before modern times they were not written down, and so there are many local differences and no fixed text. European and literate Yoruba students have only begun to write down some of the myths within the last century, and mostly in the last sixty years. Not only the myths but also the attributive and descriptive names of the divinities are valuable, in showing the character and activity of the god concerned. An African bishop, James Johnson, in 1899, collected a long list of names of Ọruñmila, and this has been followed by students ever since.[2]

Ọruñmila is a god of blessing, 'the Ruler who draws blessing or prosperity after him and who sleeps in the midst of honours'. Ọruñmila calls men and receives daily prayer: 'the Being whom all honour with the daily morning salutation, but who is above paying respect to any other being'. He is 'the Being from heaven whose constant cry to all the world is that they should come to him'.

This last sentence indicates not only the universal benevolence of Ọruñmila, but his coming from heaven and bringing joy to men. Two important titles indicate this: 'Laughing comes back to the world, or the Being whose advent has brought back the laugh of joy and gladness.' And even more ,'the Being whose advent into the world filled men with joyful and thankful surprise which caused many to ask, "Is it thou who hast come?" '

The graciousness of Ọruñmila is shown in his power over disease, for his priests (*baba'lawo*) are also doctors. So Johnson says:

> Ifa or Ọruñmila is believed to know all and everything, and is therefore consulted upon every circumstance of life, that of sickness not excluded. . . .
>
> In the traditional sayings of every Odu mention is always to be found made of sufferers from this or that form of disease and of the remedies that cured them effectively. Hence every Babalawo is necessarily a physician.

Of considerable importance is the power Ọruñmila is said to exercise over death. The titles call him, 'the Being whom death honours and pays obeisance to', 'the Being whose power is so great that he calls death to account', 'the great Changer who changes the date of death', 'the Being who, turning himself over as it were in a struggle, postpones for his client the day of death'.

This power over death is obtained by followers of Ọruñmila by blood sacrifices. When the priest has killed the victim, a cock or a goat, he dips leaves in the blood and marks the foreheads of the suppliants who chant after him. 'Ọruñmila has marked us, we shall not die again.' This optimism is based upon the great power credited to priests, when they have tended the sufferers and saved them from present death.

A common name, Ẹla, is interpreted either as an attribute of Ọruñmila or as indicating a separate entity. Bishop Johnson called Ẹla 'a contraction of Ọruñmila', and 'one of the many attributive names by which Ifa is described'. But the latest writer, Dr Idowu (1962), rather doubts this and considers Ẹla as a separate divinity, perhaps the son of Ọruñmila.[3] Whatever be the truth of the matter, Ẹla also is gracious, descends to earth, and gives power over death. 'Ẹla has descended to the earth. . . . we shall die no more.' Ẹla is called 'the offspring of a stone . . . that is the stone which gave birth to Ẹla, and will no longer die'.

In the rituals, 'Ẹla is the divinity to which harvest offerings are always presented by worshippers'. In the time of gathering the yams, 'Ọruñmila is said to come and partake of the yam with them'. It is at the yam festival that a song is sung to Ẹla of which this is the translation:

> O thou our worthy Father!
> The Son, who has descended from heaven
> to this earth,
> Who has placed us in this world.
> O thou our worthy Father![4]

Dr Idowu has recorded some of the songs still sung at Ifè in honour of Ẹla:

> Ẹla Iwori it is who saves the world from ruin . . .
> who restored order into it . . .
> Whenever Ẹlẹgbara [an evil spirit] plans to turn
> the world upside down
> Ẹla Iwori it is who obstructs him.[5]

Yet, after his coming from heaven and bestowing gifts upon mankind, men opposed Ẹla and so he returned to heaven, whither they now address their prayers for his return, in a chant sung today:

> Ẹla indeed made old age;
> Ẹla indeed made long life . . .
> After all, and in the end,
> They pronounced that Ẹla had not conducted
> the world in the right way:
> Ẹla was offended; he stretched out a rope and
> ascended into heaven;
> The inhabitants of the world changed tune and have
> since been calling out:
> Ẹla, descending, must come back to bless,
> Ẹla, descending.[6]

An ascent into heaven by a rope or chain is not uncommon in West African mythology. The chain may have been known from Sudanese traders before the coming of the Portuguese in the fifteenth century, and ropes are much older. It is doubtful whether there is any Christian influence in the descent of Ọruñmila at creation, his struggle with death, his final ascension and the plea for his return. There was a Roman Catholic mission from the fifteenth to the seventeenth centuries at Benin, not far away, and apparently a short-lived mission at Ifè which is still celebrated in a ceremony of 'burning the book'. There is a story of a heroine of Ifè, Mọremi, who sacrificed her son in payment of a vow and this has, perhaps too easily, been compared with the Christian story. There have been continuous Christian missions since the middle of the nineteenth century, and they are powerful today. But most of the myths seem indigenous and they are not hard to explain from local materials.

In occasional rituals, sacrifices and songs, Ọruñmila is believed to show his healing and guiding power. But most frequent and popular are the consultations of the oracle, through which Ọruñmila declares the will of the gods. The oracular system, it has been noted, bears the name of Ifa. The earliest references generally use the name Ifa for the oracle god. The oldest mention is found in the writings of Sir Richard Burton, in 1863. He says that Ifa is the last of the divine triad, which includes Orisha-nla and Shañgo the thunder god. Ọruñmila, or Ifa, he says,

appears to be not a person but a myth, originating at the town of Ife. He is the revealer of futurity, and the patron of marriage and childbirth. His high priest—the head of the Babbalawo, or Father of Secrets—is said to live upon a mountain near Awaye, a gigantic cone of granite eight to ten miles in circumference, seen from a distance of several days' journey towering solitary above the landscape, and surmounted, it is said, by a palm tree, bearing sixteen boughs, produced by the sixteen nuts planted by the sixteen founders of the Yoruban empire. . . . The priests are known by their bead necklaces, small strings twisted together, with ten large white and green beads, some inches apart. They officiate in white and constantly use a fly-whisk.'[7]

Burton's great granite mountain is perhaps not quite so mythical as his Ifa, for there are many remarkable granite cones that tower above the forest, though none so huge as this one. But the chief priest in Ifè lives today in a small temple on a low hill in the town. The sixteen palm nuts are those used in the Ifa divination, and hence comes the idealized palm tree.

Thirty years later Sir Arthur Ellis wrote of 'Ifa, god of divination, who is usually termed the God of Palm Nuts'. He then says that 'Ifa's secondary attribute is to cause fecundity: he presides at birth, and women pray to him to be made fruitful; while on this account offerings are always made to him before marriage'. Ellis said that 'Ifa first appeared on earth at Ife, but his parentage and origin are unexplained'. He was a diviner whose own townsmen would not listen to him, and so he travelled about the world teaching mankind. Finally he settled down and 'planted on a rock a palm-nut, from which sixteen palm-trees grew up at once'.[8]

Other stories about Ọruñmila or Ifa give him a partial or wholly human nature. One version says that his parents lived in heaven, whence Ọruñmila was sent to bring order to a troubled world. But most commonly it is said that his father lived at Ifè, and the son wandered from place to place making himself known as a diviner and herbalist and settling down eventually at Ifè to establish his divination. In different towns he is saluted by various names, which are local claims to his presence and power.

One of the earliest Yoruba writers, in a pamphlet published in 1906 and long since unobtainable, recorded this story:

Ifa was a native of Itase, near Ifè country, and of poor parentage: in his youth he had great aversion to manual labour and therefore had to beg his bread. To better his condition he applied to a sage for advice, and the latter taught him divination, traditional stories with matters relating thereto, and medicine as an easy means of obtaining a livelihood.[9]

R. E. Dennett in 1910 gave another Yoruba version:

Ifa was a human being who used to make medicine and sell it. While doing this he got to Ifè, and made that his headquarters. One day all the Ifè people joined together to fight him. Then he got vexed and went into the earth, and when they asked him to come out he refused unless they agreed to worship him. The day he entered the earth he cut four palm leaves to mark the place, and they each immediately became a palm tree. . . . Each tree had four branches or sixteen in all. He told them to pick sixteen nuts, which he said they must worship, and ask him whatever they wanted. From then anyone who got these nuts became a Babalawo and became a diviner, and these nuts teach him what leaves to pick to cure any sickness.[10]

Versions of these stories have been repeated ever since, and can be commonly heard today. A common opinion is that Ifa was a diviner, whose birthplace or centre of activity was at Ifè, and with him are necessarily associated the sixteen palm nuts used in divination. It seems that a historical person, Ifa, has become confused with Ọruñmila, the god who declares salvation through divination. It was perhaps this confusion that led Leo Frobenius, in 1913, to declare that there was no such deity as Ifa at all.[11] The deification of a hero is no uncommon thing, among the Yoruba as with other peoples. Shañgo, the god of thunder, was a historical Yoruba king who became identified with the storm deity. So Ifa is deified, and then is believed to have come from heaven previously, perhaps as the avatar of Ọruñmila.

The geomantic system of divination connected with the cult of

Ọrunmila, and known as Ifa, is deeply rooted in the life of Yoruba and neighbouring peoples. Yet it is said to have been an importation, and certainly its complicated calculations by multiples of four and sixteen resemble some of those in vogue among Sudanese peoples. One tradition is that it was introduced to the Yoruba during the reign of king Onigbogi (thirteenth–fourteenth centuries A.D.?) who was dethroned for permitting the entry of the oracle. This story says that it was brought by a blind weaver from neighbouring Nupe country, and he wandered about till he settled at Ifè. This sounds like another variant on the wanderings of the diviner Ifa.[12]

More likely is the tradition that the Ifa system was so popular among the Yoruba that the adjacent kingdom of Dahomey adopted it, at a comparatively late date. It is generally admitted that the Fa system, as the Dahomeans call Ifa, was introduced by a travelling Yoruba diviner to the capital town of Abomey during the reign of king Agadja of Dahomey in the early part of the eighteenth century. From that time Fa has been as popular with the Dahomeans as Ifa with the Yoruba. It is essentially the same system of geomancy, but the names of the local gods have been associated with it. For the Dahomean pantheon knows nothing of Ọrunmila.[13]

These legends suggest that the system of divination, so popular today, was a comparatively late introduction into Yoruba country. Research is still needed into its affinities and origins, in the Sudan or, a popular theory, in Egypt. The cult of Ọrunmila seems to have existed before the advent of Ifa. But Ọrunmila is only one among many gods. His benevolence, descent to earth at creation, conquest of death, and return to heaven, are stated in bald and general terms and it is hard to discover further details of his activities. Other gods have their myths too. Shañgo hanged himself, and then ascended to heaven. Collectively the many other gods have more followers than Ọrunmila. Ọrunmila is the favourite of some, and has his own priests; but in a polytheistic system there is fierce competition and those gods become most patronized which are successful in promoting success, curing disease, and changing 'unpregnancy'.

With the introduction of the Ifa divination and its association with Ọruñmila, perhaps by priestly manœuvre, the whole situation changes. By claiming to be the oracle of all the gods, Ọruñmila is guaranteed a place in every consultation and a share in sacrifices. He is invoked on all important occasions, at birth, adolescence, marriage and death. He declares what god a newborn child should worship. He gives the reason for sickness and trouble, and indicates which god or ancestor needs propitiation. So he has general authority, given to him by the supreme Ọlọruñ. One myth says:

Ifa was consulted for Ọruñmila once, going to receive authority from the Almighty. He sacrificed. And the Almighty gave him authority. When all the world heard that he had received authority from the Almighty they came to him. All that he said came to pass. Ever since then we say, 'It will come to pass!'[14]

While Ifa-Ọruñmila is credited with omniscience, there is a popular story which says that he received the knowledge of divination from the demonic-phallic spirit Eshu or Ẹlẹgbara. In the olden days, it is said, when men were few in number the gods were often hungry because of the paucity of the sacrifices offered to them. Ifa also was hungry and unsuccessful when he tried to work for himself. He asked Eshu what to do, and the latter offered to tell him how to get a regular supply of food for both of them. The condition of imparting the secret was that in all sacrifices the first portion should be given to Eshu. Ifa agreed and then was told to take sixteen nuts from a palm tree and was instructed how to use them for divination. This curious story simply tries to explain why in divination the first portion is set aside for Eshu. But in fact both Eshu and Ifa are intermediaries, permitting the divine messages to come to men. The myth does, however, suggest again that the geomantic system was a late introduction. Perhaps the demon Eshu is the man from Nupe.

The complex method of Ifa divination has been described many times elsewhere.[15] Suffice it here to say that manipulation of the sixteen palm nuts by the diviner produces many combinations, which all have their names, and notation which is written on a planchette. Each pattern thus produced (called an Odu) is interpreted by traditional riddles and stories. These are not obvious to the layman, and need the interpretation of the diviner who applies the example to the special need of his consultant.

> Ifa always speaks in parables,
> It is the wise man who understands.[16]

Ifa-Ọrunmila is approached with hope for blessing and success. One chant that implores his grace goes as follows:

> Ifa, fix your eyes upon me and look at me well:
> It is when you fix your eyes upon a person that he is rich;
> It is when you fix your eyes upon a person that he prospers.[17]

By his omniscience, Ọrunmila guides the destiny of men and reveals the mysteries of life to them. The diviner believes that through the many permutations of his system the unknown can be revealed. Many children at birth or adolescence have their horoscope cast for them by the diviner, and the kind of destiny that awaits them is foreshadowed. If it is evil, however, it may be changed by due offerings to the god concerned. Similarly the trials and problems that meet men in the course of their life are met by consultation of the oracle, which declares what must be done to avert evil and ensure success.

Because of his importance Ifa-Ọrunmila has first place among the days dedicated to the gods in the old Yoruba four-day week. The first day is the 'day of the secret', that of divination. On this day sacrifices of pigeons, fowls and goats are made to the god, and none of his followers should perform any other business before fulfilling this duty. It is said that in the olden days a human sacrifice might be made on exceptional and important occasions, but this was rare.

The Ifa diviner is called *baba'lawo*, 'father of mystery', or 'father of the cult'. A proverb says that the wisest priest is he who adopts the worship of Ifa. The priests usually wear white robes, though sometimes the local indigo blue dye is used for their clothes. The period of training is several years as apprentice with an old diviner, if possible at Ifè. The novice learns the Odu diagrams and the proverbs and stories associated with them. A diviner is often a herbalist as well, and some knowledge of disease is important, since Ọrunmila is looked to for the cure of disease.

The cult of Ọrunmila continues in modern times, since divination is very popular. The devotees of this cult seem to be the only ones who have tried to bring their mythology into line with the new world religions. There is a Church of Ọrunmila (*Ijọ Ọrunmila*) in Nigeria, and an Église des Oracles in Dahomey. Here the palm nuts and divining board serve as symbols instead of the Cross. A booklet published in 1943, entitled *Orunmilaism, the Basis of Jesusism*, argued that Ọrunmila was Saviour of the Yorubas as Jesus is Saviour of Christians. Another story is that Ọrunmila gave fertility herbs to Mọrowa (Mary), whence Jesus was conceived and born. Ọrunmila, it is contended, was superior to both Jesus and Muhammad since both derived from him. This is the theory of a tiny minority, though an appeal was made to the Nigerian Broadcasting Corporation to have Orunmilaism recognized as the true native religion of the Yorubas and given broadcasting time alongside Christianity and Islam. But, as Dr Idowu wisely points out, it was not hard to show 'from incontrovertible facts that Ọrunmila was just one, though a principal one, among the divinities in the Yoruba pantheon'.[18]

For those Yorubas who retain the old polytheism, and their numbers are still considerable, the ancient cults and myths are indigenous and valid. Many others neglect the old pantheons, for there is a 'twilight of the gods' owing to the great progress made by Christianity and Islam among the Yoruba in this century. But when the old gods decline magical practices often continue to flourish. Through association with Ifa it seems that Ọrunmila has a better chance than most Yoruba gods of continued existence. Perhaps the Ifa oracle is not consulted as frequently as formerly, at the birth of a child or the choice of a new village chief. But death and disease still need to be fought, and the uncertainties of the future require some kind of insurance. The old polytheists continue their devotion to the cult, but it is said that many followers of the new religions resort to the oracle, in public or in secret, in time of doubt or necessity. Fortune-telling and astrology still fascinate Europeans, and it is certain that divination will long survive in Africa. The saving deity, with his attractive mysteries, remains a powerful force in African religion.

NOTES

[1] A. B. Ellis, *The Yoruba-speaking Peoples of the Slave Coast of West Africa* (1894), 58f.
[2] J. Johnson, *Yoruba Heathenism* (1899).
[3] E. B. Idowu, *Olódùmarè, God in Yoruba Belief* (1962), 101.
[4] J. Johnson, op. cit.
[5] E. B. Idowu, op. cit., 104 f.
[6] Ibid.
[7] R. Burton, *Abeokuta and the Cameroons Mountains* (1863), 188 f.
[8] A. B. Ellis, op. cit., 57 f.
[9] Quoted in R. E. Dennett, *Nigerian Studies* (1910), 88 f.
[10] Ibid.
[11] L. Frobenius, *The Voice of Africa* (E. T. 1913), i, 228 f.
[12] S. Johnson, *The History of the Yorubas* (1921), 32 f.
[13] B. Maupoil, *La Géomancie à l'ancienne Côte des Esclaves* (1943), 50 f.
[14] S. Farrow, *Faith, Fancies and Fetich, or Yoruba Paganism* (1926), 40.
[15] E. G. Parrinder, *West African Religion* (2nd edition, 1961), pp. 138 ff.
[16] S. Farrow, op. cit., 39.
[17] E. B. Idowu, op. cit., 78.
[18] Ibid., 214.

IX

THE VENERATION OF THE PROPHET MUḤAMMAD, AS REFLECTED IN SINDHI POETRY

by

ANNEMARIE SCHIMMEL

CONSTANCE PADWICK has written that 'no one can estimate the power of Islam as a religion who does not take into account the love at the heart of it for this figure (i.e. the Prophet) . . . a warm human emotion which the peasant can share with the mystic . . .'[1]

It is a love which has been reflected in the numberless blessings (*ṣalāwāt*), expressed every day by millions of faithful Muslims over the name of him who was 'only a slave to whom it was revealed'; it is reflected in the poems setting forth, in terms of the profoundest devotion, the praise of Muḥammad, which precede every poetical composition in the Islamic countries; it is a veneration which sees in the Prophet the mild intercessor at the Day of Judgement,[2] the friend and advocate of his community, the model of human conduct, the perfect man; but also, under the influence of gnostic and neoplatonic speculations, the Perfect Man[3] who unites in himself the macro- and micro-cosmos as 'in dawn night and day are united',[4] the goal of God's creation: as God addresses him in the famous *laulāka*-traditions: 'If thou hadst not been, I would not have created the spheres', or in a later tradition—not commonly known, but used in Sufis circles at least in India: 'From the Empyrean to that which is beneath the earth, everything seeks My satisfaction, and I seek thy satisfaction, O Muḥammad!'[5] Muḥammad is the 'slave' (*ʿabd*) *katʾ exochen*, since to be 'God's slave' entails the highest bliss: that of the ascension into the immediate presence of the Lord—did not the Ḳur'ān say: 'Praised be He who travelled by night with His slave!' (Sura 17/1)?[6] Numberless miracles have been attributed to him who called the Ḳur'ān the single miraculous sign of his Prophetship—indeed theological and popular works seem to compete in enumerating his miracles.[7] Since the thirteenth century, the *maulid*, the birthday of the Prophet on 12 Rabīʿ al-awwal, has been celebrated,[8] an occasion for which, in spite of some still repeated objections from the theological side, even the most orthodox scholars have composed praises of Muḥammad,[9] which parallel the poetical descriptions of the marvellous circumstances of the Prophet's birth.[10] It has been common custom also to turn to the mild Prophet for help in every matter, and the symbol of the shelter he grants to the faithful is his *burda*, the cloak which he threw on Kaʿb ibn Zuhair when the latter recited his famous *Ḳaṣīda Bānat Suʿād*, thus imploring Muḥammad's forgiveness. The symbol became even more popular after the Egyptian poet al-Būṣīrī (d. *c.* 1296) had composed his eulogy of the Prophet who cured him of his illness by throwing, in his dream, his mantle on his shoulders: this second *burda*-poem has been learnt by heart and commented on in almost all Islamic languages, and also used as a spell against every evil.[11]

By the middle of the thirteenth century the classical veneration of Muḥammad had developed to its fullest extent: it suffices to go through Maulana Rumi's (d. 1273) *Mathnawī* and collect his wonderful verses in praise of the Lord of Messengers; his *naʿt*, the great poem in honour of Muḥammad, is still in use in the order of the Whirling Derwishes in the beautiful composition of ʿIṭrī.[12] At the same time, Ibn ʿArabī, and, somewhat later, ʿAbdurraḥīm Jīlī, worked out the theory of the Perfect Man, which was embodied in their speculations about the essential unity of being (*waḥdat al-wuǧūd*).[13]

From North Africa and Anatolia to far-away East Bengal there is no place where the poetical praise of the Prophet was not sung during the Middle Ages. Sunnites and Shiʿa poets alike contributed to it. This veneration is still as strong as ever it was: the poetry of the Indo-Muslim modernist, Sir Muḥammad Iqbal, may be cited as the most notable example of the attachment of the modern Muslim to his beloved Prophet.[14] We may also note that, already in the early period of Muslim rule in Bengal, a poet called Zainuddīn described a fantastic journey and battle of the Prophet (*Rasūl Vijay*),[15] and that his followers used this different poetical form for writing the *mi'rāǧ-nāma's* ('Book on the Ascension') and other poetical narratives about the Prophet, partly under the influence of Hindu epics, like that of Sayyid Sulṭān (d. *c.* 1648).[16] On the other hand, in the simple folksong of the riverside in Bengal Muḥammad is imagined as the great seafarer, the strong ferryman who brings the wayfarer over to the safe shore of eternity.

Urdu literature, of course, is full of the most touching poetical praises of the Prophet, and it would be amazing if the poets of the lower Indus valley, the former Province of Sind, had not produced, in their great literary output, works in praise of Muḥammad. Islam entered the country by 711, and there was no dearth of *sayyids*—descendants of the Prophet—there during the following centuries; nor of mystics who, as we can judge from the few works which have been published until now, lived in the great tradition of the Sufi orders. These mystics concentrated in their meditation upon the Prophet,[17] developing the concept of the *ḥaḳiḳa muḥammadīya* (the pre-existent Reality of Muḥammad) in long and difficult works,[18] or singing of his mysteries in verses overflowing with love—a good example is the Muḥammad-hymn in the *tafsīr sūrat al-kauṯar* by ʿAbdurraḥīm Girhōṛī (d. 1771), parts of which I have translated elsewhere.[19]

The oldest extant pieces of literature in Sind are those written in Persian, the then court language of the whole subcontinent. One of the first Persian-writing poets of the sixteenth century, Maulānā Ḳāsim Kāhī, who hailed, like many others, from Iran, had already used in his devotional poems a form which was to become very popular in both Sindhi and Panjabi, and also in Bengali religious poetry: the *sīḥarfī*,[20] i.e. the Golden Alphabet, which was often used by pious poets in order to enumerate the virtues of the Prophet. Every traditional form could express the praise of the Leader of created beings—e.g. the *maṯnawī* (the mystical *maṯnawī maẓhar al-āṯār* by Šāh Jihāngīr Hāšimī, contains no less than five *na'ts* as prelude).[21] The *rubā'ī*—otherwise vehicle of profane and mystical aphorisms, also served for extolling the Prophet,[22] and likewise the *tarǧī 'band*,[23] the long strophic poem, which by virtue of its refrain gave the poet the opportunity of repeating over and over again the formula of praise or of supplication. One of the greatest men Sind produced in those times, Mīr Ma'ṣūm Nāmī (d. 1607), the friend of Akbar, calligraphist, physician, historian and poet, was intensely attached to the Prophet, and wrote a great number of hymns and *manāḳib*, i.e. poems telling the miracles of Muḥammad:[24]

O thou whose light of Beauty displays God's mysteries,
O thou, of the grasping of whose grandeur the understanding of human beings is short!
The *kauṯar* (paradisical well) is thirsty for thy lip in the hope of life,
Riḍwān (the doorkeeper of Paradise) is disgraced in the wish of thy view.[25]

Thus runs one of his quatrains in which he does not shrink from applying the two divine attributes of *ǧamāl*, Beauty, and *ǧalāl*, Grandeur, to the Prophet, who is higher than everything in Paradise, whose lips contain the water of life even for *kauṯar* which usually grants eternal life to the blessed. Of the long *tarǧī' band* of one of his younger countrymen, Ġanī Thattawī (d. 1723), with the refrain:

Here is my hand, and the pure skirt of Muḥammad,
Here is my eye, and the collyrium of the dust of Muḥammad—

the chronicle says that 'it was immensely well received by the tongue of old and young, and was a means of help to those who wish to obtain their wants'.[26] Though, according to the classical belief, Muḥammad is only a medium through which the divine word, the Ḳur'ān, was revealed, another poet writes in a manner not uncommon in earlier Persian poets when they describe their beloved:

By the sun! is the description of thy face,
and By the Night that of thy hair—
The Ḳur'ān became completed through thy description and praise![27]

The art of *maulūd*-writing was, of course, popular among the Persian poets of Sind; poets like Fā'iz (d. 1171/1757), whose *maulūds* 'were on every tongue',[28] and Ḥakīm[29] are mentioned. From the middle of the eighteenth century the art of writing *maulūds* in Sindhi proper was introduced by Maḫdūm ʿAbdarra'ūf Bhattī (d. 1784), who used the classical Arabo-Persian metres.[30] The reason for the astonishing fact that *maulūds* were composed comparatively late in the local language may be the same as that which Ghulam Mustafa—a leading poet, and author of a *Life of Muhammad* in East Pakistan—told me in explanation of the scarcity of Bengali *maulūds* in old times: one thought the local language too unimportant, not sacred enough for expressing these holy mysteries.

The Persian poets of Sind used every available literary form—thus Muḥsin Thattawī wrote a praise-ḳaṣīda on the Prophet in the style of a spring-poem, in which all the flowers of the garden are united in a great prayer:

> Rose becomes the Imām, and the basilium prays behind her . . .[31]

And the art of composing a whole series of chronograms on some historical event by means of a praise-poem on the Prophet was found not only in Iran and Northern India, but also in the Indus valley.[32] Chronograms on Muhammad's death exist also; thus Bēdil (d. 1872) says:

> *Hū* (= He) was the chronogram of the death of the master of Prophets
> (h = 5, + u = 6 = 11 h./632 AD)
> He became united with HE; the difference in between disappeared.[33]

A religious literature in Sindhi language was composed, thanks to the efforts of Maḫdūm Muḥammad Hāšim of Thatta and his colleagues, from the beginning of the eighteenth century. Among those early works, Maḫdūm Md. Hāšim's *ḳūt alʿāšiqīn* ('The nurture of the lovers') is the most famous example, telling 'the virtues of the Prophet of God and his miracles', a work which was copied often,[34] and belonged to the first books which were printed in the Muhammadi Press in Bombay between 1867 and 1870.[35] Similar works and pieces of simple poems have been composed during the following decades, all of them in artless rhymes, just filling the last consonant with a long *a* and thus producing a rhyming effect.[36]

It was during the eighteenth century that the greatest poet of Sind appeared on the scene: Shāh ʿAbdul Laṭīf of Bhit (1689–1752).[37] In his work, the Sindhi language (of which we only know that it was long used by mystics as a means of poetical expression, although very few such verses have survived) is seen in a highly developed form, pliable and expressive and full of clever allusions and word-play. In his *Risālō*, which was printed for the first time by the German missionary Ernst Trumpp in 1867,[38] Shāh Laṭīf used the old folktales of the Indus valley as a basis for developing his mystical ideas, and singing them in the most touching way. Though sometimes the unislamic character of Sufism, especially in India, has been stressed, it seems to me that Shāh Laṭīf is one of the most brilliant exponents of Islamic mysticism at its best. There are, in his work, verses in honour of Muḥammad in which he outpours his loving feeling—he is comparatively free from the speculations about the Perfect Man, and also the pre-existent Light of Muḥammad which was such a pet subject of his contemporary mystics. He has, with a simplicity rarely met with in mystical poets of this time, sung of his sins and transgressions and expressed his hope for the friendly Lord—

Prince of Medina, hear my calling—the journey is in thy protection, thou leadst the travellers to the other shore.
Lord of Medina, hear my calling! on thee is my hope, I do not think of any other helper!
Bridegroom of Medina, hear my calling! Please, Muḥammad, come back—the sinner's hope is upon thee (*Ḍ̤ahar*, II, 1–3)

Sometimes, the sigh of the sinner who longs for Muḥammad's mild word is expressed in the words of the lonely woman who longs for her forgiving husband, and is woven again into the pattern of the old folk-stories. How touching are the *wāʾīs*—i.e. the verses with monorhyme at the end of each chapter which are sung in chorus—where the poet describes the Day of Judgement and expresses his unshakable hope in the intercession of the

Prophet, the 'advocate and intercessor, the beloved, the mercy upon the worlds'. 'Thou, only thou, art the hope of this people' he implores the Prophet in another place.[39]

But the most beautiful expression of the Prophet's mercy is *Sur Sārang*, the chapter about rain. Everybody who has been in the East knows how people long for the first clouds which bring new life to the outworn, dry, dusty country, and secure the fertility of the soil, milk to the cows, bread to the poor. The Ḳur'ān itself has called rain a sign of the mercy (*raḥmat*) of the Lord (Sūra 7/55), and still one can hear in Anatolian villages the question: 'Has there been *raḥmat* in your place?', i.e. 'Did it rain?' And since Muḥammad, too, has been called in the Ḳur'ān 'Mercy for the worlds' (Sūra 21/107), it was easy to compare him and his powers to the lifegiving cloud, the quickening rain. The comparison is not restricted to the Prophet: old Islamic poetry compares the patron to the rain,[40] and Kabīr, too, sings of the cloud of love which breaks into rain and moistens all his limbs;[41] Maulānā Rūmī has more than once shown the mystical beloved under the symbol of the rain cloud. And even in Buddhism the symbol is not uncommon; one of the finest hymns of the *Saddharmapundarika* (V, 1–27) compares the Buddha to the rain cloud which waters trees and grass alike. Thus Shāh Laṭīf did not invent anything new here; but the way in which he describes the appearing of the cloud is exquisite—its blackness reminding him of the black tresses of the beloved, i.e. Muḥammad, its pouring out of water making everybody happy; and even more exquisite is the turn he takes from this quite naturalistic description of the rain to the *wā'ī* in which the Prophet is now openly praised:

My Prince will give me protection—therefore my trust is in God,
The beloved will prostrate, will lament and cry—therefore my trust is in God,
Muḥammad, the pure and innocent, will intercede there for his people —therefore my trust is in God,
When the trumpet sounds, the eyes all will be opened—therefore my trust is in God,
The pious will gather, and Muḥammad, full of glory—therefore my trust is in God,

Will proceed for every soul to the door of the Benefactor—therefore
my trust is in God,
And the Lord will honour him, and forgive us all our sins—therefore
my trust is in God.

Besides this beautiful passage—which is followed by another, similar one (*Sārang III*)—there is one verse in the same chapter IV, where Shāh Laṭīf describes how the rain is welcomed by all countries, from Istanbul to Jaisalmer, from Dehli to Umarkot, etc. Such a description does not perhaps look like a reference to the Prophet; but when we take into consideration the later development of Sindhi prophet-hymns, we find there a special literary form which we may describe as 'geographical praise', i.e. poems in which the poet displays his whole knowledge of geographical places, from his Sindhi home village to Istanbul or even to China, in order to show how far the name of the Prophet is honoured.

There are many references to the Prophet in Shāh Laṭīf's poetry —full of pathos, for example, is the *Sur Kēdāru*, which relates the tragedy of Kerbela; but we content ourselves with mentioning one aspect which is very typical of the mystical love concerning the Prophet: the use of the Divine tradition, 'I am Aḥmad without *m*' (i.e. *aḥad*, One), which is well known to all mystics since at least the twelfth century. This *ḥadīṯ ḳudsī* is alluded to also in Shāh Laṭīf's poetry (*Sōrathi*, II, 4); but it occurs more frequently in the works of the later Sufi poets of Sind, such as Sachal (d. 1826) and Bēdil Rōhrīwārō (d. 1872), and of the Panjab, such as Bullhē Shāh (d. 1762), the reason being that it could serve as an illustration of their monistic doctrines: only the letter *m*, with the numerical value of 40, separates the Prophet (Aḥmad = Muḥammad) from the Eternal One.[42] There is a parallel tradition, namely, that God called Himself *ʿarab* without *ʿain*, i.e. *Rab*, Lord; both traditions are used alternatively. Shāh Laṭīf, however, prefers another reference to the mystical value of letters:

Put the *m* into your mind, and the *a* before it (*Yaman Kalyāṇ*, V, 28),

which means: Put the name of Muḥammad into your mind, and before it the name of Allāh (whose symbol is the straight, simple line of the Arabic *a*).[43] Hindu interpreters of the *Risālō* have found here a hint to the numinous syllable *om* as the Greatest Name of God, a view which is surely rather far fetched.[44]

In the lyrical work of the later mystics of Sind, the Prophet is praised in glowing verses; but on the whole he becomes more or less an interpreter and model of the essential unity of being. At the same time the special form of *madāḥ* (from the Arabic *madḥ*, 'praise') in the local language has developed. From about the second half of the eighteenth century it became a normal practice to sing these praise-songs in honour of the Prophet on every religious occasion, e.g. the anniversary of a saint's death, gatherings on Thursday evening, wedding-parties, etc.[45] Often first a *maulūd*, then, after a short stop, a *madāḥ* would be recited.[46] Great spiritual powers were attributed to these humble praise-poems, and though there exist many *madāḥ* extolling the first four caliphs or the saints, especially 'Abdulḳādir Gīlānī, the majority of them is composed in honour of Muḥammad 'with pure and heartfelt love and faith'.[47] Besides these *madāḥs*, which correspond to the classical *na*'*t* and *tanā*, we find also the *munāǧāt*, the prayer poems of which, again, the greatest part is addressed to the Prophet. There existed a certain class of religious poets and singers with the name *bhān*, and some of them hold that they had got this name from their connection with the famous poem *Bānat Su*'*ād* of Ka'b ibn Zuhair:

> Thou hast made me a *bhān*, O Muḥammad Mustafa,
> Reciting the ḳaṣīda *Bānat Su*'*ād*. . . .[48]

The first to start writing *madāḥ* in Sindhi was the Kalhoro prince Sarafrāz Khān, when he was imprisoned in 1774 by his successors.[49] His poem is very simple; in 30 verses he tells the aspects of the Day of Judgement and expresses his hope on Muḥammad's intercession, each stanza being followed by the refrain:

> O good prince! Listen to the prayer of this slave!

The subject was eagerly taken up by other poets. Some of the *madāḥs* contain allusions to Ḳur'ānic verses, even to classical Arabic poetry; in the rhymes Arabic and Persian words are often used for the sake of ornamentation. Among the early poets, Molla Ṣāḥib-dino of Shikarpur is especially worth mentioning.[50] All the forms which were popular in earlier Persian poetry are now used in Sindhi *madāḥ* and *maulūds*: the Golden Alphabets won special favour.[51] The general note in these poems is the stress upon Muḥammad's intercession on the Day of Judgement, and the refrains always repeat the cry for help and ask:

O put the hand of thy mercy on the head of thy slave, O Prophet![52]

or:

The rebels have hope, O Arab, in thy benevolence![53]

He is the 'leader from the *lā* (the negation in the beginning of the Muslim formula of creed) to the *illā*' (no God *but God*);[54] there are references to the miracles he has done, e.g. the healing of a sick camel:

I am sighing like the camel to the feet of the Prophet...[55]

His ascension to Heaven is a favourite subject, and so is the famous tradition: 'If thou hadst not been, I would not have created the spheres'; the refrains, which are an essential part of these poems, often contain blessings on Muḥammad; now and then the whole chain of prophets is enumerated and Muḥammad,

whose light has appeared earlier than Adam[56]

is shown as their end and seal. A peculiar subject is the wish to visit Muḥammad's resting-place at Medina, and, as Shāh Laṭīf poetically described the journey towards the Beloved in his *Sur Kunbhāt*, so another poet just sighs:

O morning breeze! Bring my greetings to the honoured Prophet,
In the high presence of His Highness confer my message:
My wish is, to see the illustrious mausoleum,
to leave this country and to live in Medina. . .[57]

Muḥammad is the prince, the lord, and he is depicted just as people in Sindhi and Baloch countryside imagined their own leaders; very simply they trust in him and see him as the King of Kings, the ruler of all places known to them:

> Thy drum is in Turan, among the Arabs and the Persians of Iran,
> In Mecca, Egypt and Multan . . .

In this geographical context (which had been mentioned in connection with the rain-motif) Ḥamal Faḳīr Lagārī (d. 1878) sings in 37 verses (out of a poem of 81 verses) the glory of the Prophet which ranges from Kairouan to Rohri, from Europe to China.[58] And another poet enumerates Ḳur'ānic and traditional hints of the glory of the Prophet:

> Thou art the caliph of creation: 'If thou hadst not been' was said in thy praise,
> There was without doubt thy mentioning several times in the Ḳur'ān,
> Thy description is in the sūras 'Star', Yāsīn and Raḥmān,
>
> Prayed upon him, the best of men, says the Great One in the Ḳur'ān.[59]

These poems are no masterpieces of poetical art, but the utterances of unsophisticated pious souls, made in such a way that even the illiterate villager could understand them and learn them by heart. Some of them were thought of as being of extraordinary merit: there is a *muʿǧiza*, a poem about Muḥammad's miracles, the poet of which promises 'innumerable future rewards' to those who read or recite it on Thursday evening.[60]

It is a strange fact that, in Sind, the art of *madāḥ* writing was not confined to the Muslims; but, as in old times, many Hindus were disciples of Muslim pirs, a Hindu poet, Ṣūfī Asūrām (d. 1941) has composed a fine prayer-poem in which he implores the grace, kindness and mercy of the Prophet of God.[61] It was also a Hindu teacher in Hyderabad/Sind who published the first *Life of Muḥammad* in Sindhi language in 1911—seeing that the children knew merely legendary facts about the founder of their religion, he thought it necessary to provide them with a biographical sketch which is very objective and written in simple prose. Three years later, a *Life of the Prophet* appeared from the pen of Ḥakīm Fatḥ Muḥammad Sehwani, who thought that it was high time to write about the benign state of the Lord of Prophets instead of composing exaggerated legend of saints, or worst of all, novels and plays.[62] Since then, the great Urdu biography of the Prophet by ʿAllāma Shiblī has been translated into Sindhi, as well as other studies on this subject. Moreover, the art of writing and singing *madāḥ*, prayers, and *maulūds* is still as flourishing as ever—not only do poetical works (like the Maṯnawī Muḥammadī of Ḥāfiẓ Basmal of Thikkuṛ, Hyderabad, 1957)[63] tell of the life and miracles of the Prophet, but the women in the villages sing these religious folk-songs, either alone or accompanied by the drum (*dhōlak*), and the children are brought up with the simple and pious songs, living in the very hope which Shāh Laṭīf had expressed in the beginning of his *risālō*:

When those who said 'He is God, alone, He has no partner'
Respect Muḥammad the intercessor, out of love with their hearts,
Then none of them is entangled in a place where there is bad landing.
(*Kalyāṇ*, I, 3)

NOTES

[1] Constance E. Padwick, *Muslim Devotions*, London, 1961, p. 145, cf. especially chap. 10b and 11a.

[2] Cf. ibid. chap. 2, and T. Huitema, *De voorspraak* (*shafāʿa*) *in den Islam*, Leiden, 1936.

[3] The essential study of the whole complex is that of Tor Andrae, *Die Person Muhammads in Glauben und Lehre seiner Gemeinde*, Stockholm, 1917. He gives an excellent account of the development of Muḥammad's veneration as based on the classical works like Abū Nuʿaims *dalā'il an-nubuwwa*, Ḳasṭallānī's *al-mawāhib al-ladunīya*, al-Baihaḳī's *dalā'il an-nubuwwa*, mystical works and widely used books like Jazuli's *dalā'il al-ḫairāt*. About the development of the idea of *insān kāmil*: H. H. Schaeder, *Die islamische Lehre vom Vollkommenen Menschen*, *ZDMG* 79.

[4] *Kalām Girhōrī*, ed. U. M. Daudpota, Hyderabad/Sind 1956, in *tafsīr kauṯar*, line 61 f. Cf. also ibid., p. 34, of the commentary, where Dr Daudpota even wants to interpret the famous verse of Shāh ʿAbdul Laṭīf of Bhit:

Do not call Him lover, nor call Him Beloved (*Ḳalyān* I 23)

as a description of the two aspects of the Perfect Man, i.d. the Prophet.

[5] *Miftāḥ rušd Allāh*, *tafsīr kalām*, part I, Karachi s.d., p. 2.

[6] On the high rank of *ʿabduhu* cf. Muhammad Iqbal, *Jāvīdnāme*, *Jupiter-Heaven*, and A. Schimmel, *Gabriel's Wing. A Study into the religious ideas of Sir Muhammad Iqbal*, Leiden, 1963, chap. II, 2.

[7] Cf. Andrae, loc. cit., about the development of prophetical miracles, and Baḳillānī, *kitāb fī iʿğāz al-Ḳurʾān*.

[8] Andrae, p. 368; Ibn Ḥallikān, II, (about *maulid* in Arbela in 604/1207; Maḳriẓi, *Hiṭaṭ*, I, 433, 466; art. 'Maulid' in *Handwörterbuch des Islam*, Leiden, 1942.

[9] Cf. Ibn Katīr (d. 774/1372), *maulid rasūl Allāh*, ed. Dr Ṣalāḥaddīn al-Munağğid, Beirut, 1961.

[10] Perhaps the finest example is Suleyman Çelebi's *maulūd-i-šarīf* in Turkish poetry, which has been popular in Turkey since the 14th century; cf. Lyman MacCallum's translation, London, 1936; I. Engelke, Süleyman Tschelebis *Lobgedicht auf den Propheten*, Berlin 1926.

[11] Cf. EI s.v. 'burda'.

[12] Text and melody in A. Gölpinarli, *Mevlana'dan sonra Mevlevilik*, Istanbul, 1953, p. 503 f.

[13] Cf. A. Affifi, *Ibn ʿArabi*, Cambridge, 1936; R. A. Nicholson, *Studies in Islamic Mysticism*, Cambridge, 1921; H. S. Nyberg, *Kleinere Schriften des Ibn al-Arabi*, Leiden, 1919.

[14] Cf. A. Schimmel, *The Place of the Prophet in the Thought of Iqbal*, Islamic Studies, Karachi, 1962.

[15] Enamul Haq, *Muslim Bengali Literature*, Karachi, 1947, p. 56.

[16] Ibid., pp. 111 ff.

[17] S. M. Muṭīʿullāh Rāšid Burhānpūrī, *Burhānpūr kē Sindhī Auliyā*, Karachi, p. 152.

[18] A very important source is the still unpublished Persian work of Abū'l-Hasan Ḍāhirī, *yanābiʿ al-ḥayāt al-abadīya*, cf. Kalām-i Girhōrī, notes, p. 30.

[19] *Oriens*, XVI: 'Sindhi Translations and Commentaries of the Ḳurʾān'.

[20] Cf. *IC* 1953; a complete edition of Kāhī's poetry is being published by Hafeez Hoshyarpuri, in Sindhi Adabi Board, Hyderabad.

[21] *Matawi mazhar al-āṭār*, ed. Sayyid H. Rashdi, Karachi, 1955.

[22] Cf. Mīr ʿAlī Šīr Ḳāniʿ, *maḳālāt aš-šuʿarā*, ed. H. Rashdi, Karachi, 1956, pp. 193, 180.

[23] Ibid., p. 159; cf. *Dīwān-i ʿAṭā*, ed. Rāšid Burhānpūrī, Karachi s.d., pp. 338, 340.

[24] H. I. Sadarangani, *Persian Poets of Sind*, Karachi, 1956, p. 30; Ḳāniʿ, loc. cit., p. 801.

[25] *Sadarangani*, loc. cit., p. 30.

[26] Ḳāniʿ, loc. cit., 478; Gulām ʿAlī Māʾil, *Dīwān*, ed. M. A. ʿAbbāsī and M. H. Rushdi, Karachi, 1959, pp. 191 ff.; *Sadarangani*, loc. cit., p. 290; *Kulliyāt-i Gadā*, ed. Rashid Ahmad Lashari, Karachi, 1957, pp. 283 ff.

[27] Mahdūm Ibrahīm Ḥalīl, *takmilat maḳālāt aš-šuʿarā*, ed. H. Rashdi, Karachi, 1959, p. 44.

[28] Ḳāniʿ, loc. cit., 483.

[29] Ibid. p. 183.

[30] Sayyid H. Rashdi, *Sindhi Adab*, Karachi s.d., p. 58.

[31] Ḳāniʿ, loc. cit., p. 714.

[32] Ibid., p. 516: 3600 chronograms for the day of Miyan Muhammad Murādyāb Khān's ascension to the throne; cf. *Dīwān-i Māʾil*, p. 199 ff., a similar praise-poem in chronograms; and Rückert-Pertsch, *Grammatik, Poetik und*

Rhetorik der Perser, Gotha, 1870, p. 253, a similar poem by Muḥammad Bāḳir Gīlānī about Aurangzēb's reign.

[33] Bēdil, *Diwan*, ed. Abdul-Ḥusain Šāh Mūsawī, Karachi, 1954, p. 348.

[34] Cf. H. T. Sorley, *Shah Abdul Latif of Bhit*, Oxford, 1940, p. 216, and R. Burton's remarks about the religious education of boys in Sind (*Sind and the races that inhabit the Indus valley*). The *ḳūt al-āšiḳīn* was printed again in 1950 in Hyderabad.

[35] Al-Ḥāğğ Allāh Baḫš Uḳailī, *Sindhi čhapā'ī ğī muḫtaṣar ta'rīh*, in *Mihrāṇ jā mōtī*, Karachi, 1960, p. 217.

[36] Cf. British Museum, Sindhi MSS., Or. 6533, Or. Add. 26335 which contains, *inter alia*, a 'Praise of Muhammad', a *maulūd*, a poem of the marriage of Muhammad and Ḫadīğa.

[37] H. T. Sorley, *Shah Abdul Latif of Bhit* is the best book on this subject. The edition used by the present writer was that of K. Aduwani, Bombay, 1958.

[38] About the first investigator of Sindhi language see: A. Schimmel, *Ernst Trumpp. A Brief Account of his Life and Work*, Karachi, 1962.

[39] *Sur Bilāwal*, IV, *wā'ī*; *Sur Barwō Sindhī* III, *wā'ī* 2; cf. *Sur Sārang* III *wā'ī*, *Sur Kunbhāt* I, *wā'ī*, etc.

[40] U. M. Daudpota, *The Influence of Arabic Poetry on the Development of Persian Poetry*, Bombay, 1934, p. 93.

[41] Ch. Vaudeville, *Kabir Granthavali* (*Doha*), Pondichéry, 1957, p. 4, No. I, 34.

[42] On these monistic trends in Sindhi poetry cf. A. Schimmel, The Martyr-Mystic Ḥallāj in Sindhi Folk-poetry in *NUMEN. IX* 3

[43] Cf. also *Sur Suhṇi*, III, 9, *Sur Pūrab*, II, wā'ī.

[44] Jethmal Parsram, *Sufis of Sind*, Madras, 1924, p. 120.

[45] A fine collection of these poems is—after some smaller Bombay prints—made by the Sindhi Adabi Board in its Folklore Series: *Madāḥūn ain munāğātūn*, ed. Dr N. B. Baloch, Karachi, 1959; there is a good collection of *muʿğizā*, ed. Dr N. B. Baloch, Karachi, 1960, and of *manāḳibā*, ed. Dr N. B. Baloch, Karachi, 1960, which together form the basis for further research. Cf. *madāḥūn*, p. 1, 13.

[46] Ibid., p. 14.

[47] Ibid., p. 5.

[48] Ibid., p. 8.

[49] H. Rashdi, *Sindhi Adab*, p. 59, cf. p. 63; *Madāḥūn*, pp. 11, ff.

[50] H. Rashdi, loc. cit., 74.

[51] A special collection of these religious Golden Alphabets is: *Ṭīh akariyūn*, ed. N. B. Baloch, Karachi, 1960, which belongs to the same Folklore Series as the above-mentioned books.

[52] *Madāḥūn*, p. 20, in the refrain.

[53] Ibid., p. 192, cf. p. 98. Arabic formulas like a repeated *al-ġiyāṯ*, help!, and others are frequently found.

[54] Ibid., p. 95.

[55] Ibid., p. 25, cf. especially the *manaḳibā* and the *muʿğizā*. Shāh Laṭīf also alludes once to a miracle, i.e. that the elephant, at the time when Abraha besieged Mecca, prostrated before Muḥammad's ancesṭor ʿAbd al-Muṭallib when he saw the light on his forehead (*Sur Sārang*, III, wā'ī).

[56] *Madāḥūn*, p. 231.

[57] Ibid., p. 180. The motif is very common in Islamic poetry, and is also found, for instance, in Muhammad Iqbal's poetry.

[58] Ibid., p. 121, cf. ibid. 310. For the first time it is used in a praise-poem in honour of ʿAbdulḳādir Gīlānī by Mēnghī Faḳīr Šar Balōch, ibid., 160.

[59] Ibid., p. 253.

[60] *muʿǧizā*, p. 176.

[61] *madāḥūn*, p. 313.

[62] *ḥayāt an -nabī*, Hyderabad, 1914, 1959[5].

[63] *Naieṇ Zindagī*, June 1960.

X

REMARQUES SUR LA SOTÉRIOLOGIE DU NOUVEAU TESTAMENT

par

MARCEL SIMON

LE christianisme a été mainte fois, et à juste titre, défini comme le type même de la religion de salut.[1] Le terme de comparaison normal, à cet égard, est fourni par les cultes à mystères qui, nés comme lui dans le Proche Orient, se sont propagés dans le temps même où il se diffusait à travers le monde méditerranéen et constituent une partie de son contexte historico-religieux.[2] Certains chercheurs ont pensé trouver de ce côté non seulement des parallèles au «mystère chrétien», mais le prototype même dont le christianisme ne serait qu'un démarcage plus ou moins précis. On connaît les vues exposées par tel ou tel représentant de la *religionsgeschichtliche Schule* au début du siècle,[3] les controverses qu'elles ont suscitées et la réaction qui est intervenue par la suite. Elle a été parfois jusqu'à nier toute espèce d'affinité, sinon de pure apparence, entre cultes à mystères et christianisme. L'on s'est alors tourné volontiers vers le judaïsme, pour y chercher des points de comparaison plus probants ou des influences plus plausibles.[4]

Il n'est dans mon intention ni de rouvrir le débat, ni de l'arbitrer. Je voudrais, beaucoup plus modestement, compte tenu de l'emprise indéniable et persistante des cadres de la pensée juive sur la théologie chrétienne, et les ressemblances entre le christianisme et les religions à mystères étant un fait, plus difficile à mesurer et à apprécier exactement qu'à constater, proposer, un peu à bâtons rompus, quelques réflexions sur certains traits de la sotériologie chrétienne primitive et sur la problématique particulière qu'elle implique.

Si l'on confronte le christianisme naissant avec les mystères, la différence la plus frappante, la plus immédiatement apparente réside dans le fait que le Sauveur chrétien est un personnage de l'histoire, tandis que les sauveurs païens sont des figures mythiques. Alfred Loisy, pervenu au terme de son évolution spirituelle, exprimait son scepticisme radical vis-à-vis des dogmes chrétiens en disant qu'il ne se sentait plus capable de souscrire qu'à un seul article du *credo*: «Il a souffert sous Ponce Pilate». De fait, le christianisme n'est pas concevable sans l'historicité du Christ. Essayer, comme l'ont fait les tenants de l'école dite mythologique, de démontrer qu'elle n'était qu'un leurre, c'était s'attaquer aux fondements mêmes de la foi.[5] Et toute l'apologétique chrétienne contemporaine, soucieuse d'arracher Jésus à des rapprochements jugés compromettants et dangereux, n'a pas manqué de souligner l'opposition qui sépare à cet égard le mystère chrétien et les mystères païens.[6] Elle est en effet, pour nous modernes, fondamentale et irréductible. Il n'est pas certain que l'optique des anciens ait été exactement la même que la nôtre. On doit noter en effet que ni, bien entendu, la masse des païens, ni même parfois les chrétiens de l'époque n'ont mis en doute la réalité historique des figures divines et plus particulièrement — ce sont les seules qui nous intéressent ici — des divinités salvatrices.

Sans doute, la position des auteurs chrétiens n'est pas sur ce point uniforme. Il y a bien chez eux une critique de l'idolâtrie, dont les éléments sont empruntés à l'Ancien Testament et à la polémique juive antipaïenne: «Leurs idoles sont de l'argent et de l'or, ouvrage de la main des hommes».[7] Mais, conscients que, au moins pour les païens éclairés, la statue du dieu n'est qu'un symbole, certains d'entre eux admettent eux aussi qu'il existe, derrière les images cultuelles, une réalité spirituelle. «Elles portent le nom et sont faites à la ressemblance de ces démons mauvais qui apparurent autrefois».[8] L'argument qu'ils opposent à leurs adversaires n'est pas, en général, «vos dieux n'existent pas», mais plutôt «ce ne sont pas de vrais dieux». On les identifie parfois aux anges déchus de la Bible, mais parfois aussi on y reconnaît, à la suite d'Evhémère, des hommes, souverains pour la plupart, et bienfaiteurs de l'humanité, que la gratitude de leurs congénères éleva au ciel. L'évhémérisme, parce qu'il fournissait à l'Eglise ancienne une arme fort précieuse, a connu dans ses rangs une fortune considérable. «Ceux que vous adorez n'étaient jadis que des hommes» écrit Clément d'Alexandrie.[9] Et Firmicus Maternus, qui explique le paganisme par le culte des éléments, fait cependant une exception à propos des mystères isiaques: «Cet Osiris et ce Typhon furent sans doute rois et souverains de l'Egypte. Mais l'un fut juste, sauf dans le crime (d'inceste) qu'il commit avec sa soeur, tandis que l'autre fut violent, emporté et orgueilleux. Aussi Osiris est-il vénéré, Typhon redouté. Voilà l'essentiel de la religion d'Isis».[10] L'auteur s'en prend ensuite aux païens allégorisants qui «donnent de ces rites une interprétation fondée sur la nature. A leurs dires, Osiris n'est autre que le grain, Isis la terre, Typhon la chaleur». Il les réfute en affirmant que «ces funérailles et ce deuil ont été réellement célébrés autrefois» et en rappelant «qu'un tombeau d'Osiris existe toujours en Egypte».[11]

Dans une telle perspective, les différences par rapport à Jésus s'estompent considérablement. Comme lui, les dieux sauveurs du paganisme sont des hommes qui ont vécu sur terre. Certes, pour un fidèle de l'Eglise ancienne, ce ne sont que des hommes, indûment divinisés, tandis que le Christ est le Dieu fait homme. Mais cette opposition se situe sur le plan subjectif de la foi et non pas, comme celle qui apparaît à l'historien moderne, sur celui des réalités objectives. Dès lors qu'on admet l'existence terrestre des sauveurs païens, la différence essentielle réside dans le fait que la passion du Christ se place dans un passé encore tout proche, tandis que celle de ses rivaux appartient aux lointaines origines de l'histoire humaine. Et elle se solde en définitive, pour le christianisme qui cherche à se répandre en milieu païen, par un handicap assez sérieux. Car la mentalité païenne fait volontiers de l'ancienneté un critère de vérité. On reproche au christianisme sa nouveauté par rapport au *mos majorum* et même à la tradition juive, à laquelle on reconnaît quelques titres de noblesse, précisément parce qu'elle est faite de l'apport des siècles.[12] Par surcroît, le Sauveur chrétien est mort dans le supplice infamant de la crucifixion, comme un criminel de droit commun, et l'autorité romaine a eu quelque part dans sa condamnation. Les dieux souffrants du paganisme au contraire ont péri victimes soit de quelque fatalité, soit des forces mauvaises qui sont à l'oeuvre dans l'univers. Leur mort n'est point ignominieuse. A ceux des païens que rebutait la grossière crudité de certains mythes, l'allégorie — Firmicus Maternus nous le rappelait à l'instant — offrait une possibilité de transposition et de réinterprétation, dans la ligne d'un panthéisme naturaliste. Aucune allégorie n'était possible en revanche dans le cas d'un homme qu'on savait avoir été supplicié en Palestine, sous le règne de Tibère. Nous avons, certes, quelque peine à nous persuader que tel ait pu être l'état d'esprit des païens confrontés au christianisme. Il ne fait guère de doute cependant que tel il a été effectivement, plus d'une fois. Il n'est pour s'en convaincre que de feuilleter Celse, à travers Origène, ou Julien l'Apostat.[13]

Le caractère tardif de la passion du Christ soulevait en outre un problème théologique que les cultes à mystères, si du moins ils se le sont explicitement posé, ont pu résoudre plus facilement. Pour ces derniers en effet, puisque la passion du dieu se situe aux origines de l'histoire, l'instauration des rites qui la commémorent est censée se placer elle-même aussitôt après. C'est dire que dès la naissance de l'humanité, les moyens de salut sont mis à la disposition de ceux qui voudront bien y recourir. Il n'y a pour les cultes à mystères, tout au long de l'histoire humaine, qu'une seule division, celle qui oppose les initiés à ceux qui ne le sont pas. Pour le christianisme au contraire, à cette coupure qu'on pourrait appeler verticale, qui sépare ici en deux catégories l'humanité postérieure au Christ, s'en ajoute une autre, horizontale: elle oppose ceux qui, nés après le Christ, ont pu s'intégrer à son Eglise, et ceux qui, morts avant sa venue, ne l'ont pas connu. Le problème du salut des infidèles revêt ainsi, pour la pensée chrétienne, un double aspect, puisqu'il concerne deux catégories différentes d'individus. Il a beaucoup préoccupé les théologiens des premiers siècles. Les tentatives diverses faites pour vieillir le christianisme et pour démontrer qu'il n'est en fait que l'épanouissement ou la résurgence de la religion primordiale de l'humanité visent sans doute non seulement à lui conférer des quartiers de noblesse et à réfuter l'accusation de nouveauté qu'on lui opposait,[14] mais aussi à fournir une réponse satisfaisante à un problème que les païens eux-mêmes n'ont pas manqué de soulever: «Pourquoi le Christ serait-il venu si tardivement, après avoir laissé l'humanité privée pendant tant de siècles du bienfait de la révélation? Pourquoi aurait-il permis que se perdent sans secours d'innombrables âmes?»[15]

La question revêtait d'ailleurs une acuité très différente selon qu'elle s'adressait à des milieux de tradition paulinienne ou à des éléments plus ou moins teintés de judéo-christianisme — et je pense pour ma part qu'il en a existé dans la Grande Eglise jusqu'à une date assez avancée. Le christocentrisme radical de Paul ne laissait à l'Ancienne Alliance qu'une place assez modeste dans l'économie du salut, puisqu'il allait jusqu'à établir une connexion très étroite entre le règne de la Loi et celui du péché.[16] Pour le judéo-christianisme de toutes nuances, la Loi offrait, avant que vînt le Christ, un moyen de salut: la division verticale que je mentionnais à l'instant remontait ainsi jusqu'à la période pré-chrétienne. Il y a dans le Nouveau Testament des traces de cette sotériologie sans sauveur qui est celle du judaïsme. Au jeune homme ou au docteur de la Loi qui l'interrogent sur ce qu'ils doivent faire pour accéder à la vie éternelle, Jésus rappelle tout simplement la pratique du Décalogue ou de la loi d'amour de Dieu et du prochain. Il propose en outre au premier de renoncer à ses biens et de le suivre, «ayant pris la croix» ajoute Marc.[17] Nous sommes ici dans la ligne de cette majoration par rapport aux exigences de la Loi morale juive qui paraît avoir été caractéristique de la prédication de Jésus. Mais le rôle qu'il s'assigne est celui d'un guide et d'un modèle, non pas d'un sauveur à proprement parler. C'est à son imitation, mais non par son sacrifice rédempteur que le disciple sera sauvé. L'instrument véritable du salut, c'est encore la Loi, interprétée, précisée et pratiquée de façon exemplaire par Jésus.

Même dans les milieux, devenus rapidement majoritaires, de l'Eglise ancienne qui ne s'en sont pas tenus à cette conception, et qui assignent au Christ seul la fonction salvatrice reconnue par les

Juifs à la Loi, la sotériologie chrétienne reste étroitement tributaire du judaïsme. Elle le reste en particulier du fait de la relation étroite, et en quelque sorte organique, dans laquelle elle se trouve par rapport à l'eschatologie. C'est là une autre différence fondamentale avec les religions païennes de salut, à la seule exception, semble-t-il, du mithriacisme, où l'eschatologie mazdéenne paraît avoir tenu une place assez analogue à celle que l'eschatologie juive a continué d'occuper dans le christianisme.[18] Selon le schéma le plus habituel dans les cultes à mystères, c'est immédiatement après sa mort que le myste accède à l'immortalité bienheureuse, après, avoir triomphé d'épreuves, diversement imaginées par les divers mystères, et affronté peut-être, comme dans ceux d'Osiris, un jugement individuel. Au contraire, dans la tradition de pensée juive et chrétienne, et dans le mithriacisme, le sort des élus comme celui des réprouvés ne sont définitivement réglés qu'à la fin des temps, dans le cadre d'un renouvellement cosmique total, par la résurrection et le jugement dernier. D'où la nécessité d'une période d'attente, d'un état intermédiare. Celui-ci peut être soit neutre et qualitativement indifférencié, soit fait de souffrances ou de joies qui annoncent, pour l'âme encore désincarnée, ce que sera son sort lorsqu'elle aura à nouveau revêtu une enveloppe corporelle.

Il est certain que ce schéma posait des problèmes inconnus des cultes à mystères, mithriacisme exclu. La résurrection des corps est difficile à imaginer. Pour un païen, surtout s'il est plus ou moins frotté de platonisme, elle est une impossibilité et un non-sens. Les porte-parole du paganisme ne se sont pas fait faute d'en rire, non sans lourdeur. Porphyre propose à ses adversaires chrétiens le cas suivant: un homme meurt dans un naufrage; les poissons de la mer dévorent son corps; ils sont à leur tour mangés par des pêcheurs; ceux-ci périssent et leurs cadavres sont dévorés par des chiens, qui sont enfin la proie des vautours. Qu'est devenue la chair du naufragé, et comment imaginer qu'il puisse ressusciter un jour?[19]

En fait, la croyance à la résurrection des morts, telle que l'entendent le christianisme primitif et le judaïsme de l'époque, trouve son contexte le plus naturel dans la vieille conception israélite du *schéol* où l'existence souterraine des défunts, indistinctement mêlés, qu'ils soient justes ou pécheurs, est celle de pâles fantômes, plongés dans une torpeur ou un sommeil assez voisins de l'annihilation totale.[20] Dans cette optique, le retour à la lumière du jour et à une vie digne de ce nom par une résurrection corporelle apparaît effectivement comme le seul moyen d'accéder à la félicité, une félicité qui se situe sur terre. A partir du moment où l'on admet, comme le faisaient au début de notre ère d'importants secteurs de l'opinion juive, que cet état intermédiaire désincarné non seulement n'entraîne pas la perte de la conscience, mais préfigure déjà, étant soit heureux, soit malheureux, le sort final de chaque individu, la question se pose immanquablement de savoir ce qu'une résurrection corporelle, même et surtout si ce n'est pas celle du corps de chair, peut y ajouter de vraiment spécifique. Elle s'est posée déjà pour le judaïsme, dont certains éléments paraissent avoir opté, sans doute sous l'influence de conceptions grecques, pour l'immortalité sans résurrection, tandis que d'autres, les plus nombreux, s'efforçaient d'accorder les deux notions.[21] Pour le christianisme, le problème se compliquait du fait de la résurrection de Jésus, affirmation centrale de la foi. Jésus étant le premier-né d'entre les morts, ses fidèles devaient necessairement sortir un jour du tombeau comme il l'avait fait lui-même, revêtus d'un corps glorieux, pour être ensuite, comme lui, élevés dans les cieux.[22] Que la pensée chrétienne primitive ait connu à ce sujet quelques hésitations et ait été parfois tentée d'opter elle aussi pour une béatitude définitive, suivant immédiatement la mort corporelle, le Nouveau Testament l'illustre amplement. Rien par exemple, dans la parabole de Lazare et du mauvais riche, ne suggère que leurs situations respectives ne sont que provisoires.[23] La notion johannique d'une vie éternelle qui pour les fidèles commence dès ici-bas, et dont il est généralement parlé au présent, se plie assez mal aux cadres de la pensée juive dans lesquels elle s'exprime.[24] Elle ne laisse guère de place à ce sommeil qui même pour Saint Paul, sépare le mort de la résurrection.[25] Lorsque, dans le Quatrième Evangile, le Christ déclare «celui qui mange ma chair et boit mon sang a la vie éternelle, et moi je le ressusciterai au dernier jour»,[26] on ne peut se défendre de l'impression que le second membre de phrase atteste l'emprise durable des schémas juifs pré-chrétiens plutôt qu'il ne prolonge la ligne de pensée exprimée dans le premier.[27] Dans l'épisode de la résurrection de Lazare, l'affirmation de Jésus: «je suis la résurrection et la vie; celui qui croit en moi, quand même il mourrait, vivra, et quiconque vit et croit en moi ne mourra jamais»[28] semble bien corriger, et réfuter, la profession de foi, très traditionnellement pharisienne, de Marthe: «Je sais que mon frère ressuscitera lors de la résurrection, au dernier jour».[29] La parole que Luc prête à Jésus s'adressant au bon larron: «aujourd'hui encore tu seras avec moi dans le Paradis»[30] paraît refléter, bien que l'auteur la fasse suivre du récit de la résurrection, un état de la pensée chrétienne où l'ascension de Jésus et, à sa suite, l'assomption de son compagnon de supplice étaient conçues comme immédiatement consécutives à leur mort.[31] Il n'est pas sûr enfin que la pensée paulinienne elle-même soit à cet égard aussi assurée et aussi immuable qu'on l'admet souvent et qu'elle n'ait pas évolué dans le sens de ce qu'on pourrait appeler une hellénisation croissante.[32]

Plusieurs ouvrages récents, soucieux de dégager l'originalité du christianisme vis-à-vis de la pensée grecque, ont insisté sur des antinomies à coup sûr réelles, mais non point aussi radicalement irréductibles qu'ils ne les présentent.[33] Ni l'hellénisme, ni la tradition biblique, ni la pensée chrétienne ne sont parfaitement uniformes et homogènes et ne se sont développés en vase clos. Il y a, de l'un à l'autre, des interférences indiscutables. La pensée grecque ne se réduit pas au seul platonisme, que l'on prend souvent comme pierre de touche. Opposer sans nuances l'immortalité de l'âme, notion grecque, et la résurrection, conception chrétienne héritée du judaïsme, c'est méconnaître les influences du milieu hellénistique qui se sont exercées sur le christianisme dès ses premiers pas, tout comme elles s'étaient exercées déjà sur le judaïsme. Elles rendent compte, au moins pour une part, des hésitations dont je viens de relever quelques exemples. Au reste, peut-on parler encore, quatre siècles après Alexandre, de «Grecs», et les opposer en bloc aux Juifs et aux Chrétiens? La civilisation et la pensée du monde hellénistique sont faites de bien d'autres apports encore que celui de la seule Grèce classique. Or ce sont elles, et non pas les écoles athéniennes du IVème siècle, qui représentent le contexte du christianisme naissant. Dire que pour «les Grecs» l'âme est immortelle par nature, tandis que pour la Bible et le christianisme la vie éternelle est un don de Dieu, c'est oublier que, pour un nombre considérable — la majorité peut-être — de «Grecs», c'est-à-dire en définitive de païens, au début de l'ère chrétienne, la mort ne donne accès qu'aux ténèbres de l'Hadès et à une survie aussi blafarde et fantomatique que celle du *schéol*, ou plus simplement encore, ne s'ouvre que sur le néant: les nombreuses épitaphes désabusées du type «*non fui, fui, non sum, non curo*» témoignent d'un scepticisme assez commun touchant l'au-delà.[34] C'est oublier aussi, à l'inverse, que dans la perspective des cultes à mystères, assez analogue à celle du christianisme, la véritable immortalité, loin d'être un attribut naturel de l'âme, est le privilège de ceux qui se sont fait initier, et par conséquent un don du dieu sauveur. Opposer la vision verticale des Grecs — vie d'ici-bas et vie dans l'au-delà — à la vision horizontale de la Bible et du christianisme — monde présent et monde à venir — c'est simplifier à l'excès une réalité infiniment complexe. Il existe un messianisme païen, tendu vers les promesses d'un futur radieux — *veniet felicior aetas* — ; pour les chrétiens le «ciel» est une réalité présente, aussi indiscutable que le Royaume des temps ultimes; et la théologie ecclésiastique s'est toujours efforcée de faire le raccord entre les deux.[35]

Le problème qui se posait à elle relativement à la survie des fidèles devait nécessairement se poser aussi par rapport au Christ lui-même: sa réponse, mentionnée plus haut, au bon larron en fait foi. Vainqueur de la mort, pour lui-même et pour l'humanité rachetée, était-il concevable qu'il eût été asservi, ne fût-ce que trois jours, au sommeil de la mort? Son destin n'était-il donc en rien supérieur è celui des sauveurs païens qui, eux, étaient morts d'une mort totale, avant de renaître à la vie éternelle? Il semble bien, ici encore, que les catégories juives traditionnelles aient parfois infléchi la pensée chrétienne dans un sens qui n'était peut-être pas le plus naturel. Elles font apparaître le séjour du Christ dans la tombe, si bref qu'il ait été, comme l'équivalent de cet état d'attente ou de dépouillement qui, pour de commun des hommes, doit séparer la mort corporelle de la résurrection finale. Mais alors il introduit dans le déroulement du plan divin une coupure déconcertante. Car la théologie chrétienne n'a cessé d'affirmer, à la suite de Saint Paul, que l'acte rédempteur du Christ, le tournant décisif, c'est-à-dire sa victoire sur le péché, les puissances mauvaises et la mort, se situe non pas au matin de Pâques, — la Résurrection n'est que le signe et la conséquence de cette victoire — mais sur la croix, au moment même où il expire: «Il a dépouillé les principautés et les puissances, et les a livrées hardiment en spectacle en triomphant d'elles par la croix».[36] Il était impossible d'admettre, dans ces conditions, que son passage dans la tombe ait pu être un moment d'annihilation totale. L'idée d'une entrée immédiate dans le Paradis, telle qu'elle s'exprime dans la réponse au bon larron, pouvait résoudre le problème. Mais du même coup elle en posait une autre, en rendant difficilement explicable, parce que superflue, la Résurrection. Certains secteurs de l'Eglise primitive ont eu très tôt conscience de ces difficultés. Les spéculations relatives à la descente aux Enfers en apportent la preuve.[37]

Elles s'efforcent de combler de façon satisfaisante le vide qui sépare la mise au tombeau du Christ et son retour triomphal à la lumière et de rétablir ainsi, entre sa vie terrestre et sa vie glorifiée, cette continuité qui seule peut sauvegarder l'unité du plan divin. Du même coup elles fournissent une solution au problème qui se pose relativement aux justes morts avant le Christ.

Le Christ est «descendu aux Enfers», soit pour leur annoncer la bonne nouvelle de leur salut et de la résurrection à venir, soit pour accomplir d'emblée à leur bénéfice, parfois au prix d'un combat avec Satan et ses hordes, l'acte rédempteur.[38] Sans doute, c'est dans des Apocryphes du Nouveau Testament, de date relativement tardive, que cette conception du «descensus», sous l'une ou l'autre forme, trouve son expression la plus nette et ses développements les plus étoffés.[39] Mais l'on peut tenir pour assuré qu'elle est très ancienne. Le R. P. Daniélou estime qu'elle est étrangère au Nouveau Testament et qu'elle est proprement judéo-chrétienne.[40] Je serais, sur l'un et l'autre point, moins catégorique que lui. On peut admettre que le sort des saints de l'Ancien Testament ait préoccupé spécialement les chrétiens venus d'Israël. Mais les alliances conclues avec Abraham, puis avec Moïse, ne fournissaient-elles pas au peuple élu, jusqu'à la venue du Christ, les moyens de salut nécessaires? Il n'est pas sûr que la majorité des judéo-chrétiens ait partagé sur ce point le pessimisme de Paul. A l'inverse, la question ne pouvait laisser indifférents non plus les chrétiens de la Gentilité, dès lors qu'ils revendiquaient eux aussi l'Ancien Testament. Le caractère judéo-chrétien des écrits où s'exprime la croyance au «descensus» n'est pas établi de façon absolument indubitable dans tous les cas, sauf si l'on accepte la notion très élargie et très personnelle que le R. P. Daniélou propose du judéo-christianisme, qu'il définit par des catégories de pensée et considère comme coextensif à l'Eglise depuis les origines jusqu'au milieu du IIème siècle. «La localisation de l'habitat des morts dans un lieu situé dans les profondeurs de la terre» est païenne autant que juive: le terme de Hadès traduit communément, dans la Septante, l'hébreu *schéol*. Par ailleurs, il paraît difficile d'admettre que les nombreuses descentes aux Enfers de dieux ou de héros païens, celle d'Hercule par exemple, n'aient eu aucune influence sur la fixation de la croyance chrétienne et sur son adoption généralisée: il y avait, si l'on peut dire, des précédents du côté païen, il n'y en avait pas du côté juif.[41]

D'autre part, pour ce qui est des racines néotestamentaires de la doctrine, il semble en effet assuré que des textes souvent invoqués à l'appui du «descensus» n'ont pas le sens qu'on leur prêtait.[42] Mais même si l'on en néglige d'autres, qui paraissent y faire allusion, il reste en tous cas le texte de Matthieu, 27, 52–53, que Daniélou signale, mais sans s'y arrêter. Au moment de la mort du Christ, «les sépulcres s'ouvrirent et les corps de beaucoup de saints défunts ressuscitèrent. Et sortis de leurs tombeaux après sa résurrection, ils entrèrent dans la ville sainte et apparurent à beaucoup». Les exégètes ne sont pas d'accord sur la signification exacte de ces versets. Certains d'entre eux refusent de mettre le prodige qu'ils relatent en rapport avec la descente du Christ aux Enfers.[43] Ils le placent sur le même plan que les ténèbres et le tremblement de terre mentionnés juste avant, et invoquent à l'appui de cette interprétation tel parallèle païen.[44] D'autres au contraire pensent que l'Evangéliste y a reconnu une manifestation de l'oeuvre rédemptrice du Christ.[45] Une étude attentive du texte semble leur donner raison. Si le voile du Temple se déchire, ce ne peut être là une simple conséquence du tremblement de terre, puisque celui-ci n'est mentionné qu'après. Il faut plutôt y voir le signe que les rites de l'Ancienne Alliance sont désormais caducs. Le tremblement de terre signifie que la nature entière est affectée par le drame du Calvaire. Quant à l'apparition des morts, elle est bien, si l'on veut, liée, et de façon assez naïve, au séisme, en ce sens que, fissurant le sol, il leur donne la possibilité matérielle de remonter à la lumière. Mais il est clair que ce phénomène de géophysique, lui-même miraculeux, ne suffit pas à expliquer le fait: pour utiliser la porte de sortie qui leur est offerte, il faut que les morts aient été préalablement ressuscités. Et s'ils l'ont été, c'est que le Christ en mourant est allé leur porter la vie.

La façon même — primitive ou consécutive à un remaniement rédactionnel, peu importe — dont l'évènement est présenté est à cet égard très caractéristique. La résurrection des saints s'accomplit, si l'on peut dire, en deux temps: rappelés à la vie à l'instant où le Christ expire, ils n'apparaissent dans Jérusalem que lorsque lui-même s'est manifesté à ses disciples.[46] Deux idées sont ainsi coordonnées tant bien que mal: celle du Christ premier-né d'entre les morts,[47] et celle de sa victoire, acquise par sa mort même. Les saints sont «réveillés» au moment précis où il descend vers eux, parce que pour lui la mort corporelle, loin de déboucher sur la torpeur ou l'anéantissement, donne accès à la vie totale et promeut l'action rédemptrice, manifestée «aux Enfers» par sa descente avant de s'affirmer sur terre par sa résurrection. Notre texte suppose donc bien la descente aux Enfers. Et Ignace d'Antioche en apporte un écho très fidèle lors qu'il écrit: «Comment pourrions-nous vivre sans lui, quand les prophètes eux-mêmes, ses disciples en esprit, l'attendaient comme leur maître? Voilà pourquoi celui qui était l'objet de leurs espérances les a, par sa présence (*παρῶν*)ressuscités des morts».[48]

Notre texte ne dit pas ce qu'il est advenu par la suite de ces ressuscités. L'auteur ne s'est peut-être pas posé la question. Nous avons néanmoins le droit de nous demander comment il y aurait répondu. Il est évident que cette résurrection ne saurait être un épisode éphémère, après lequel les défunts retombent dans leur sommeil ou leur attente. Elle ne les ramène pas davantage à la condition de ceux qui sont encore en vie sur terre. Elle doit se traduire par un changement définitif de résidence ou tout au moins d'état: normalement, cette résurrection devrait être suivie d'une assomption, puisqu'aussi bien elle souligne la parfaite identité entre le destin du Christ et le sort de ceux qui, avant sa venue, ont cru en lui.[49]

Ce n'est pas là, cependant, la seule façon dont le christianisme antique a conçu l'action rédemptrice du Christ par rapport aux générations disparues. Dans une perspective plus ritualiste, c'est le baptême qui est pour les vivants l'instrument ou tout au moins la condition indispensable du salut. Il doit donc l'être aussi pour les défunts. D'où l'idée du baptême des justes, dans les Enfers même, par le Christ ou, à un stade ultérieur du développement de cette idée, par les Apôtres, descendus à sa suite dans le monde souterrain.[50] D'où aussi l'idée connexe du baptême pour les morts, par personne interposée, dont Saint Paul mentionne l'usage en passant.[51] Dans un cas comme dans l'autre c'est en vue de la résurrection générale que le rite est accompli; il ne change rien pour le moment à la situation des défunts, mais leur donne simplement la garantie du salut à venir. Selon la conception sous-jacente au texte de Matthieu, au contraire, le changement est immédiat. Elle ne laisse de place à l'état intermédiaire, d'attente et de nudité, qu'avant la mort du Christ. Plus explicite, plus dégagée des cadres de l'eschatologie traditionnelle, elle devrait normalement associer aussi, et a fortiori, les fidèles défunts à cette identité de destin qui unit les justes de l'Ancien Testament à l'expérience de vie du Christ vainqueur. On est fondé, semble-t-il, à ajouter ce texte à ceux que je rappelais plus haut et qui attestent l'existence, dans la sotériologie chrétienne primitive, à côte du courant de pensée issu de l'apocalyptique juive et du pharisaïsme, d'un autre courant qu'on peut, en simplifiant, et avec les réserves formulées précédemment, appeller «grec»: celui qui ne connait pas de hiatus entre la mort corporelle — du chrétien — et la naissance à la vie éternelle.

A coup sûr, l'immortalité bienheureuse est toujours, pour les écrivains néotestamentaires, un don divin, lié à l'action salvatrice du Christ: les ouvrages signalés plus haut ont parfaitement mis ce point en lumière. Mais sur les modalités de cette action les textes ne sont pas entièrement concordants. Immortalité immédiate dans «le ciel» ou résurrection finale, les deux notions ont toujours coexisté dans l'Eglise: la liturgie catholique des défunts, entre autres, en apporte une illustration fort éloquente.[52] Elles sont déjà dans le Nouveau Testament, la seconde à coup sûr plus appuyée et plus voyante, la première esquissée ou ébauchée plutôt qu'entièrement élaborée. Il suffit cependant qu'elle y apparaisse çà et là pour qu'il devienne difficile à l'historien de la déclarer étrangère à la tradition chrétienne authentique.[53]

NOTES

[1] Ainsi, tout récemment, S. G. F. Brandon, *Man and his Destiny in the great Religions* (1962), 223.

[2] L'ouvrage fondamental sur les cultes a mystères reste toujours celui de F. Cumont, *Les religions orientales dans le paganisme romain*[4] (1929).

[3] En particulier à propos de la pensée paulinienne: R. Reitzenstein, *Die hellenistischen Mysterienreligionen*[3] (1927); A. Loisy, *Les mystères païens et le mystère chretien*[2] (1930). Sur les relations cultes à mystères — christianisme, F. Cumont, *Les mystères de Mithra*[3] (1913), 199 ss. Critique de la position comparatiste, K. Prümm, *Religionsgeschichtliches Handbuch für den Raum der altchristlichen Umwelt* (1943), 308–56, qui n'est d'ailleurs pas exempt de préoccupations apologétiques; cf. F. C. Grant, *Roman Hellenism and the New Testament* (1962), 76 ss.

[4] C'est encore autour de Paul que tourne le plus souvent le débat: W. D. Davies, *Paul and Rabbinic Judaism* (1949); H. J. Schoeps, *Paulus* (1959). La découverte des Manuscrits de la Mer Morte a jeté une lumière nouvelle sur les racines et l'arrière-plan juifs du christianisme; elle ne paraît pas avoir apporté d'élément d'explication décisif touchant plus particulièrement la sotériologie.

[5] Cf. en particulier les ouvrages de P. L. Couchoud, dont les dernier est *Le Dieu Jésus* (1951), caractérisé d'ailleurs par une curieuse religiosité centrée sur un Christ non incarné.

[6] K. Prümm, op. cit., 310.

[7] Psaume 115:4; 135:15.

[8] Justin, *I Apol.*, 9, 1–2.

[9] Clément d'Alexandrie, *Cohort. ad Gentes.*

[10] *De Errore profan. relig.*, II, 3, trad. G. Heuten.

[11] Op. cit., II, 6. Sur les différentes conceptions professées par les ancien chrétiens touchant les dieux païens, M. Simon, *Hercule et le Christianisme* (1955), 17 ss.

[12] «*Hi ritus, quoquo modo inducti, antiquitate defenduntur*», Tacite, *Hist.*, V, 5. Cf. Origène, *Contre Celse*, II, I.

[13] Sur la critique que ces deux auteurs font du christianisme, P. de Labriolle, *La réaction païenne* (1934), 111 ss. et 369 ss.

[14] M. Simon, *Verus Israel* (1948), 105 ss.

[15] P. de Labriolle, op. cit., p. 274; cf. Origène, *Contre Celse*, IV, 7.

[16] Rom. 7:7–25; Gal., 3:10–29; 4:3 ss. cf. G. B. Caird, *Principalities and Powers* (1956), 40 ss.

[17] Matth. 19:16; Marc 10:17; Luc 10:25.

[18] Sur l'eschatologie mazdéenne et mithriaque, F. Cumont, *Les mystères de Mithra*, 147 ss.

[19] P. de Labriolle, op. cit., p. 276; cf. les réactions des Athéniens (Actes 17:32) lorsque Paul leur parle de la résurrection.

[20] R. Martin-Achard, *De la mort à la résurrection d'après l'Ancien Testament* (1956).

[21] Sur les différentes conceptions de l'au-delà dans la pensée biblique et juive, H. H. Rowley, *The Faith of Israel* (1956), 150 ss. et S. G. F. Brandon, op. cit., en particulier 137 ss.

[22] Formulation classique en I Thess., 4:13–18; cf. I Cor. 15:20–52.

[23] Luc 16:19–31: Brandon, op. cit., 209.

[24] Sur la notion de vie èternelle dans le Nouveau Testament, et spécialement chez Jean, C. Alington, *The Life Everlasting* (1947).

[25] Lorsque Paul parle de ceux qui dorment (I Cor. 15:20, I Thess. 4:13, etc.) il y a là plus, semble-t-il, qu'une simple métaphore et qu'une comparaison purement verbale avec le sommeil vulgaire.

[26] Jean 6:54.

[27] Certains commentateurs considèrent le second membre de phrase comme une adjonction rédactionnelle: Loisy, *Le Quatrième Evangile*[2] (1927) 243.

[28] Jean 11:25–26.

[29] Jean 11, 24.

[30] Luc 23:43.

[31] M. Goguel, *La Vie de Jésus*, (1932), 523; *La Naissance du Christianisme* (1956), 54; cf. W. Bousset, *Kyrios Christos*[3] (1926), 63.

[32] S. G. F. Brandon, op. cit., à propos de II Cor. 5:1–4; cf. Phil. 1:21–23.

[33] Entre autres Ph. Menoud, *Le sort des Trépassés* (1945); G. van der Leeuw, *Unsterblichkeit oder Auferstehung* (1956); O. Cullmann, *Immortalité de l'Ame ou Résurrection des Morts?* (1956).

[34] E. Rohde, *Psychè*, II[3] (1903), 395 ss. Sur les croyances populaires païennes relatives à l'au-delà, A. F. Festugière, *L'idéal religieux des Grecs et l'Evangile* (1932), 143–160. Sur les formes diverses de l'espérance païenne, F. Cumont, *Lux Perpetua* (1949).

[35] H. A. Wolfson, 'Immortality and Resurrection in the Philosophy of the Church Fathers', in *Religious Philosophy. A Group of Essays* (1961), 69–103, critique les vues développées par Cullmann et souligne que pour les Pères de l'Eglise unanimes, et fidèles en cela, estime-t-il, à la pensée de Jésus lui-même, immortalité et résurrection étaient inséparablement liées: 'To them, the belief that Jesus rose on the third day after the crucifixion meant that his soul survived the death of the body and was reinvested with his risen body' (70).

[36] Col. 2:13–14.

[37] Etude d'ensemble, W.. Bieder, *Die Vorstellung von der Höllenfahrt Jesu-Christi* (1949). Sur l'intégration de cette notion dans le symbole de foi, J. N. D. Kelly, *The Early Christian Creeds* (1950), 378–83.

[38] Sur les différentes formes revêtues par cette croyance, J. Daniélou, *Théologie du Judéo-Christianisme* (1958), 257–73.

[39] P. ex. l'Evangile de Nicodème, 2ème partie: M. R. James, *The Apocryphal New Testament* (1924), 117–46. Autres textes mentionnes ou cités dans J. Daniélou, op. cit., 259 ss.

[40] Op. cit., 257; cf. W. Bousset, op. cit., 26.

[41] J. Kroll, *Gott und Hölle. Der Mythos vom Descensuskampfe* (1932).

[42] En particulier I Petr. 3:19 ss. et 4: 6; Eph. 4:9, etc.: W. Bieder, op. cit., 33 ss.; cf. Bo Reicke, *The Disobedient Spirits and Christian Baptism* (1946); H. Schlier, *Christus und die Kirche im Epheserbrief* (1930).

[43] Ainsi E. Klostermann, *Das Matthäus-Evangelium*² (1927), 225.

[44] Ovide, *Métamorph.*, 7, 205–206:

> «Et silvas moveo jubeoque tremescere montes
> Et mugire solum manesque exire sepulchris.»

[45] P. ex. M. Goguel, *Naissance*, 54: 'On est conduit à voir dans la résurrection des saints une conséquence de la victoire remportée par Jésus sur la mort, non pas au matin du troisième jour, mais a l'instant même où il expire'; cf. J. Daniélou, op. cit., 261.

[46] La leçon, très mal attestée, *αὐτῶν* au lieu de *αὐτοῦ* est visiblement aberrante et défigure le sens réel de la phrase: E. Klostermann, loc. cit.

[47] Col. I:18; I Cor. 15:20.

[48] Magn. 9:2, commenté par Daniélou, op. cit., 261.

[49] Il est à noter que la résurrection du Christ (*ἔγερσις*, seul emploi du terme dans le Nouveau Testament) et celle des saints (*ἠγέρθησαν*) sont désignées dans ce passage de façon identique.

[50] J. Daniélou, op. cit., 262 ss.

[51] Cor. 15:29.

[52] On notera en particulier les termes de la Préface: '... In quo (J. C.) nobis spes beatae resurrectionis effulsit; ut quos contristat certa moriendi conditio, eosdem consoletur futurae immortalitatis promissio. Tuis enim fidelibus, Domine, vita mutatur, non tollitur, et dissoluta terrestris hujus incolatus domo, aeterna in caelis habitatio comparatur'. On doit noter par ailleurs que, dans la perspective catholique, la conception de la vie future est rendue encore plus complexe par un dédoublement de l'état intermédiaire en Purgatoire et Paradis ou Ciel.

[53] L'ouvrage de R. H. Charles, *A Critical History of the Doctrine of a Future Life*² (1913) 401 ss. continue de rappeler fort utilement qu'il n'y a pas unité rigoureuse de vues sur la question dans le Nouveau Testament. Si, avec certains théologiens, on remplace l'idée d'une resurrection générale à la fin des temps par celle d'une résurrection individuelle immédiatement consécutive à la mort, la différence par rapport á l'immortalité conçue 'à la grecque' devient, malgré l'insistance sur la notion de 'corps spirituel', bien ténue et subtile. A lire la littérature récente sur la question on a quelquefois l'impression d'une simple querelle de mots. Cf. le chapitre très nuancé consacré à ce sujet dans *Doctrine in the Church of England*² (1950), 202–20, et en particulier les conclusions, d'une sage réserve, formulées p. 211.

XI

THE WORK OF THE BUDDHA AND THE WORK OF CHRIST

by

NINIAN SMART

I

THE aim of this paper is to set out the likenesses and differences between Christian and Buddhist conceptions of the way in which the Buddha and Christ bring about salvation or liberation. Since systems of religious belief and practice are organic,[1] similarities between features of two systems have to be seen in the perspective of crucial divergences elsewhere. The present investigation, then, aims to throw light not only on the particular similarities and dissimilarities between beliefs about the work of the Buddha and the work of Christ, but also upon the underlying dynamics of the two systems.

In a way, though, it is an over-simplification to speak of only two systems, since the changes and developments within Buddhism especially must make our comparisons multiple. This in turn means that a treatment confined to a single essay must be impressionistic and selective: nevertheless, this may turn out to be an advantage rather than the reverse, in letting us go to the heart of the matter.

II

At first sight, Theravāda Buddhism has no concept of a saving god. Not only is it agnostic about a Creator, so that there is no

Supreme Being for an earthly figure such as Gotama to embody or manifest in his person, but also the Buddha himself is not, strictly, an object of worship. It is true that the expression *devātideva* ('god above gods') is used of him in the Pali writings;[2] and he is also said not to fit into human categories.[3] But the former epithet is a way of signifying that the Buddha transcends in value the gods, who are not spiritually important. For this reason, H. Zimmer coined the term 'transtheistic' to describe Buddhism and Jainism[4] (though it would be more natural to refer to them as 'transpolytheistic': the gods, in the plural, are not denied, but the highest truth and salvation cannot be obtained from them—'transtheism' would be a term more appropriate to Advaita Vedānta, where it is theism which is transcended[5]). And the Buddha's not fitting into human categories is at least partly a means of expressing the transcendental nature of the attainment of *bodhi* and *nirvāṇa*. It would thus be a considerable misrepresentation of the Theravāda to think of the Buddha as a kind of incarnate deity. Since salvation in the Christian tradition essentially involves a relationship with God, there can be no question of a strict parallel between the Christian and Theravādin conceptions of the work respectively of Christ and the Buddha.

Nevertheless, the Buddha did do something which looks like a 'saving work': he provided a prescription for liberation from the world's ills. As the spiritual doctor, he provided a diagnosis and a therapy.[6] Still, this is essentially saving men through *teaching*, not, as most Christian theories of the Atonement claim, through the performance of an act which has a cosmic effect, the benefits of which are available to the faithful. This is in line with an important strand of Indian thought, namely that men and other beings owe their sufferings and dissatisfactions ultimately to ignorance, rather than to sin or moral evil—so that the cure essentially involves knowledge, rather than repentance. For this reason, when the Buddha said that after his passing the faithful would still have the *dhamma*,[7] he was not, according to the Theravādin tradition, affirming the identity between himself and a transcendent principle, as the Mahāyāna *trikāya* doctrine asserts, but pointing only to the continued importance and saving power of his teachings.

These are efficacious in themselves, and are in a sense only contingently related to the historical Buddha: for the charismatic authority of the Buddha is qualified by the injunction to his followers to test the teachings in their own experience (in this way, Buddhism is much more 'experimental' in its flavour than Christianity—the truth is *ehipassiko*, not just authoritatively revealed). The emphasis upon the saving work of the Buddha's *teachings* contrasts with the main Christian theories of Christ's saving work: it is not so much Christ's words which help us, but Christ as the Word. If Jesus' teachings were detached from their historical context and significance, and regarded as a sufficient prescription for salvation, then the result would be the kind of ethical theism found in Unitarianism; but it would be notably different from Christianity as traditionally understood.

It should be noted that the concept of the liberating power of knowledge in Buddhism, and to be found in other strands of Indian religion, is mainly a result of two factors. First, the absence of belief in a divine Being, and the relative insignificance of the gods, mean that there can be no special place for the notion of sin as separation from, and as the converse of, the Holy. Notions of ritual and moral 'uncleanness' and the sense of unholy inadequacy before the *mysterium tremendum et fascinans* are not evident in the central tradition of the Theravāda.[8] Second, the essential concentration, in the Theravāda, upon contemplative or mystical experience gives the concept of *knowledge* an obvious importance. For mystical experience is like a direct acquaintance with something (*Brahman*, God or the state of *nirvāṇa*, etc.) and this has analogies with one sense of 'knowing' (e.g. 'He knows Macmillan, Loch Lomond, etc.'). Again, it brings a kind of certitude, and knowledge as contrasted with belief is like this. Finally, one sees the 'point' of the doctrines associated with the path through which one attains the experience: one knows *that* such-and-such is the case on the basis at least in part of direct experience.[9] But of course, all this must not be conceived merely as intellectual, like seeing the truth of the Binomial Theorem, partly because the emptiness of mystical states precludes discursive knowledge;[10] and partly because the path typically involves some degree of asceticism,[11] since the right total view of the world itself requires the taming of desires which lead to attachment to, and implication in, empirical reality. By contrast with Buddhist yoga, theism stresses belief and a personal relationship to God through faith. Not unnaturally wrong belief tends therefore to be traced to sin, or wrong relationship to God. But wrong belief in the Theravāda is conceived ultimately as the product of a failure in spiritual perception.

Nevertheless, it might be thought that there was some analogy between the Buddha's defeat of Māra and the 'classical' theory of the Atonement.[12] Just as the Buddha, at the time of his Enlightenment, defeated Māra, so Christ, through his life, death and resurrection, overcame Satan. In an excellent recent work, Dr T. O. Ling has surveyed the Pāli material on Māra; and his conclusion is plainly correct: 'the figure of Māra represents an *approach* to the Dhamma (from animism), but is no part of the Dhamma itself . . .; he is a doctrinal device, not an item of doctrine.'[13] Māra shows that the ills of life are not to be dealt with piecemeal, in an animistic manner. But the symbol is transcended, as indeed is animism and polytheism, in the realization of the peace and insight of *nirvāṇa* and in the formulation of doctrine which expresses that insight. Indeed, the essential Theravādin view could be said to rest on the text of *Dhammapada* 276:

> *tumhe hi kiccam ātappam, akkhātāro tathāgatā,*
> *paṭipannā pamokkhanti jhāyino mārabandhanā.*

Thus the virtual absence of Māra from the Abhidhamma is no accident.[14] Now it is true that Satan has come in for symbolic treatment, and is now liable to be demythologized.[15] But of course he has been regarded much more as a metaphysical reality, partly because his existence has a doctrinal function to play in connection with the problem of evil—whereas agnostic Buddhism does not have to concern itself with reconciling God's goodness to the ills of the world.

Still, though at the doctrinal level Māra is not ultimately significant, the symbol of the Buddha's overpowering is not without similarity to the defeat of Satan. Māra, both etymologically and mythologically, is associated with death, and his defeat, like that of Satan, means the overcoming of death, in so far as death is looked upon as the finishing of a life still stained with evil.[16] Again, both Satan and Māra represent the forces hostile to men's endeavour to lead a truly religious life, and therefore try to deflect the respective Teachers from their path, only to find that the attempt is unsuccessful. But in the New Testament, the ultimate victory over Satan is through the performance of an act, namely the sacrifice on the Cross;[17] but it is the knowledge of Māra, i.e. of the real nature of evil, which is the key to the Buddha's victory.[18] Thus the concept of Māra illustrates clearly the centrality of contemplative insight in the Theravādin tradition.

So far, then, there is no strong analogy between the work of Christ and the work of the Buddha, But it is worth noting that there is an exemplarist strand in Buddhist soteriology. There was evidently too some feeling that the docetic ideas associated with the Lokottaravāda undermined this exemplarist position, for then 'we are mere men and unable to reach the state of a god'.[19] This no doubt is the main reason for the Sarvāstivādin insistence on the humanity of the Buddha. However, the like orthodox Christian insistence on Christ's humanity has largely a different cause, namely that Christ's reconciling sacrifice, in so far as it is expiatory or propitiatory, requires his solidarity with mankind, so that a phantom Christ would be sacrificially irrelevant.

III

The absence of a concept of God as a supreme object of worship precludes the Theravāda from having any doctrine of reconciliation and from any idea of salvation as some kind of intimate union with God. Mahāyāna developments partly altered the situation. First, the cult of Bodhisattvas and celestial Buddhas made these beings, phenomenologically considered, divine. Not only from the side of the devotee is *bhakti* important, so that the inner aspect of worship complements the externals—the cult of images, etc.; but also these beings acquire mythologically the attributes characteristically ascribed to numinous powers elsewhere. The sword of Manjuśrī and the thunderbolt of Vajrapāṇi express the *tremendum* on its fiercer side; the supernatural marvels of the *Saddharmapuṇḍarīka* express its dumb-founding and fascinating side. And though the total cosmos remains uncreated, in accordance with the Buddha's ban on undetermined questions and agnosticism, Buddhas are now conceived as partially creative, through the idea of the *buddhakṣetra* or 'Buddha-field'.[20] Not only this, but their celestial habitations are psychologically distant enough to function as virtually transcendent places, not so different from the ordinary Christian's conception of heaven as where God is and as the goal of salvation.

Unification of this complex pattern of belief and practice was brought about from two directions. the religious and the metaphysical. This indeed was no accident. E. J. Thomas has written:

> Two aspects of Mahāyāna doctrine, which seem to show no relation to each other, stand out in great contrast. There is the religious side of the worship of saintly beings with the ideal of a succession of lives of heroic virtues, and the philosophical side developing the boldest speculations in logic and epistemology. The cause of this contrast was inherent in Buddhism from the beginning—the division into the monastic order and the laity.[21]

But this judgement is most misleading: for the Mādhyamika and Yogācāra systems, for instance, are not purely intellectual. As nearly everywhere else in the field of Indian philosophy, the determinative ideas in these systems are born of religious experience. Buddhist metaphysics is ultimately concerned with defending a spiritual view of the world. Thus the unification of Mahāyāna belief and practice was achieved both at the religious and metaphysical level in a harmonious way. First, this was done through what was later systematized as the *trikāya* doctrine. Thus the multiplicity of celestial and earthly Buddhas has a transcendent unity in the *dharmakāya*. Whereas *dhamma* in the Pāli canon refers to a body of propositions, the Mahāyāna evolved a doctrine analogous to what happens elsewhere, which can be called 'identification with the reference': i.e. the propositions no longer constitute the *dharma*, but the *dharma* essentially *is* the being or state which the propositions centrally allude to.[22] Likewise, *śruti* in the Hindu tradition is sometimes thought of as what propositional *śruti* refers to; and rather recently, for partly different reasons, revelation has been treated by some Christian theologians in a similar manner.[23] But the *dharma* referred to by scriptures is somehow specially manifested by, and taught by, the celestial and earthly Buddhas; and so it cannot simply be viewed as a state to be achieved, like *nirvāṇa* in the Theravādin sense. In a more substantial sense it underlies the numinous Buddha-figures. Thus, from the point of view of popular religion, the doctrine of the *dharmakāya* achieves something like the unification of polytheism expressed in the famous lines of the Dīrghatamas hymn, *Ṛgveda*, I, 164, 46: the one reality has different names.

It is against this background that the Mādhyamika and Yogācāra should be viewed. The *śūnyavāda*, for instance, is not a restatement of the virtual pluralism of the Theravādin ideal (with its affinities to pluralistic Jainism); yet neither on the other hand does it try to express something quite foreign to the Theravāda. For both these Mahāyāna schools and the Theravāda have as their central concern the mystical or contemplative experience which is the starting-point of Buddhist doctrine. It seems superfluous to postulate radically different kinds of mystical experience to account for the variation in Indian doctrines, whether Hindu, Buddhist or Jain, and in particular within Buddhism, in view of the methodological distinction between experience and interpretation,[24] and in view of the phenomenological principle that the goal is in some degree affected by the path leading to it.[25] Thus the Mahāyāna stress upon *karuṇā* may well give a special flavour to what is found in contemplation, without however affecting its essential nature. In general, in the Indian context at least, there seems reason to suppose that the interpretation of mystical experience is only partially determined by the nature of the experience itself, but is normally also affected by the weight given to other forms of religious experience. For instance, the experience of a personal Being, expressed in the reaction of loving adoration or *bhakti*, affects theological attitudes to mystical experience and to its doctrinal interpretation.

This last point could be expressed in a very crude way by the following equations, where the numbers roughly estimate the weight given to the different kinds of experience. The left-hand side gives the kind of experience or associated activity considered relevant to the perception of the highest truth about reality, and the right-hand side gives the correlated doctrines.

0 *bhakti* + 2 *dhyāna* = agnostic/atheistic pluralism (Jainism, and the virtual pluralism of the Theravāda)
1 *bhakti* + 2 *dhyāna* = transtheistic monism (e.g., Advaita)[26]
2 *bhakti* + 1 *dhyāna* = transmonistic theism (e.g. Rāmānuja)[27]

One can indeed generalize such equations, by contrasting the numinous and the mystical in their many modes of combination (and failure to combine), and by observing the correlation between the intensity and importance attached to these two kinds of experience and the doctrines associated with the relevant religious movements.[28] It is often because of its association with *bhakti* or with a prophetic tradition that mystical experience is not given that minimal doctrinal interpretation which the Theravāda represents (putting it crudely: you have to have the concept of God already if mystical experience is to be interpreted as a kind of union with the divine).

These general remarks show how the monism of the Mādhyamika and of the Yogācāra can be explained. The substitution of the *śūnya*, *tathatā*, etc. as a kind of substance—albeit a pretty shadowy one—for the Theravādin *nirvāṇa* conceived as a *state*, i.e. the introduction by the Mahāyāna of an Absolute,[29] is in line with the need to accommodate the religious concept of the numinous as somehow concealed behind phenomena and yet as being a personal object of devotion.[30] Thus, the Theravāda stands to the Mādhyamika roughly as Sāṃkhya-Yoga stands to Advaita. It is not fortuitous, even apart from historical connections, that both in Advaita and in the main stream of Mahāyāna thought which we are now considering at least a secondary place is given to *bhakti* in the religious quest and to the experience of numinous beings. The many Buddhas, then, have a concealed, mysterious unity in the *dharmakāya*, even if this unity is ultimately viewed as a kind of non-dual (*advaya*) Emptiness, in accordance with the deliverances of the contemplative consciousness. But, as in the Theravāda, the latter remains supremely important: in this, both Lesser and Greater Vehicles are, largely, at one, and where they differ is as to whether anything else is important, i.e. whether *bhakti* has any basis or significance. The Mahāyāna doctrines are a means of synthesizing two forms of religion, with the religion of worship in second place. This balance is altered in some phases of the later development of the Mahāyāna, notably in the Far East, so that eventually there can arise sects which stress faith only, and where the underlying Buddha-principle is conceived as essentially personal: thus bhakti and paradise are substituted for *prajñā* and identification with the Absolute as the soteriological means and ends.

This excursus into the dynamics of Mahāyāna doctrines, and of the Mādhyamika and Yogācāra schools in particular, as centrally representing 'main-stream' Mahāyāna, is necessary for the understanding of the comparison between Christian and Mahāyāna soteriology. With the evolution of the idea of the Buddha as a divine being, it could be expected that salvation would be seen as a kind of communion with the Buddha, and the overcoming of the gulf fixed between the worshipper and the object of worship. Now it is true that the colourful picture of Amitābha's paradise reflects the hope of something analogous to the beatific vision of God, even if in theory the Pure Land is merely a place specially favourable for the attainment of *nirvāṇa*. Nevertheless, the different dynamics of Mahāyāna doctrine mean that in the last resort the communion is differently conceived: for ultimately the devotee attains the highest goal, the contemplative goal with its non-duality. And because of this non-duality, there can be no distinction between the devotee and the Absolute: which in religious terms means that the devotee is indeed the Buddha. There being no overriding concept of a personal Lord to check the mystical tendency towards non-dualism,[31] the devotee in highest truth is, in worshipping, only worshipping his future self.[32] It happens too that there were other forces impelling the Mahāyāna towards the same conclusion—principally the emphasis on morality and compassion, for the attachment of these ideals to the figure of the

Bodhisattva meant that the universal requirements of goodness and self-sacrifice could be seen as presupposing the future Buddhahood of all men.

But though the provisional nature of the distinction between men and the divine Reality (as contrasted with the radical distinction presupposed in most of the Judaeo-Christian tradition, which sharpens the Christological paradox) means that the work of the Buddha still centres on his teaching and that it is contemplative knowledge that ultimately saves, nevertheless the provisional truth incorporated soteriological elements which have some analogies to Atonement doctrine. The most famous of these is, of course, the concept of *puṇyapariṇāmanā* or the transference of merit. The self-sacrificing Bodhisattva can out of the treasury of his merit, the *guṇa sambhāra*, convey some of it to the otherwise unworthy devotee. This gives to Buddhist mythology a strong flavour of the Christian idea of Christ's sacrifice as bringing about an immense or infinite abundance of merit available to the faithful. Thus St Thomas Aquinas writes: *Christo data est gratia non solum sicut singulari personae, sed in quantum est caput Ecclesiae, ut scilicet et ipso redundaret ad membra*; . . . *manifestum est autem quod quicunque in gratia constitutus propter iustitiam patitur, ex hoc ipso meretur sibi salutem* . . .[33] But there remain differences between the two doctrines. First, the Buddhist concept has as its background the doctrine of *karma*, so that the acquisition of merit has a kind of causal effect; but by contrast the Christian counterpart, in theory at any rate, is the direct activity of God. Second, the acquisition of merit by Christ was conceived as a consequence of his self-sacrifice upon the Cross,[34] and 'sacrifice' here had a ritual sense. Although Old Testament concepts of ritual sacrifice were transcended in the New, their transcendence presupposed their initial acceptance. But the self-sacrifice of the Bodhisattvas is essentially moral, and has little of a ritual background to be transcended and given new significance. It perhaps may be that one or two instances of a moralizing of ritual sacrifice occur in the *Jātakas* and elsewhere, e.g. the hare's famous self-immolation;[35] but this does not involve an explicit acceptance of the quasi-causal effects of ritual sacrifice. And although a ritual significance is given to self-offering through the *pūjā* involved in following the path of Bodhisattvahood,[36] the ultimate emphasis remains on treating this as a means rather than an end—whereas worship by contrast in the Judaeo-Christian tradition is the intrinsically appropriate response of men to the Holy One.

Furthermore, in both the Mādhyamika and the Yogācāra, the empirical world is in a sense illusory—for where there is in essence only one reality the multiplicity of the cosmos as viewed from the ordinary common-sense standpoint must ultimately be an illusion. This means that the docetic tendencies of the Lokottaravāda are reinforced in the fully-fledged Mahāyāna. The plurality of earthly Buddhas likewise puts pressure in the same direction: for where the divine Being 'appears' in many forms, it is a natural inference that these are *mere* appearances; while the Christian insistence on the uniqueness of Christ preserves two features which Atonement doctrine requires, namely Christ's simultaneous humanity and divinity. It is as though, in having only one Incarnation, God fully commits himself to the earthly life, and is not just arranging a theophany in human form.

The docetism of the Mahāyāna and its relative unattachment to historicity is signalized by the concept of *upāya-kauśalya* or 'skill in expedients' (Edgerton also suggests a nice translation, 'diplomacy' [37]). The Buddha is essentially a pragmatist, engineering human relations so that men will be brought to the truth. At one stroke the Mahāyāna has a piece of apologetic *contra Hinayanistas* and an explanation of the secondary importance of *bhakti* and the whole elaborate scheme of popular Buddhist cults. These are only means, both from the side of the individual and from the side of the Buddha-principle itself, for bringing about a certain spiritual result.

In turn this reminds us that Christian soteriology has always been conceived as closely tied to history. God's saving work is thought of as manifested in history (i.e. in the flow of human events) and as grounded in history (i.e. in historical evidences). On both counts, and in both senses of 'history', Buddhism has a different attitude. The general backcloth of the cyclical immensity of time makes the brevities of human life seem unimportant, and in so far as Buddhism speaks of a direction of events in our epoch it is one of decline rather than progress. And historical evidences are not vital where the truth is seen in inner experience.

IV

In brief, the picture of the crucified Christ and that of the suffering Bodhisattva may appeal to the same stirrings in the human heart; but the moral hero and the mediator diverge precisely because in the one system the ultimate reality is the contemplative intuition of Emptiness, while in the other it is a personal God. Both the Theravāda and 'main-stream' Mahāyāna are at one in stressing the centrality of *prajñā*, even if they differ about whether or not the religion of worship and devotion should be given doctrinal recognition. The Buddha's liberating work is bringing men to a type of *gnosis*; Christ's is the reconciliation of men with a numinous Object of worship. The Buddha bridges the gap between men and *nirvāṇa*; Christ bridges the gap between men and the Father.[38]

NOTES

[1] That is, in a sense analogous to that in which a work of art is organic: see my *Reasons and Faiths* (1958), p. 12; H. Kraemer makes a similar point in speaking of a 'totalitarian' approach (*The Christian Message in a Non-Christian World* (1938), p. 145), but the term 'organic' seems for various reasons more suitable.

[2] *Niddesa*, ii, 307, etc.

[3] *Anguttara Nikāya*, ii, 38, etc.

[4] See *Philosophies of India* (1951), pp. 181–2.

[5] The concept of transcendence in *this* sense is of considerable importance, and implies that where the concept of A is transcended by the concept of B, the former concept is not denied to have spiritual value, but is subordinated to, and ultimately interpreted in terms of, the latter concept. Here 'transcendence' is not meant to express, but only to describe, a value-judgement, which the comparative religionist need neither endorse nor fail to endorse. For the senses of 'transcendence', see my 'The Transcendence of Doctrines' in *Sri Aurobindo Circle*, No. 16 (1960), pp. 93–8.

[6] 'The so-called Four Noble Truths of Buddhism correspond exactly to the four successive problems which the Hindu doctor is taught to face in treating a patient.' H. Zimmer, *Hindu Medicine* (1948), pp. 33 ff.

[7] *Dīgha Nikāya*, ii, 154, etc.

[8] For which reason, Rudolf Otto's analysis of religion is not entirely successful: see my 'Numen, Nirvana and the Definition of Religion', *Church Quarterly Review*, March, 1959, pp. 216–25. Of course, it is true that numinous elements enter into popular belief, but they have little or no significance at the level of the *Abhidhamma*. Moreover, rituals are of little importance (cp. *Saṃyutta Nikāya*, ii, 99), though, as Keith points out, there are references to ritual bathing, etc. (*Buddhist Philosophy in India and Ceylon* (1923), p. 114, n. 2.

[9] *Reasons and Faiths*, pp. 176–7.

[10] Thus the contrast between *jñāna* and *yoga* in the Indian tradition is more a matter of emphasis than a radical distinction: as Eliade points out, 'the two methods, that of the "experimentalists" (the *jhains*) and that of the "speculatives" (the *dhammayogas*), are equally indispensable for obtaining arhatship' (*Yoga: Immortality and Freedom* (1958), p. 176). The teachings are tested in contemplative experience and in turn are used to interpret it.

[11] For this reason, there is not a firm division between *tapas* as a soteriological technique and *yoga*: it is true that the Jains, because of a materialistic view of *karma*, stressed *tapas* very strongly, but the interior quest of the Jain ascetic is clearly analogous to that of *yogins* in other traditions. Thus *dhyāna* is used in Jainism, and the Buddha's condemnation of *tapas* extends only to extreme self-mortification. *Tapas* is praised as meaning *brahmacariyā* and *saṃvara* (see *Pali Text Society's Pali-English Dictionary* (1922), p. 131a).

[12] To use Gustav Aulen's term (see *Christus Victor* (Eng. trans., 1953)).

[13] *Buddhism and the Mythology of Evil* (1962), p. 94.

[14] Ibid., p. 163.

[15] See, e.g., a rather Buddhist approach in Don Cupitt's 'Four Arguments against the Devil', *Theology*, vol. LXIV, No. 496 (Oct. 1961).

[16] Ling, op. cit., pp. 56 f.

[17] As in, e.g., Colossians 2:15.

[18] Ling, op. cit., p. 63.

[19] *Lalitavistara*, 100, preserving Sarvāstivādin doctrine according to E. J. Thomas in *History of Buddhist Thought* (1933), p. 174.

[20] Indeed, Buddhas take on the attributes of Hindu creators, so that it becomes hard to draw a firm line between the ontological status assigned to the great gods and Buddhas in the Hindu and Mahāyāna traditions respectively.

[21] Thomas, op. cit., p. 198.

[22] Thus in the *Lankavātāra Sūtra*, the distinction is made between word (*ruta*) and reference (*artha*). Words are subject to intellectual understanding, but their essential reference (i.e. the reference of the scriptures in particular) is an experience; the relation between *ruta* and *artha*, and that between *akṣara* and *tattva*, are like that between the finger and the moon (D. T. Suzuki, *Studies in the Lankavatara Sutra* (1920), p. 109). Thus the *dharma* is no longer propositional, no longer *akṣarapatita*, but is the 'object' of contemplative experience.

[23] For a Hindu example of 'identification with the reference', see P. N. Srinivasachari, *The Philosophy of Bhedābheda* (2nd edn., 1950), pp. 11–12; for the history of the new Christian concept of revelation, see J. Baillie, *The Idea of Revelation in Recent Thought* (1955). But whereas in the Indian context it is typically experience, or the Absolute or divine Being as experienced, which is what the scriptural words point to, the Christian case is complicated by the fact

that God's self-revelation occurs in a concrete historical process, so that Christ rather than the New Testament, is what is essentially meant by 'revelation'.

[24] The distinction is clearly stated by W. T. Stace in *Mysticism and Philosophy* (1960), pp. 31 ff. See also my 'Mystical Experience', in *Sophia*, vol. i, no. 1 (1960), pp. 19–26.

[25] This in two ways: both through the current doctrinal interpretation put upon the mystical experience, which will affect the manner in which the believing contemplative will see his own experience; and through the kind of training involved in the path, which may reflect the doctrinal milieu—e.g. Buddhist compassion influences Buddhist meditative techniques.

[26] I use 'transtheistic' in the unZimmerian sense suggested above: Advaita does not deny theism, but considers it only a provisional and secondary truth.

[27] That is, Rāmānuja is close to the doctrine of the *Bhagavadgītā*: 'Though the Brahmam is again and again referred to as the highest abode . . . , yet God in his super-personality transcends even Brahman' (S. N. Dasgupta, *History of Indian Philosophy*, vol. ii (1932), p. 476).

[28] *Reasons and Faiths*, chap. v.

[29] I use 'Absolute' not in the sense in which Dr Conze uses it in *Buddhist Thought in India* (1962) (by the term he means that which is unconditioned or out of relation with anything else); but as that which underlies, embraces or is the essential nature of reality. This brings out the similarity between Śankara and Nāgārjuna, and makes the equation *nirvāṇa* = *saṃsāra* meaningful.

[30] *Reasons and Faiths*, p. 35.

[31] That is to say, because of the fact that the mystic is—in the interior vision—withdrawn from ordinary perceptions, the normal sense of a duality between perceiver and what is perceived is absent; hence the mystic, if he conceives himself as having an experience of Something tends to think that he is identical with that Something. Thus the division between subject and object is likely, in this context, to be abrogated; but where on other grounds the mystic regards the distinction between men and God as fundamental, he is more inclined to use such images as that of spiritual marriage, which combines a sense of distinctness with a feeling of the greatest possible intimacy. See my *Theology, Philosophy and the Natural Sciences*, University of Birmingham (1962), p. 12.

[32] See T. R. V. Murti, *The Central Philosophy of Buddhism* (1954), p. 202.

[33] *Summa Theologica*, iii, Q. xlviii, art. 1.

[34] *Cur Deus Homo?*, ii, 11 and 14.

[35] *Jataka*, iii. 51. Butnote that the term used, *pariccajati*, has no ritual significance (as in the English 'self-sacrifice').

[36] See Bhikshu Sangharakshita, *A Survey of Buddhism* (2nd edn., 1959), pp. 446–8, following Sāntideva.

[37] *Buddhist Hybrid Sanskrit Grammar and Dictionary*, vol. ii (1953), p. 146b.

[38] I am grateful to Dr Conze for sending me a copy of his essay for the present volume, while I was in process of writing my own. Thereby I have avoided some errors and (I trust) too much overlapping in our treatments of a very similar theme.

XII

SAVIOUR GODS IN CHINESE RELIGION

by

D. HOWARD SMITH

BY the early part of the fifth century A.D. Mahāyāna Buddhism had spread throughout China, exerting a strong religious influence over all sections of the population. The numerous Buddhas and Bodhisattvas appealed to the Chinese as saviour-gods, who brought comfort amidst the ills and misfortunes of life, release from the guilt and retribution of sin, and promise of a happy destiny in some blessed paradise beyond the grave. Confucianism, in spite of its noble ethical teachings, was practically devoid of an eschatology. It offered cold comfort to the sinful and bereaved and held out little hope of a satisfying existence beyond the grave. Before Buddhism gained a hold in China religious Taoism had attempted to satisfy a deep-seated need, but its concepts of salvation and saviour-gods were almost invariably associated with the magical and occult techniques of shaman-diviners and Taoist adepts. It was hard to find any really spiritual conception of a state of existence beyond death.

From earliest times the Chinese, no less than other peoples, in facing the problems of evil, sickness, misfortune and death, have turned to supernatural agencies to find help and deliverance. Most frequently worshipped for their ability to ensure well-being to their own offspring were the spirits of deceased ancestors, so that the roots of indigenous Chinese religion are found in a primitive animism and a cult of ancestor worship. Yet there is evidence from the second millennium B.C. that already the concept of a supreme and all-powerful deity, who dwelt above and who ruled over the whole universe, was accepted at least among the nobility. The solidly-constructed and elaborately furnished tombs of this period witness to the belief in a continued existence within the tomb. Yet the evidence of oracle-bone inscriptions from the Shang dynasty (*c.* thirteenth century B.C.) points to a belief that a ruler, on his decease, went up on high to be associated with a primaeval ancestor-spirit who was conceived of as a supreme deity.[1] There seems to be no evidence that this supreme deity acted in the role of saviour-god except on behalf of his own descendants. As first ancestor he was concerned to receive their worship and sacrifices, and in return rewarded them with prosperity and happiness and the hope of a happy destiny. The good life, here and hereafter, resulted from the meticulous performance of magico-religious rituals. Common people could look forward to nothing better than a temporary post-mortem existence within the grave until, on the corruption of the physical elements, the soul-forces mingled with the mysterious source of creative energy within the earth.

With the establishment of the Chou dynasty (*c.* 1022 B.C.) a great change gradually took place in religious thinking. Though the ancestor cult and the religious beliefs and practices of the previous dynasty were taken over and elaborated, the royal ancestor-spirits were now relegated to a position inferior to, though in association with, a supreme deity known as Shang Ti or T'ien, and from the evidence of contemporary documents we learn that this supreme deity T'ien was conceived of as a powerful saviour-god.[2]

T'ien as a saviour-god

The Chinese concept of T'ien as a saviour-god in the period of the Western Chou (*c.* 1022–722 B.C.) has some points of similarity to that of the early Hebrews, who thought of Yahweh pre-eminently as a saviour who, regarding the miseries of an enslaved people in Egypt, out of his great compassion determined to save them by a series of mighty acts, and set them up as a people for whom he had a special and peculiar regard. To accomplish this purpose Yahweh raised up and 'called' his servant Moses to be a deliverer. In a similar way, according to early Chou theology, as revealed in the *Book of Odes* (*Shih Ching*) and the authentic chapters of the *Book of Documents* (*Shu Ching*), T'ien looked down with compassion on the Chinese people suffering under the licentious rule of the last king of the Shang dynasty, and determined to deliver them. To this end T'ien surveyed the whole land in order to find a man whose strength and great virtue were equal to the task. None virtuous could be found, save only Fa, chieftain of the powerful Chou clans which lay in the north-west. T'ien 'called' this man, laid upon him the mandate to overthrow the Shang, gave him supernatural assistance, and set him up as a virtuous ruler over all the Chinese people.[3]

Numerous passages in the *Shih Ching* and the *Shu Ching* leave us in no doubt as to the saving power of T'ien, supreme over all the universe, and deeply concerned with the well-being and happiness of his people. Again and again stress is laid on the fact that the ruler is only T'ien's vice-regent on earth, holding his mandate to rule from T'ien and responsible to T'ien. He, in turn, will merit T'ien's wrath and be deposed if he departs from the way of virtue. But, if he is obedient to T'ien's mandate, he may look forward after death to a position of dignity and power in association with T'ien on high.[4]

During the dark centuries of the Ch'un Ch'iu period (*c.* 722–489 B.C.), when China was split up into virtually independent states, and even more during the period known as the Warring States (*c.* 465–221 B.C.), when state rulers 'did what was right in their own eyes', the ambitions and rivalries of the nobility brought about social disintegration, economic collapse and political instability. This had a marked effect on religion. Though the idea of a compassionate T'ien as the saviour of his people was never entirely obliterated, the idea of T'ien as an all-powerful saviour-god receded into the background. T'ien was cruel. T'ien was indifferent. He no longer concerned himself with the people's welfare.[5] As Shigeki Kaizuka has written,

Belief in a spirit or god, a personification and deification of Heaven, was for the most part shattered in the course of the Ch'un Ch'iu period, and in its place there already existed in some measure the idea that Heaven was not a human being possessed of a form: Heaven's will was to be revealed in the will of humankind as a whole.[6]

Leading thinkers arose who referred to T'ien more and more in naturalistic terms, as the principle of cosmic order. T'ien's action is pre-determined. T'ien neither sees nor hears. As the author of the *Tao Te Ching* puts it, 'Heaven and Earth are not humane (*jen*): they treat the ten thousand things like (sacrificial) straw dogs.'[7]

After the time of Confucius, salvation, conceived of in terms of an ordered society, a good life here and now, and freedom from suffering and evil, was thought of as achievable by human effort alone; but only through conformity with the cosmic law which pervades the universe. Mo-tzu among post-Confucian thinkers is almost unique in holding to a more anthropomorphic concept of deity. But even in Mo-tzu, though T'ien loves the people and seeks their happiness and well-being, there is no thought of T'ien's saving grace. Salvation is the result of human effort as man models himself on T'ien and seeks to do the will of T'ien.

Thus in the whole range of philosophical and religious literature before the Christian era and the advent of Buddhism, the main concern is with salvation of the individual and of society in the here and now. Whatever good destiny is attainable beyond the grave is the result of man's own efforts and 'virtue' in this life, and is not attributable to the saving and redeeming acts of some divine being. The cult of ancestors, which had been practised from the earliest historical times and which continued to have paramount significance throughout Chinese history, laid stress upon the family as a cohesive unit rather than on the individual. Consequently, the total obliteration of the family was conceived to be the greatest calamity. The ancestor spirits were worshipped, not only because they were thought to possess supernatural powers by which to bring prosperity and happiness to the family, but because they were themselves 'involved' in the continued existence of the family group.

The extant literature from this early period reflects the attitude of the scholar-class, and hardly anywhere reveals the hopes and fears, the longings and aspirations of the common people. There seems to be no parallel to the Hebrew and Christian concern with the heinousness of 'sin', and no attempt at a mythological explanation as to how sin entered the human race, so that man became a sinner in need of salvation. The statement of A. Reville that 'Les Chinois n'a jamais connu le besoin de rédemption parce qu'il n'a jamais eu l'idée ni de la chute ni d'un état de péché inhérent à la nature humaine'[8] needs some qualification, but it is true that in Confucian literature as a whole there is no adequate realization of human depravity and the consequent need for divine initiative in salvation. Of the three commonly used characters for sin, '*o*' means 'evil, bad or hateful'; '*kuo*' has the meaning 'to transgress or go beyond what is right', and '*tsui*', though coming nearest to the idea of sin has also the meanings of 'crime, punishment, penalty' and is even applied to breaches of decorum or the laws of etiquette. As J. Dyer Ball writes, 'The idea of sin was vague, and the opinion has been expressed that it might be said to have no well defined existence at all. . . . It has been said that the task of tasks is to bring home to the native mind (of the Chinese) the sense of what sin is.'[9] According to early Confucian teaching man's status in life and his 'length of days' are decreed by T'ien. His fate or destiny is something which is ordained by the nature of things, yet he does possess the power to fall short of or overpass the norm or standard which is decreed for him. By doing so he becomes enmeshed in misfortune and calamity. Thus, though 'Heaven's decrees are unceasing and unfathomable, it is not T'ien who destroys men. They by their evil doings cut short their own lives.'[10] The part of wisdom is to give the gods and ancestor spirits their due, but to keep them at a distance.

There are, however, indications of a wide-spread longing, not only to be freed from the evils of this life, but to attain personal significance and immortality beyond the grave. To this end the populace at large sought the aid of shaman-priests, who not only practised magical techniques but pointed to powerful divine beings whose assistance could be solicited.[11] Sorcerers, serving as mediums between men and gods, gave an empirical witness to the existence of deities who were powerful to save. One could enter into personal relationship with them. Religion was no longer just the affair of the ruler or territorial magnate seeking the well-being of land and people. It was the business of each one to seek from the gods a spiritual happiness in this life and the next. The official religion did not concern itself with the problems of the after-life, but it was of greatest importance to the individual that he should ensure for himself a good destiny hereafter. The rise of Taoism as a popular religion in the early centuries of the Christian era seems in large measure due to the fact that it provided a soteriology. The Taoists sought to make the body immortal, for it seemed to them that only in that way could the different essences which composed a human being be held together. Often technique took the place of true religion.

The saviour-gods of early Taoism

The term 'Taoism', as Zürcher reminds us, is extremely ambiguous. 'To call it a religion at all is misleading because, though it includes a religion, its other elements were equally important.'[12] These other elements were oddly assorted. There were, for example, 'the science of alchemy; maritime expeditions in search of the Isles of the Blest; an indigenous Chinese form of Yoga; a cult of wine and poetry; collective sexual orgies; church armies defending a theocratic state; revolutionary secret societies; and the philosophy of Lao-tzu.'[13] The pursuit of immortality was a strong element in Taoism, but as the personality was considered to be a composite of several complementary souls which dispersed at death, immortality was thought of in physical terms as the perpetual union of these soul-elements in harmonious relationship.

Already in the third century B.C., in the books of *Chuang-tzu* and *Lieh-tzu*,[14] there were numerous references to sages who, having perfected themselves in the Tao, had attained to immortality. Lieh-tzu speaks of the Isles of the Blest, inhabited by immortal sages (*hsien*).[15] These immortals, as Welch writes, 'took over the centre of the stage in Taoism. They became celestial officials who governed the world from Heaven, and who, though born as men, had won magical powers and immortality through the practice of hygiene; . . . if only the adept could win their favour, they would teach him how to follow in their footsteps.'[16] Chuang-tzu ridiculed these 'professors of hygiene, who lived in marshes or in the wilderness, exhaling and inhaling, getting rid of the old and assimilating the new, stretching like a bear or craning like a bird . . . who try to preserve the body to the age of P'eng-tzu (the Chinese Methuselah)'.[17] For Chuang-tzu

> life and death belong to destiny. Their sequence, like day and night, is of God, beyond the interference of men, and inevitable law. . . . To have attained to the human form must always be a source of joy. And then to undergo countless transitions, with only the infinite to look forward to,—what incomparable bliss is that! Therefore the truly wise rejoice in that which can never be lost, but always endures.[18]

The stories of Chuang-tzu and Lieh-tzu should, as Welch suggests, be taken allegorically and not literally;[19] but they do, I believe, indicate that in the folk-beliefs of their time there was an ardent concern for immortality, and a widespread belief in powerful divine beings whose assistance would render immortality possible.

As early as the reigns of dukes Wei and Hsüan of Ch'i and duke Chao of Yen (378–279 B.C.) frequent expeditions were being sent out to discover the islands of P'eng Lai, and find the drug or plant which prevented death. The first emperor, Shih Huang Ti, (*c.* 221 B.C.) had an almost fanatical concern for immortality, and not only experimented with alchemy, sent out maritime expeditions, and prepared an elaborate tomb to represent the universe in miniature, but sought the aid of several powerful divinities, of whom the god of T'ai Shan is noteworthy.[20]

Among the numerous gods to whom appeal was made for assistance and protection in this life and the next, two of the most significant were *The Grand Unity* (T'ai I) and *The Master of Destinies* (Ssu Ming). The co-operation of such gods was considered essential if salvation, in the Taoist sense, was to be achieved. As the *Songs of Ch'u* indicate, powerful shaman-diviners (*wu*) acted as intermediaries between the human and the spiritual world.[21]

T'ai I seems to have been regarded as a supreme god, similar to Shang Ti or T'ien, and, as A. Waley indicates,[22] he had a tremendous vogue during the second and first centuries B.C. In or around 133 B.C. the emperor Wu of the Han dynasty was prevailed upon to make the imperial cult centre in this deity.

The earliest of the saviour-gods of Taoism, who seems to have gained prominence before Buddhism gained a foothold in China, was Tsao Chün, the god of the stove, who was identified with Ssu Ming, the Master of Destinies. He held the records of the destinies both of men and immortals. He alone, in obedience to the supreme ruler of the universe, could transfer a name from the mortal to the immortal register. Therefore Tsao Chün became an object of worship and intercession.

It was not until late Han times, in the second century A.D., that Taoism developed as an organized religion. As such it gradually formed a pantheon of innumerable saviour-gods who were graded into a fantastic hierarchical structure. The basic aim of this Taoism, writes Zürcher, 'was to acquire bodily immortality, to obtain the state of a *hsien*, an Immortal who leads a life of everlasting bliss in a kind of light and indestructible *astral body* formed during his lifetime by following a prescribed course of physical and moral conduct.'[23] This early Taoism, being an amorphous mixture of hygiene techniques, alchemy, magic, medicine and religion, had little distinctive to offer in respect of the idea of salvation. It appealed to the masses mainly as a cult of faith-healing; but the healing was a catharsis of the whole personality, in which great prominence was given to confession of sins, fervent prayers to the gods, the proclamation of forgiveness and the imposition of penances. The rapid spread of Taoism among the populace towards the end of the second and throughout the third centuries A.D. witnesses to a deep-seated feeling of need for salvation. There was a fervent longing for deliverance from evil retribution and for the attainment of a blessed immortality beyond the grave. It was only later, in reaction to Buddhism, that Taoism developed a belief in heaven and hell and a vast pantheon of saviour-gods, for whom it claimed superiority over the Buddhas and Bodhisattvas of the *foreign* religion. It found in the mythical and semi-mythical heroes and sages of ancient times the divine instructors whose teachings were believed to direct the adept towards the achievement of immortality. But it was Buddhism, for a long time gravely misunderstood and which finally emerged in a distinctively Chinese form, which came to China with the fervour of a missionary religion, and provided in its Mahāyāna sects the saviour-gods to whom the populace at large could give unstinted devotion.

The saviour-gods of Chinese Buddhism

Buddhism, when it reached China, had had more than five hundred years of historical development. Some three hundred years of extensive missionary effort were to pass before Buddhism could be said to be truly indigenized, making its appeal on the one hand to the highly intellectual scholar-class, and on the other to the illiterate peasant. Buddhism, as Zürcher writes,

> widened the mental horizon of its cultured devotees. . . . It revealed to them a universe of staggering proportions evolving through a sequence of cosmic periods of inconceivable length, the figure of a completely super-human saint who in transcendent wisdom, love and power infinitely surpassed any of the earthly-minded sages of Chinese tradition, and a moral and seemingly logical explanation of the problem of universal suffering, as well as a detailed and systematic method of escape from it.[24]

To ordinary men and women, conscious of their own frailty and sinfulness, Buddhism brought the concepts of the compassionate Buddha and the innumerable Bodhisattvas. These powerful divine beings were worshipped as saviour-gods, who not only assured salvation to the faithful, but were ever ready to bring succour in all times of distress. They were gods of mercy and compassion who answered prayers for protection and success, but who also exercised control over those heavens to which the good hoped to be translated on death, and to which even souls undergoing purgation in hell might eventually aspire. A. F. Wright, referring to the time when Buddhism reached the apogee of its influence in the T'ang dynasty, writes,

> The notion that the compassionate Bodhisattvas could intervene in the lives of men to save them from danger, to help them to felicity, and—above all—to guide them to bliss beyond the grave, was present

in numerous texts of the Mahāyāna. It was popularized for the common people in the sermons of lay and clerical preachers, in tales of the Bodhisattvas' saving interventions, in forged popular 'sutras' written to Chinese tastes, and in collections of cases of the working of karmic retribution and divine grace. Each of the many Buddhist deities presided over a heaven which was colourfully and appealingly described and contrasted with the torments of innumerable hells. . . . In contrast to the shadowy *immortals* of religious Taoism and its psycho-physical regimens, Buddhism offered a rich iconography and mythology which would fire even the most sluggish imagination.[25]

Two facts are of great significance in Chinese Buddhism. First, the figure of the historical Gautama, though usually occupying a central place in the Buddhist temple, did not appeal as powerfully to Chinese popular imagination as did the galaxy of saviour-gods of whom O-mi-t'o-fo (Amitābha), Mi-lei-fo (Maitreya), Kuan-yin (Avalokiteśvara), Ta-shih-chih (Mahāstāma), Pi-lu-fo (Vairocana) and Wen-shu (Mañjuśrī) were the most noteworthy. Secondly, though according to Buddhist doctrine these saviour-gods were merely hypostases of the Buddha-nature, the Buddha-mind or the Buddha-principle, by the populace at large they were worshipped as gods, and hope was directed not so much to attainment of Nirvāna as entrance into some paradise. Certain factors help to explain the peculiar developments in Chinese Buddhism. Buddhism went a long way in seeking to accommodate itself to indigenous thought, and to give ancient sages and heroes a place in its pantheon. Then again, Buddhism entered China not so much directly from India as from places in Western Asia where syncretistic tendencies had already greatly modified Buddhist belief and expression. Also it must be remembered that very few Chinese, and only the highly intellectual, ever really understood the highly metaphysical doctrines and penetrating psychological analysis which had already developed in Indian Buddhism.

Of the innumerable saviour-gods of Chinese Buddhism it is only possible here to refer briefly to three, which are chosen, not only because of their widespread influence, but because any consideration of the role which they exercised in China raises interesting, if sometimes insoluble, questions.

O-mi-t'o-fo (*Amitābha*)

Where did this Buddha of boundless light have his origin? According to Eitel 'the dogma of Amita reached China (*via* Tibet) from Cashmere and Nepal, which had been greatly influenced by Persian ideas'.[26] Helmut Hoffmann writes that

the figure of Buddha, 'immeasurable light', Amitābha, with his paradise Sukhāvatī, regarded as being in the West, strongly suggests the influence of Iranian religious ideas. Originally conceived in the spirit of Zoroastrianism, Amitābha's character could readily be incorporated by Manichaeism in its mythological identifications.[27] ... Southern Buddhism knows no Amita, neither are there traces of a Brahminical or Vedic origin of this doctrine.[28] ... He is unknown in Siam, Burma and Ceylon.[29] ... Amitābha is only known in Northern Buddhism.[30]

As the sovereign teacher of the Western Heaven, of great mercy and infinite compassion, he is by far the most popular saviour-god in Chinese and Japanese Buddhism.

According to Zürcher, a late tradition connects the beginnings of the Amitābha cult in China with the name of an early third century A.D. Buddhist scholar, Wei-shih-tu, but

the first mention in early literature of a ceremony in which the devotee takes refuge in the saving power of the Buddha Amitābha, and before an icon of this Buddha makes a solemn vow to be reborn in the Western Paradise, occurs in the *Kuang Hung Ming Chi*, where we find a number of eulogies by Chih Tun (A.D. 314–366), extolling the qualities of several Buddhas and Bodhisattvas.[31]

The Amitābha sutra was translated into Chinese about A.D. 402 by Kumārajīva,[32] and from this time onwards the worship of Amitābha became increasingly popular. Undoubtedly the influence of the famous monk Hui Yüan (A.D. 334–417), and the rise of the Pure Land school, led forward to great developments throughout the fifth century A.D. 'On 11th September 402 A.D. Hui Yüan assembled the monks and laymen of his community before an image of Amitābha, and together they made a vow to be reborn in the Western Paradise, where Amitābha was believed to reside. ... The vow was accompanied by offerings of incense and flowers, and a solemn covenant between the participants to help each other to reach their goal.[33]

Through the writings of Shan-tao (*ob.* A.D. 681) the thought of eternal life and of a vicarious Saviour were added to the concept of Amitābha.[34] As Shan-tao lived near to the sphere of Nestorian activity, the unresolved question of how far Buddhism was influenced by Nestorianism arises. Reichelt maintains that through Nestorian influence masses for the dead were introduced into Buddhism in the eighth century by Amogha Vajra (*ob.* A.D. 772).[35] They became a most important element in Chinese Buddhism. By this means the souls of the dead, suffering torment in hell, were translated to the Western Paradise through the infinite merit and mercy of Amitābha. A verse which Reichelt translates from '*Masses for the Dead*' reveals Amitābha as a supreme saviour-god.

Thou perfect master
Who shinest upon all things and all men,
As gleaming moonlight plays upon a thousand waters at the same time!
Thy great compassion does not pass by a single creature.
Steadily and quietly sails the great ship of compassion across the sea of sorrow.
Thou art the great physician for a sick and impure world,
In pity giving invitation to the Paradise of the West.[36]

As Doré writes,

Amitābha rules over this (Western) paradise, and admits thereto all those who trust in his abounding power and pity, and who faithfully repeat his holy name.[37] . . . The powerful name of Amitābha is the mysterious sword, which overcomes all doctrines opposed to that of the Western Paradise; it is the antidote whereby all fear of Hades is banished from the mind; it is the brilliant light which dispels the darkness of the understanding; it is the merciful craft, whereby mortals are wafted across the ocean of misery and suffering, and borne to the happy land of the West.[38]

Kuan-yin (*Avalokiteśvara*)

This great Bodhisattva, whose name might be translated as 'The Lord who looks down', was introduced into China about the fifth century A.D. Kumārajīva is reputed to be the first to render the Hindu name by its Chinese equivalent, Kuan-shih-yin. Under the name Kuan-yin, 'contemplating sounds', hence 'the One who hears prayers', this deity rapidly became and has remained the most widely revered of all the Bodhisattvas. He (or she) is the great assistant of Amitābha, and mythologically conceived of as Amitābha's son. He originated as an Indo-Tibetan deity. His name is found for the first time in a sutra written about the first century A.D. As the Lord of mercy he looks down on all mankind to save men from every kind of distress, and lead them to Amitābha's paradise. He is the 'All-pitying One'. 'People pray to him more than to any other Bodhisattva, and not only for release from future rebirths, but in all cases of bodily danger, and domestic affliction.'[39] In the *Lotus Sutra* (chap. 25) it is claimed that those who hold fast to the name of Kuan-yin will be saved from every kind of peril, affliction or danger. Those possessed of carnal passions, anger or infatuation, will be set free. Women desiring children will have their wish granted. 'The merit attained by worship of other Bodhisattvas . . . just equals the merit of him who but for one moment worships the Regarder-of-the-Cries-of-the-World.'[40]

There seems to be no doubt that, when Kuan-yin first came to be revered in China, this deity was represented with male attributes. But at least from the twelfth century onwards, and probably considerably before that time, it is in the form of a great female deity that Kuan-yin is mainly depicted and worshipped. How the change of sex came about and the reasons for it have been the subject of considerable controversy. Edkins pointed out that 'in the *Fa-hwa-ching*, Kuan-yin is described as being able to assume any form at pleasure, whether that of Buddhas, Devas, men or others, and as being guided in such voluntary metamorphoses by a constant desire to proclaim the Buddhist doctrine to those who need it, in the form most likely to effect the object'.[41] He believed that the feminine form did not appear in China before the early part of the twelfth century, about which time a Buddhist monk wrote the romantic story of Miao-shan, and identified this remarkable princess and Bodhisattva with Kuan-yin. Yet Doré points out that some paintings of the seventh and eighth centuries are markedly feminine. Doré has summarized the main reasons which have been suggested for this transformation of Kuan-yin into a beneficent and compassionate goddess, the Queen of Heaven, the Guardian Goddess of the Southern Seas, the patron of sailors, the protector of mothers, the bestower of children, the goddess of a thousand arms and eyes.[42]

It is probable, as Reichelt has pointed out, that a number of goddesses were known and dear to the Chinese from old times, and that the all-embracing Kuan-yin absorbed the functions of these goddesses. So also, in later times, new features were added to the picture of Kuan-yin. 'It is almost certain', writes Reichelt, 'that the idea of the Holy Virgin, the merciful Madonna of the sixteenth and seventeenth centuries has also influenced this Kuan-yin picture.'[43]

Mi-lo-fo (*Maitreya*)

It might appear strange, at first sight, that in a discussion of the many saviour-gods of Chinese Buddhism, prominence should be afforded to this pot-bellied, smiling, good-natured Bodhisattva, whose image is often erected in the outer hall of the temple, and who seems to have exercised the functions of a tutelary deity. Yet, as Reichelt writes, 'some of the deepest thoughts and liveliest hopes of Buddhism are bound up with this figure'.[44] There was a period, during the fourth and early fifth centuries A.D., when Maitreya occupied an even more prominent place than Amitābha. The ardent hopes and expectations which were aroused by the thought that on the completion of a thousand years after Gautama's enlightenment some new revelation would appear on earth, coupled with a belief that human society was rapidly deteriorating, no doubt stimulated faith in Maitreya, the Coming One, who, at the command of Buddha, would descend from the heaven of the blessed and establish a great millennial kingdom. In China Maitreya was spoken of as 'Mi-lo-fo who is to come', the Messiah of Buddhism. In the *Mi-lo-hsia-sheng* sutra a description is given of Maitreya's descent into the world at a time when the powers of evil are at their height and everything is tending to ruin. Dwelling in the Tuchita heaven, he is thought of as controlling the progagation of the Buddhist faith.[45]

The worship of Maitreya witnesses to a strong element of Messianism in the Chinese. This is seen also in the semi-religious revolutionary movements which have throughout nearly two thousand years of history been inspired by Taoism, and by the appeal which Christian millennary teachings have had in modern times among the peasantry of China. As among other peoples, misery and distress occasioned by war, famine and government oppression have, in China, proved a fertile field for ideas of a saviour-god who would come down to earth to establish a kingdom of peace and righteousness. Maitreya has occupied the role of such a saviour in the imagination of the Chinese.

There is no space in this essay to discuss the role of Mani and that of Jesus Christ in the development of the Chinese ideas of salvation and saviour-gods. From such observations as we have made the conclusion may be drawn that the Chinese people are not so irreligious and materially-minded as some scholars have been led to believe. Throughout their history the feeling of a need for salvation has been as prominent among the Chinese as among many other peoples. Though often this need has been expressed as a desire to be freed from the ills, sorrows, misfortunes and dangers of this life, there has also been expressed a fervent longing for a better life in a world-to-come. The hold which Taoism and Buddhism gained over the populace is in large measure due to the fact that they encouraged belief in powerful saviour-gods, who were ever ready to save and bless. Though these saviour-gods have often been presented in crude and fantastic imagery, it is undoubtedly true that the great saviour-figures of Chinese religion have symbolized some of the most profound religious concepts, whilst at the same time these saviour-gods have been the focus of fervent devotion and aspiring faith on the part of millions of people.

NOTES

1 D. H. Smith, 'Chinese Religion in the Shang Dynasty', *Numen*, vol. viii, Fasc. 2, p. 147. Cf. Fu Ssu-nien, *Hsing-ming Ku-hsün Pien-chang*, 1947, vol. 2, pp. 4 ff.

[2] D. H. Smith, 'Religious Development in Ancient China prior to Confucius', *Bull. Rylands Library*, July 1962.

[3] *Shu Ching*: To Fang, 17–19; K'ang Kao, 4; To Shih, 2–3.

[4] *Shu Ching*: Chiu Shih, 2, 4; *Shih Ching*: 4:3; 2, 1; 3:1; 1.

[5] *Shih Ching*: 3:3; 10, 1; 3:3; 11, 1; 3:3; 2, 12; 2:4; 10, 1; 2:4; 7, 5–6.

[6] Shigeki Kaizuka, *Confucius*, 1956, p. 81.

[7] *Tao Te Ching*, Chapter 5. Cf. J. J. L. Duyvendak, *The Tao Te Ching*, 1954, p. 28 n. 'The moral principle of *Jen* is not inherent in heaven and earth; that is, the processes of nature. There every-thing and every being is treated with complete ruthlessness merely to the purpose that each may play "its part in the scheme of things".'

[8] *La Religion Chinoise*, p. 199.

[9] 'Sin (Chinese)', *E.R.E.*, 1920, vol. 11, p. 535.

[10] *Shih Ching*: 4:1; 2, 6.

[11] Holmes Welch, *The Parting of the Way*, 1957, pp. 100 ff. For the significance of shaman-priests cf. A. Waley, *The Nine Songs*, 1955, Intro.

[12] E. Zürcher, *The Buddhist Conquest of China*, 1959, p. 288.

[13] H. Welch, p. 88.

[14] Lieh-tzu is attributed to the third century A.D. by numerous Chinese scholars, but is undoubtedly based on earlier sources. Cf. *The Book of Lieh-tzu*, transl. by A. C. Graham, 1960, Intro.

[15] *Lieh-tzu*, chap. 5.

[16] Welch, p. 92.

[17] *Chuang-tzu*. Transl. by H. Giles. Rev. Ed. reprinted 1961, p. 152.

[18] Ibid., pp. 75–6.

[19] Welch, p. 92.

[20] L. Wieger, *Hist. of Rel. Beliefs and Phil. Opinions in China*, 1927, p. 253. See also Wieger, *Textes Historiques*, 1929, Tome 1, pp. 209–31.

[21] D. Hawkes, *The Ch'u tz'u*. transl. 1959, pp. 8 and 9.

[22] Waley, p. 24.

[23] Zürcher, p. 289.

[24] Ibid., p. 268.

[25] A. F. Wright, *Buddhism in Chinese History*, 1959, pp. 81–2.

[26] E. J. Eitel, *Handbook of Chinese Buddhism*, 1870, pp. 6–7.

[27] Helmut Hoffman, *The Religions of Tibet*, 1961, p. 52.

[28] Eitel, p. 7.

[29] J. Edkins, *Chinese Buddhism*, 1893, p. 171.

[30] H. Doré, *Researches into Chinese Superstitions*, 1920, vol. vi, p. 106.

[31] Zürcher, p. 128.

[32] Doré, vol. vi, p. 109.

[33] Zürcher, pp. 219–20.

[34] K. L. Reichelt, *Truth and Tradition in Chinese Buddhism*, 1927, pp. 131–132.

[35] Ibid., pp. 88–9.

[36] Ibid., p. 137.

[37] Doré, vol. vi, p. 112; Edkins, pp. 208, 233; Johnston, *Buddhist China*, p. 98; Beal, *Buddhism in China*, p. 129.

[38] Doré, vol. vi, p. 113.

[39] Ibid., p. 197; J. H. Chamberlayne, art. 'The Development of Kuan Yin', *Numen.*, vol. 9, Fasc. 1, Jan. 1962.

[40] W. E. Soothill, *The Lotus of the Wonderful Law*, 1930, p. 248.

[41] Edkins, p. 208.

[42] Doré, vol. vi, pp. 200 ff.

[43] Reichelt, p. 184.

[44] Ibid., p. 187.

[45] Eitel, p. 70.

XIII

THE MUSLIM YEARNING FOR A SAVIOUR: ASPECTS OF EARLY 'ABBĀSID SHĪ'ISM

by

W. MONTGOMERY WATT

The problem and the starting-point

THE study of the earlier history of the Shī'ite form of Islam is peculiarly difficult. In the course of a century or two considerable changes took place, and the accounts of the early period were written in the light of what subsequently happened. This article is an attempt to develop in certain directions a reappraisal of early Shī'ism begun elsewhere,[1] and will be specially concerned with the years from 750 to 925.

In the turmoil which followed the first wave of Muslim conquests it became apparent that among certain sections of the Arabs, preponderantly among those from South Arabia, there was a deep yearning for a deliverer of more than human stature. It would be only natural that in an era of insecurity following on rapid changes in their manner of life men should turn to look for some contemporary equivalent of the divine kings who had guided the civilization of South Arabia for centuries. The first actual person to whom they turned was 'Alī, the cousin and son-in-law of Muḥammad. By about the middle of the seventh century A.D. this longing for a saviour or charismatic leader had been linked up with politics. It was not the only religious urge among the Muslims, however. Among other Arabs there was a vigorous belief that they were members of a charismatic community, and the need to ensure that the existing Islamic community retained its charismatic character also led to political action. This belief was indeed the basis of the Sunnite form of Islam; and the conflict within Islam between Sunnism and Shīʿism may be said to be due in the last resort to a failure to discover forms of political activity that satisfy both the religious urges simultaneously.

In this confusion of religion and politics that is characteristic of all communities in the Middle East and not simply of the Muslims, one guiding principle on which a firm grasp must be maintained is that Shīʿism is not simply a political movement, but arises, at least in part, from a genuine religious urge. The primary aim of the present article is to indicate the ways in which politicians have tried to make use of the energies underlying the religious urge in order to achieve political aims. A second guiding principle is that the interminable discussions under the ʿAbbāsids whether Abū-Bakr or ʿAlī should have succeeded Muḥammad did not proceed from an interest in history as such, but were in some way relevant to contemporary ʿAbbāsid politics. It is not always easy for us to see in what this relevance consisted. Under an autocratic government, it was presumably advisable not to express political opinions too obviously; and, of course, even when ideas were clearly understood by contemporaries, there was no guarantee that they would be effective.

Yet a third guiding principle to be kept in mind is that one of the most important political contrasts in a situation such as that in the ʿAbbāsid caliphate is between the activists who are plotting to overthrow the existing régime and the quietists who are prepared to accept it, at least for the visible future. This contrast can be illustrated by the various developments of Shīʿism up to the fall of the Umayyad dynasty. It was in the first place activists who thought they had found in ʿAlī an inspired leader who could guide them safely through the perils of the contemporary situation; but they were gravely disappointed by the actual achievements of ʿAlī and his sons, al-Ḥasan and al-Ḥusayn (d. 680). Before long, however—in 686—another activist, al-Muḫtār, though unable to claim charismata for himself, attracted Shīʿite support by asserting that he was the accredited emissary of a son of ʿAlī (not by Fāṭima) known as Muḥammad ibn-al-Ḥanafiyya. Whether the assertion was true or false is uncertain, but the fact that it was made is of importance. Many other such assertions were made towards the end of the Umayyad period and later. There were also some risings headed by men who themselves claimed to be charismatic leaders as members of the 'family' (*ahl al-bayt*); the best known of these is the rising of Zayd, a grandson of al-Ḥusayn, in 740.

From a political point of view it was unsatisfactory that a large number of people should be able to claim charismata. A multiplicity of leaders meant that the religious feeling, of which the politicians hoped to make use, was being dissipated in different directions. If any member of the clan of Hāshim could claim charismata, there was little hope of creating a single strong movement. It therefore became usual to claim that a particular person became imam (as the Shī'ites tended to call the inspired leader) through the 'designation' (*naṣṣ*) of a previous imam, usually the immediate predecessor. Even this device failed to achieve unity, of course, for it was easy to invent a claim to have been designated. The original basis of the 'Abbāsid claim to the caliphate (presumably made public only in 750) was that about 716 the son of Muḥammad ibn-al-Ḥanifiyya had designated as his successor the father of the first 'Abbāsid caliph. It may be noted in passing that in the caliphate of al-Mahdī (775–85) or earlier[2] this claim was abandoned, and instead it was asserted that the rightful imam after the Prophet was his uncle al-'Abbās, the ancestor of the dynasty. Perhaps this change was due to the difficulty of substantiating one claim to designation over against another.

Before the activists made their attempts to overthrow the Umayyads there had been a peaceful half century, from the defeat of al-Muḫtār in 687 until 737, when the quietists were predominant in the Shī'ite movement. Under their influence the conception of the 'hidden imam' was developed. In particular it was asserted that Muḥammad ibn-al-Ḥanifiyya had not died, but was in concealment (*ġayba*), and that one day he would return as the Mahdī to set wrongs right and establish justice on earth. These assertions are in accordance with religious rather than political needs. They constitute a faith that gave men some comfort and assured them that their lives were not meaningless; despite contrary appearances and the impossibility of political activity to improve their circumstances, all would eventually be well. In practice the conception of the hidden imam seems to have been chiefly linked with political quietism, but there is always the possibility of a change to activism. If the times appear to be propitious, someone may put himself forward either as the hidden imam returned or as his emissary, and in this capacity may demand the active support of all the believers in the hidden imam. This in fact happened in Ismā'īlism, but not till about 900 (as will be mentioned below). We may conclude, then, that during the Umayyad period, though the conception of the hidden imam held a potential threat to the régime, the religious aspect was primary.

The Rāfiḍites and Imāmites

The later Imāmite accounts (of which the early chapters of D. M. Donaldson's *The Shi'ite Religion* present a version) make it seem that there was an active Imāmite or moderate-Shī'ite movement from the death of al-Ḥusayn in 680 onwards, that each of the imams recognized by the later Imāmites duly designated his successor, and that there was a considerable body of men who acknowledged them as imams during their lifetime. This is almost certainly not the case. Any attempt to assert in any public fashion that a particular person was the rightful imam of the Islamic community would have been tantamount to an act of rebellion against the 'Abbāsid dynasty. The dynasty had suspicions about some of the 'Alid imams and kept a careful watch over them, even making some of them undergo a light form of imprisonment. If the 'Abbāsid agents were unable to uncover any subversive movement with wide ramifications, there is a strong presumption that no such movement existed. The Imāmite sources themselves, too, are devoid of factual material to support the great claims made for the imams. A possible exception to this is Ja'far aṣ-Ṣādiḳ, who is reckoned as having been imam from his father's death in 731 until his own in 765. This was the period of the break-up of the Umayyad caliphate and its replacement by the

'Abbāsid; and it may be that he, as head of the descendants of al-Ḥusayn, thought there might be some good fishing for his family in the troubled waters. If he engaged in political intrigues, however, he must have realized by the time of his death that the 'Abbāsids were not to be easily dislodged, and he had doubtless prudently accepted a policy of quietism.

In 817 the 'Abbāsid caliph al-Ma'mūn made an ingenious attempt to strengthen the ruling institution and remove whatever Ḥusaynid menace there was by declaring the most prominent of the Ḥusaynids, known as 'Alī ar-Riḍā, to be his heir and marrying him to his daughter. Unfortunately 'Alī died in 818, and his son Muḥammad—not, of course, by al-Ma'mūn's daughter—was only seven or nine; and nothing came of the move. This series of events tends to confirm the view that the leaders of the Ḥusaynids were not serious rivals to the 'Abbāsids, and that, though they might be able to rouse some popular enthusiasm, had no *organized* following. Anything in the nature of a closely-knit party would have threatened at least some part of the existing ruling institution. All efforts to enlist the support of the unorganized moderate-Shī'ite feeling came to an end about 849, and instead the régime committed itself to a mainly Sunnite policy. The Ḥusaynid leader of the time, the tenth imam, was shortly afterwards imprisoned, at least to the extent of being kept under surveillance. On his death in 868 his son, the eleventh imam, was at first treated similarly, but after a short time set completely free. When this imam in turn died in 874, he was supposed to have been succeeded by his son, the twelfth imam, who was a mere boy. The twelfth imam is further supposed to have gone into concealment. What exactly happened must remain mysterious; he may have died, or —as some sceptics have suggested—may never have existed.

All that has just been said points to one conclusion. It was shortly after 874 that the Imāmite form of Shī'ism (as it may properly be called from this time onwards) took the definite shape with which we are familiar from the source-material; the latter is nearly all subsequent to 874, and whatever is earlier is interpreted in terms of the later. Not long after 874, then, some politician, who must have been essentially a quietist, applied the conception of the hidden imam to the Ḥusaynids, and probably at the same time established the sequence of twelve imams. The names are known of various Imāmite leaders who were active about this time. Abū-Ğa'far al-Ḳummī (d. 903) is regarded as the founder of Imāmite jurisprudence, while Abū-Sahl an-Nawbaḫtī (d. 923) was head of the Shī'ites in Baghdad for some time before his death.[3]

To discover the significance of this constitution of the Imāmites as a definite party or sect we must turn back to the previous period. There were moderate-Shī'ites during the first half of the ninth century, for the most part called Rāfiḍites by their contemporaries. A prominent theologian was Hišām ibn-al-Ḥakam, who probably died about 825. He and others like him were on good terms with the ruling institution, and were certainly not plotting to replace the 'Abbāsids by 'Alids; according to al-Aš'arī[4] they held that insurrection was wrong, unless their imam appeared. The most distinctive point in their views was apparently their rejection of the caliphates of Abū-Bakr and 'Umar and their insistence that 'Alī was the rightful imam after the Prophet. How were such assertions relevant to the politics of the early ninth century? It seems most likely that what the Rāfiḍites were interested in was a more autocratic form of government. In particular this would mean that all decisions should be taken by the caliph and his advisers, and that they should not be restricted by the views of Sunnite jurists on what was commanded by the *šarī'a* or revealed law. The Rāfiḍite belief in the charismata of 'Alī seems to have implied a belief that the state would be best governed when its affairs were directed by a gifted leader. Ordinary ungifted people, they held, were always liable to error. In rejecting Abū-Bakr and 'Umar they were virtually impugning the majority of the Companions; and it was on the testimony of the Companions that the Traditions depended which were the basis of Sunnite jurisprudence. This is a view which makes sense in the circumstances of the time. That it was held by many does not mean that it was effective, but it probably exercised some pressure on the thinking of the actual wielders of power.

The change of governmental policy about 849 meant a consolidation of the influence of the Sunnite jurists, and thus to a great extent the defeat of the autocratic ideas of the Shī'ites. It was doubtless this situation which caused certain leaders towards the end of the ninth century to organize Shī'ite opinion as it had never been organized before, and to do so round the conception of twelve imams, of whom the twelfth had gone into concealment. This definite theological conception transformed into a definite movement what had previously been a vague climate of opinion. It was thus primarily a reaction to their discomfiture by the Sunnites. It is also possible that the Imāmite leaders were anxious lest the main body of Shī'ite sympathizers should be carried away by Ismā'īlite propaganda. Ismā'īlite propaganda was gaining momentum towards the end of the ninth century, and was essentially activist or revolutionary. Such propaganda must therefore have been most distasteful to the Imāmites who were political quietists. Once again the discussion of a contemporary political question would appear to have taken the form of arguments about what happened a century and a half earlier just before the death of Ǧa'far aṣ-Ṣādiḳ in 765. The new Imāmite organization led to the attainment by quietist Shī'ite opinion of an established place in the caliphate. Under the Buwayhid war-lords, who professed Imāmism, official recognition was given to the distinctive Imāmite legal rite.

Whatever political influence the Imāmites may have had, their doctrines certainly had religious importance. The attempt to have the 'Abbāsid caliphs accepted as divinely inspired or charismatic leaders was almost necessarily foredoomed to failure. In an empire as large as that ruled by the 'Abbāsids there was bound to be some discontent. It did not help a discontented person to know that the head of the state was divinely inspired; if his present unsatisfactory circumstances were brought about by divine power, there could be little hope of improvement.[5] On the other hand, if one day there was to be an inspired deliverer who would set everything right, the discontented had some comfort and a ground for hope—just sufficient to make his present unsatisfactory situation bearable.

The Ismāʿīlites

The line of thought indicated above suggests that the essential break between the Imāmites and the Ismāʿīlites took place towards the end of the ninth century, and not shortly after the death of Jaʿfar aṣ-Ṣādiḳ in 765. The break was primarily a break between quietists and activists, and it was accompanied by a theological process in which a definite form was given to the theories of the twelve and seven imams respectively. There had, of course, been a considerable volume of Shīʿite thinking between 765 and 900, but it had been very diffuse. Small groups had worked out and applied Shīʿite conceptions in their own way, and there had been little agreement. The later part of the ninth century seems to have witnessed the concentration of this diffuse thinking in two main streams, together with a definite cleavage between these two streams.

In an article such as the present this view can only be put forward as a suggestion or hypothesis, and it requires to be substantiated or rejected by a careful examination of the early sources. One small point in support of it is that the Zaydite writer al-Ḳāsim ibn-Ibrāhīm (d. 860) regards as Rāfiḍites all who acknowledge Ǧaʿfar aṣ-Ṣādiḳ, and the slightly later Sunnite writer al-Ašʿarī (d. 935) likewise includes various Ismāʿīlite groups among the Rāfiḍites.[6] Without finally deciding about this hypothesis, however, it is possible to notice how the transition from quietism to activism was made by the branch of the Ismāʿīlite movement which achieved the establishment of the Fāṭimid dynasty.

A German scholar, Wilferd Madelung, in an article entitled 'Das Imamat in der frühen ismailitischen Lehre' has recently examined some Ismāʿīlite books which appear to have been written before the Fāṭimids became openly active.[7] One of the themes of these books is that the era of the Mahdī or promised saviour is already here. In one of the books, *Kitāb al-kašf*, the words 'a call-to-prayer from God' in *Ḳur'ān*, 9.3 are interpreted as referring to the man who will give the call to prayer and prescribe the forms of prayer as imam; and he is asserted to be none other than 'Muḥammad, our master and Lord, who wields the sword and speaks openly in his age'. Madelung thinks that this originally referred to Muḥammad ibn-Aḥmad (d. 896 probably), and that at one time he had hoped to be in a position to come forward publicly as imam. Whoever the person intended, this book shows how it is possible to move towards a claim that the hidden imam has appeared, provided care is taken and one does not move too rapidly. Madelung further thinks that the leadership of the movement might at first have been in the hands of a group of men, each of whom might be known as a 'proof' (*ḥuǧǧa*), but that in course of time one man became dominant.[8]

To prevent misunderstandings some of the points of difference between the present hypothesis and current views may be underlined. As representative of current views we may take *The Origins of Ismā'īlism* by Bernard Lewis (Cambridge, 1940), especially the recapitulations on pp. 42 f. and 66 f. This current view accepts the implication of most of the sources that from about 750 there was an extremist or revolutionary wing of the Shī'ite movement, and that this had a sufficient degree of organization to be able to carry on propaganda with a view to political action in the foreseeable future. The new hypothesis does not deny developments in Shī'ite thinking between about 750 and 870, but insists that they were primarily religious and were directed towards men's religious needs; that is to say, they were politically quietist and not activist. It would further suggest that the degree of organization has been exaggerated, and that connections have been alleged between persons where none existed in reality. In other words, most of the statements in the sources which imply that there was an activist underground movement are later inventions with a view to legitimizing Ismā'īlism, especially as against Imāmism; and the Imāmites also tended to speak as if they had a rival underground movement.

It must be conceded that there existed some activism shortly before and after 750. The case of Abū-'l-Ḫattāb, who was executed by the 'Abbāsid authorities in 755 (probably), is an instance; but the accounts of his teaching and that of his followers in *Firaḳ aš-Šī'a* (ascribed to an-Nawbaḫtī) suggest that their interests were primarily religious. On the other hand, assertions about underground activities that do not lead to public action must only be accepted after the closest scrutiny. An important example of this is the assertion that Maymūn al-Ḳaddāḥ and his son ʿAbd-Allāh were active propagators of the Ismāʿīlite movement before and round about 800. One fact that makes this assertion dubious is that the two men were Traditionists of the circle of Ǧaʿfar aṣ-Ṣādiḳ, accepted by the later Imāmites. This fact is difficult to square with the current view, but is easily understood on the new hypothesis. Here, however, the matter must be allowed to rest so far as the present article is concerned.

The Zaydites

The Zaydites are in some ways the most difficult to understand of the Shīʿite sects. The difficulty is in seeing the point or practical significance of the doctrines they are alleged to have held. To reduce the problem to manageable proportions four phases of Zaydism may be distinguished. Firstly, there is the rising of Zayd himself in 740. Secondly, there are a number of scholars who may be presumed to have been active during the first thirty years of ʿAbbāsid rule; among these are: Muḳātil ibn-Sulaymān (d. 767), Sufyān aṯ-Ṯawrī (d. 777), al-Ḥasan ibn-Ṣāliḥ ibn-Ḥayy (d. *c.* 785).[9] Thirdly, there were other scholars in the first half of the ninth century, of whom the best known is Sulaymān ibn-Ǧarīr (probably d. *c.* 840). Fourthly, there are the movements later in the ninth century which led to the establishment of small Zaydite states in Daylam (at the south of the Caspian Sea) and in the Yemen.

Of these phases the first is essentially activist. Its distinctive feature doctrinally is that no member of the 'family' is to be recognized as imam until he actually puts himself at the head of an insurrection. Zayd was the first ʿAlid to do so for many years. He and his followers were thus opposed to the quietism associated with the conception of the hidden imam. Whether there was any extensive continuity of personnel between this first phase and the later phases is doubtful. The main continuity would seem to be in the realm of ideas. A number of unsuccessful revolts led by ʿAlids —by Muḥammad an-Nafs az-Zakiyya in 762, by Muḥammad ibn-al-Ḳāsim in 834, and by Yaḥyā ibn-'Umar in 864—had probably little connection with Zayd and possibly none with the later Zaydite scholars. (It is noteworthy that after each of these three revolts there was a group which regarded the unsuccessful leader as a hidden imam who would one day return—instances of political failure leading to quietism; al-Aš'arī regards these groups as belonging to the Zaydite sect of the Ǧārūdiyya.[10]) The successful revolts which led to the establishment of Zaydite states in Daylam and the Yemen (the fourth phase), or at least the second of them, had some effective contact with the scholars. It must also be remembered that the movement which led to the 'Abbāsid caliphate was an insurrection led by activists of 'the family' (in the wide sense) which proved successful.

Apart from the revolts just mentioned the Zaydite movement in its second and third phases was politically quietist. The scholars named cannot even be suspected of underground plotting. Doctrinally this means that the principle that the imam must be activist is no longer distinctive of Zaydism.[11] Instead another principle, apparently also held by Zayd himself, becomes the distinguishing mark, namely, that although 'Alī was the best (*afḍal*) of the Muslims after Muḥammad, he allowed Abū-Bakr and 'Umar to have supreme authority, and therefore their caliphates are to be recognized. This principle is often called 'the imamate of the inferior (*mafḍūl*)'. It is at bottom a compromise. It acknowledges the charismata of 'the family' (restricted to the descendants of 'Alī and Fāṭima), but it avoids branding Abū-Bakr, 'Umar and other leading Companions as dishonest because they did not at once do homage to 'Alī in accordance with Muḥammad's alleged designation of him as his successor. That is to say, it endeavours to satisfy men of Shī'ite sympathies without antagonizing those inclined to Sunnism; for the latter group any criticism of the uprightness of the Companions was virtually an attack on the corpus of Sunnite Traditions, since these were all in the first place related by Companions.

Even when all this has been said, it is still not clear what it meant to be a Zaydite in 765 or 825. Presumably there was no desire to overthrow or replace the 'Abbāsids. So it would seem that the main concern must rather have been for the precise nature of the caliph's position and authority. The compromise would then be an attempt to mediate between those who favoured autocracy, especially the civil service with its enduring links with the old Persian traditions, and those who might be described as 'constitutionalists', represented above all by the majority of the Traditionists and jurists. Though these ideas might be widely held, it does not follow of course that they were correspondingly effective in influencing those who took the big decisions. Ideas may have had some effect, however, and perhaps some of the discussions were an attempt to make the appointment of the caliphs conform more closely to an ideal. The normal theory was that each imam 'designated' his successor (or even more than one successor). But some of the Zaydites are found saying that this is not the only method, and suggesting a small committee instead (*šūrā*).[12] Another suggestion—that 'Alī was designated by 'description', *sc.* that a description was given of what the character of the imam must be—might merely be a way of avoiding the difficulty that the assertion that Muḥammad designated 'Alī was not generally accepted; but it might also be an endeavour to ensure that the caliphate was restricted to suitably qualified men. During the ninth century succession to the caliphate came to be more and more determined by the intrigues of members of the administration or Turkish officers.

There seems to have been some connection between the Mu'tazilites of the first half of the ninth century and some of the later Zaydites. Al-Aš'arī[13] notes that many of the Zaydites take similar positions to the Mu'tazilites on such matters as the divine attributes and man's capacity for acting. The scholar, al-Ḳāsim ibn-Ibrāhīm (d. 860), whose grandson founded the Zaydite state in the Yemen, stood particularly close to the Mu'tazilites.[14] Whatever the reason for this connection or mutual sympathy, both were working for a political and religious compromise, though they had a slightly different formula.[15] The Mu'tazilites had a measure of actual power from about 825 to 849. At the latter date, however, a great change in policy was made, and the government decided to abandon compromise and give definite support to Sunnism. This change was doubtless due to the fact that it had been found in practice that compromise gave the rulers the worst of both worlds; they satisfied neither side and failed to enlist enthusiastic support. The complex of factors which told against Muʿtazilism would also affect Zaydism. In addition the Zaydite principle of the imamate of the inferior was unfortunate in its form of expression. When it was coupled with the restriction of the imamate to the descendants of Fāṭima, it was difficult to avoid the conclusion that the ʿAbbāsids were inferior. Thus the Zaydites were unlikely ever to share the favour at court enjoyed by the Muʿtazilites. The story of how some people were converted from Zaydite to Muʿtazilite views shortly before 850[16] suggests that about this time Zaydism in the heartlands of the caliphate was absorbed by Muʿtazilism which, though itself declining, was much more vigorous.

Conclusion

In the period from 750 to 925 the politicians had a number of successes in manipulating the deep religious yearning for a saviour in order to attain their political ends. Towards the end of the period the Imāmite party was organized, the Ismāʿīlites established a small state in Tunisia and the Zaydites states in Daylam and the Yemen. One incident has been recorded in Tunisia which suggests that political success was followed by disillusionment, and it would be interesting to know whether this phenomenon was widespread. What is relatively clear is that the activities of the politicians by no means exhausted the religious urge. At times they found it recalcitrant and not easily bent to their purposes; and now that much of their political achievement has disappeared something of the same religious urge is seen to be still alive.

NOTES

1 *Islam and the Integration of Society*, London, 1961, especially chap. 4; 'Shiʿism under the Umayyads', *JRAS*, 1960, 158–72; 'The Rāfidites', *Oriens*, xv (1962); *Islamic Philosophy and Theology*, Edinburgh, 1962, especially chap. 6; *Muslim Intellectual*, Edinburgh, 1963, especially chap. 4.

2 D. S. Margoliouth, *Lectures on Arabic Historians*, Calcutta, 1930, 127, says that according to aṭ-Ṭabarī this new claim was made by al-Manṣūr.

[3] Cf. *GALS*, i, 319.

[4] *Maḳālāt*, 58.

[5] Less than a year after the establishment of the first Fāṭimid ruler in Tunisia, presumably because all his decisions did not show the expected inspiration, his leading henchman began to question his claim (*Der Islam*, xxxvii, 66).

[6] Wilferd Madelung, *Der Islam*, xxxvii (1961), 61 n.; *Maḳālāt*, 26, etc.

[7] *Der Islam*, xxxvii (1961) 43–135. The passage referred to below is from p. 56.

[8] Ibid., 63 n.

[9] Ibn-an-Nadīm, *Fihrist*, 178 f.; cf. Šaš-ahrastānī, *Milal* (ed. Cureton), 115–21, 145 (includes Abū-Ḥanīfa; and mentions other respected Traditionists among the Imāmites), etc.

[10] *Maḳālāt*, i, 67.

[11] The conception of a distinctive Zaydite doctrine or position is probably what is meant by the *tazayyud* mentioned by Lewis, 63 n. In the mouth of an Imāmite author it would mean opposition to Imāmite or Rāfiḍite views, possibly acceptance of the caliphates of Abū-Bakr and 'Umar.

[12] *Maḳālāt*, 67.

[13] *Maḳālāt*, 164, 172 f., 177, 181; 72 f.

[14] Cf. *GALS*, i, 314 f.; R. Strothmann, art. 'al-Zaidīya' in *EI*(*S*).

[15] Cf. 'The Political Attitudes of the Mu'tazila', *JRAS*, 1963.

[16] Al-Ḫayyāṭ, *K. al-Intiṣār* (ed. H. S. Nyberg), 89.

XIV

BAPTISM AND ENTHRONEMENT IN SOME JEWISH-CHRISTIAN GNOSTIC DOCUMENTS

by

GEO WIDENGREN

IN another connection an attempt has been made to distinguish between the coronation of a king and his enthronement.[1] The ceremonies of coronation in ancient Near Eastern religion obviously took place in the temple, whereas the scene of enthronement was envisaged as situate in heaven. Enthronement may be said to be the mythical counterpart of the coronation ritual. Enthronement in its ritual form served as a visualization of the mythical action, of which the king was the centre. Accordingly, we meet in the coronation ceremonies with the same interplay between myth and ritual as elsewhere in the Near East, and, to facilitate a distinction between a purely mythical action and its ritual performance, the use of the terms enthronement and coronation is convenient. Other expressions might be used; but what really matters is the fact that the distinction between myth and ritual be kept in mind.

The pattern of enthronement, as well as that of coronation, can be traced back to ancient Mesopotamian times; early forms also occur in the West-Semitic, especially the Israelite, civilizations, and from there its developments can be followed on into Hellenistic-Jewish times.[2] It is but natural that this pattern should admit of certain variations, however, its main proportions were firmly established and they may be reconstructed as follows overleaf.[3]

1. Ascent to heaven.
2. Ablution.
3. Unction.
4. Communion.
5. Investment with a holy garment.
6. Handing over of the ruler's attributes.
7. Participating in the heavenly secrets.
8. Sitting on the throne of God.

In the following pages an endeavour will be made to trace out this pattern of enthronement in some Gnostic texts, above all in those belonging to Jewish-Christian Gnosticism. Mandaean texts, however, are not subjected to any analysis here, since they are reserved for special study in the future.[4]

The two most important texts concerned with our theme are the so-called *Naassene Sermon*[5] and Justin's *Book of Baruch*,[6] both being products of a Jewish-Christian Gnosticism in which the Jewish background is strongly evident.

In the first text, generally held to belong to the sect of the Ophites, which was a Syrian-Egyptian type of Gnosticism,[7] it is stated that the saviour is Adam.[8] Thus one of our sources of information records: 'For the Samothracians explicitly relate as a tradition that in the mysteries celebrated with them Adam is the Primordial Man, ἀρχάνθρωπος' (Hippolytos V 8, 9). In a manner quite common in Gnostic piety and in mystery religions, the pneumatic Gnostic in every respect is identified with this Saviour, the archetypal. The following passage is significant: 'And in the temple of the Samothracians stand two statues of naked men. But the aforesaid statues are the images[9] of the Primordial Man and of the reborn Pneumatic, in everything of the same substance, ὁμοούσιος, with that Man' (Hippolytos, V, 8, 10).

Of the ascension of this saviour Adam the *Naassene Sermon* gives the following account:

But concerning his ascension, that is (his) rebirth, that he may be born spiritual (pneumatic), notfleshly (sarchic), he says, the Scripture speaks:

Lift up the gates, ye archontes,[10]
and be ye lift up, ye everlasting doors,
and the King of Glory shall enter in.
(Hippolytos, V, 8, 18[11]).

Of the spiritual man, the Pneumatic, who is 'the perfect man', *τέλειος ἄνθρωπος*,[12] we also have the following important piece of information:

Therefore, he says, the perfect man will not be saved unless born again by entering in through this gate.
(Hippolytos, V, 8, 21)

This gate into which the Pneumatic shall enter in order to be reborn[13] is the gate of heaven, a statement which is corroborated by a quotation from *Gen.* 28:17:

The same entrance and the same gate, he says, Jacob saw when journeying to Mesopotamia—and he wondered at the heavenly gate, saying: 'How terrible is this place. It is none other than the house of God and this is the gate of Heaven.'[14]
(Hippolytos, V, 8, 20)

It is further emphasized that it is the pneumatic man, not the sarchic one, who will be reborn:

This, he says, is the resurrection which comes through the gate of the heavens, through which, if they do not enter, all remain dead.[15]
(Hippolytos, V, 8, 24)

Then the following sentence:

And the same Phrygians, he says again, say that this same one (i.e. the pneumatic Gnostic) is by reason of the change a god. For he becomes a god, when he arises from the dead and enters into heaven through the same gate. This gate, he says, Paul the Apostle knew.
(Hippolytos, V, 8, 24–5)

There follows here the well-known quotation from 2 Cor. 12, 3–4. In the sequel we are instructed that the word about the good fruit of the tree (Matt. 3: 10) is applicable to a certain class of people, i.e. the 'rational', *λογικοί*, living men who enter into the third gate (V 8, 31). Now, we must ask whether this gate, 'the third gate', is identical with 'the gate of heaven' or not. On the point we have the following statement:

But we are, he says, the Pneumatics who have chosen out of the living water, the Euphrates flowing though the midst of Babylon, that which is ours, entering in through the true gate which is Jesus the blessed. And we alone of all men are Christians, whom the mystery in the third gate has made perfect, and have been anointed there with silent oil from the horn like David.

(Hippolytos, V, 9, 21–2[16]).

Of this, the living water Euphrates, it is further said:

This Euphrates, he says, is the water above the firmament concerning which, he says, the Saviour spake: 'If thou knewest who it is that asks thou would have asked of him, and he would have given thee to drink living, rushing water' (John 4:10).

(Hippolytos, V, 9, 18)

Accordingly, the river Euphrates here on earth is only an image, a *typos*, of the heavenly one with its living water, the Water of Life.[17]

Of this Water of Life the Pneumatic partakes when entering through the true gate, Jesus. In this case the language is possessed of a cultic orientation, although the technical term 'gate' is interpreted allegorically as referring to the Saviour. It is interesting to note that Mandaean literature has preserved the expression 'the upper Euphrates', which would seem to indicate the Euphrates as being 'the water above the firmament'.[18]

We receive further information about the water above the firmament in the *Book of Baruch*, ascribed to the Gnostic Justin, where it is said in one passage:

For there is a distinction, he says, between water and water, and there is the water below the firmament of the bad creation, wherein receive ablution, *λούονται*, the earthly and psychic men, and there is the living water above the firmament of the Good One in which receive ablution the pneumatic and living men.

(Hippolytos, V, 27, 3)

In the water which is above the firmament, accordingly, the Pneumatic, the 'living man', receives a kind of baptism. It was stated in the *Naassene Sermon* that the pneumatics had chosen out of the living water, the water of Life, said to be the heavenly Euphrates, the water above the firmament. Therefore the Pneumatic is baptized in the water of Life above the firmament of the Good One, i.e. the Highest God.[19]

According to what is said in the *Naassene Sermon*, the Pneumatic enters into heaven through its gate and is then transformed into a divine being, for he arises from the dead by sharing in 'the resurrection which comes through the gate of the heavens'. That this gate is identical with the third gate is shown by the fact that, on the one hand, it is said that the perfect man, i.e. the Pneumatic, cannot be saved except by means of the rebirth, thanks to the entrance into the gate of heaven. On the other hand, it is said that the Pneumatics by means of the mystery of the third gate have become perfect and have chosen out of the living water, and thus have been reborn, got (a new) life. Accordingly, it is stated that the pneumatic man will be reborn and that this is the resurrection which comes through the gate of the heavens. This gate is, therefore, identical with the so-called third gate. We have obviously before us a conception of the world where there are three spheres, each provided with an entrance through a special gate. The third gate is the highest one, conducting to the heavenly abode where the highest god is enthroned. This picture of the world is not the old Near Eastern, but the Iranian idea.[20]

In the mystery of the third gate the Pneumatic not only is purified in the water of Life, but also anointed with oil. This part of the ritual, however, we shall leave for the time being and concentrate on some other passages in the *Book of Baruch*. Here it is related that the father of all, Elohim, who is the creator, aspires to ascend from the earthly world, which he has produced, up to the highest regions of heaven. When he came to the upper limit of heaven he said:

> Open unto me the gates,
> that I may enter in and acknowledge the Lord.
> For I thought that I was the Lord.[21]

Then a voice from the light said to him:

> This is the gate of the Lord,
> the righteous enter through it.[22]

The gate is opened, and Elohim enters in through it, to stand before the Good One, the Highest God, and he sees 'what eye has not seen nor ear heard, nor has it entered into the heart of man'. Here we observe the quotation from 1 Cor. 2, 9.[23] The quotation from Ps. 117 (118): 19–20, we also meet with in the so-called 'Prayer of Cyriacus', where, however, the first part of it has disappeared.[24] What is important to note is the fact that the two verses in question are part of the Israelite-Jewish royal ritual.[25]

The Good One then addresses Elohim in the following words:

> Sit thou on my right hand.[26]
> (Hippolytos, V, 26, 14–17)

At the end of the *Book of Baruch* there is further an account of the oath sworn by Elohim in the presence of the Good One, and this oath is quoted. Shortly before, it is said that they who are about to hear the mysteries and to be perfected—or initiated[27]—by the Good One swear the same oath. When this formula of the oath has been reproduced, it is further told how Elohim entered into the presence of the Good One:

> And when he has sworn that oath he enters into the presence of the Good One and sees 'what eye hath not seen nor ear heard, and it has not entered into the heart of man', and he drinks from the living water, which is for them an ablution, λουτρόν, as they think, a well of living, gushing water.
>
> (Hippolytos, V, 27, 1–3)

Here there follows the already quoted saying about the two kinds of water, the water above, and that below the firmament.

We observe how the Pneumatic, who has been initiated into the mysteries and made perfect, in everything is acting with Elohim as his pattern. He swears the same oath, he enters like him into the presence of the Good One, and partakes of mysteries, which in both cases—that of Elohim and that of the Pneumatic—are described in the words of Paul in 1 Cor. 2:9. He drinks of the living water, in which the Pneumatic is said to have his ablution (Hippolytos, V, 27, 3). However, it is expressly stated that he drinks of this living water, which nevertheless is styled a *λουτρόν* and which is mentioned as the water in which Elohim underwent his purification, as well as that wherein the Pneumatic gets his bath of purification. The baptism in this water accordingly means at the same time an ablution in the water of Life and a drinking thereof, hence a kind of communion.

This same ritual practice is found in other gnostic circles. Among the Sethians the Logos of God, according to Hippolytos:

> after entering into the foul mysteries of the womb, performed ablution and drank of the cup of living, gushing water, which he must needs drink who was about to put off the slave-like form and put on a heavenly garment.
>
> (Hippolytos, V, 19, 21)

Here we find the same combination of baptism and water-communion as we met with in both the *Naassene Sermon* and the *Book of Baruch*. It is obvious that the saying in John 4: 10 ff. appears as a scriptural basis of the idea of the Water of Life, of which the Pneumatic partakes in communion, and in which he is baptized.[28] It is however doubtful if this saying really is taken from the Gospel of John.

What is new in the last-quoted passage is the idea of changing the garment, to 'put on a heavenly garment'. This is the well-known gnostic symbol,[29] which was represented in baptism by the white garment put on by the newly baptized.[30] Because of the correspondence of inner value and outward form, as we have been able to ascertain from our texts, there was presumably a special rite also among the Gnostics concerning a garment that was put on after baptism, reminiscent of the practice in both the Christian church and the Mandaean community.[31]

Before leaving the question of the water of Life above the firmament as constituting the element of baptism and communion, it should be pointed out that a parallel to this idea is found in the writings of Origen, who speaks of some form of water in the heavenly places:

For that reason we hope that, after the troubles and fights here, we shall come to the heavenly heights, and, after partaking of the springs of the water which is gushing forth to eternal life, according to the teaching of Jesus, we shall drink from the rivers of knowledge(s) at the so-called 'waters above the heavens'.

Contra Celsum, VI, 20

How much of concrete imagery we are entitled to ascribe to this statement is difficult to ascertain. At any rate the wording itself demonstrates that 'the water above the firmament', as a source from which the Gnostic drinks, has been a standard expression of an idea that was widely known both in Gnostic and Christian quarters. Confirmation of this is found in the Adam-book of Gnostic-Jewish-Christian content, edited by Renan more than 100 years ago. Here we find the same 'waters which are above the heavens'.[32]

If we turn again to the description of Elohim's ascension, we can see at once that the last moment of that ascension was the act of enthronement itself, which took place by using the formula of the royal proclamation: 'Sit thou on my right hand.' This formula fits in exactly with the other royal formula from Ps. 117 (118) used in the text. The ascent of the Saviour-God has been pictured in accordance with the ritual of the enthronement of the ruler in ancient Israel.

Because of the parallel structure of the Saviour-God's ascension and that of the Pneumatic, we are conceivably entitled to make a supplementary addition. In the *Naassene Sermon* it is expressly stated that in the 'third gate', the gate of heaven, where ablution in the water of Life, and hence rebirth, takes place, there also the 'perfect man' is anointed with oil.

The ritual of the last part of the ascent, thanks to the comparison between the *Naassene Sermon* and the *Book of Baruch*, may accordingly be reconstructed as follows:

1. Ascent to the gate of heaven.
2. Exhortation to open the gates.

3. Entrance into the presence of the Highest God.
4. Ablution-baptism in the water of Life and communion.
5. Unction.
6. Partaking of the heavenly mysteries.
7. Royal proclamation together with enthronement.

These observations concerning the various elements of the enthronement ritual, which has been thus reconstructed in above, may receive some supplementation from other Gnostic texts, most of them possessed of a Jewish-Christian background. The fifth element, anointing with oil, in the *Naassene Sermon*, as we may recall, was mentioned very briefly. Origen, however, tells us that among the Valentinian Gnostics anointing was supposed to be carried out by means of oil from the Tree of Life. According to Origen, the Valentinian Gnostic says:

> I am anointed with light oil from the Tree of Life.
> (*Contra Celsum*, VI, 27)[33]

As the Pneumatic is baptized in the Water of Life, so the Gnostic is anointed with oil from the Tree of Life.

This idea of an anointing with oil from the Tree of Life is found in a pregnant form in the Ps. Clementine writings, from which some quotations may be given. In the passage concerned the author (or rather his original source)[34] discusses the problem of the Primordial Man as Messiah. He is represented as stressing the fact that the Primordial Man is the Anointed One:

> But the reason of his being called the Messiah (the Anointed One) is that, being the Son of God, he was a man, and that, because he was the first beginning, his father in the beginning anointed him with oil which was from the Tree of Life.
> *Ps. Clem. Recognitiones syriace*, ed. Frankenberg, I, 45, 4

Primordial Man, who had received the anointing, thanks to which he had been installed in the threefold office of king, high priest, and prophet, is then paralleled with every man who has received such anointing:

> The same, however, is every man who has been anointed with the oil

that has been prepared, so that he has been made a participant of that which is possessed of power, even being worth the royal office or the prophet's office or the high priest's office.

Ps. Clem. Recognitiones syriace, ed. Frankenberg, I, 46, 3[35]

The book then renders a dialogue which wants to demonstrate that the Primordial Man is both a prophet and the Anointed One (Messiah):

I remember, O Peter, that you have told me concerning the Primordial Man that he was a prophet, but that he was anointed you have not told me. If accordingly a man cannot be a prophet without being anointed, how could the Primordial Man then be a prophet when he had not been anointed? (Peter answers:) . . . If the Primordial Man prophesied, it is clear that he was also the Anointed One (Messiah).

Ps. Clem. Recognitiones syriace, ed. Frankenberg, I, 47, 1–3

From these allusions we are conceivably entitled to draw the conclusion that there were in Gnostic circles certain speculations current about the Primordial Man as being also the Primordial King, provided with prophetical and priestly functions, and who had received an initiation to his office by being anointed with oil from the Tree of Life. It is this Primordial Man, who is called the Anointed One (Messiah, Aramaic *mᵉšīḥā*), who is the Son of God. He is the *typos* of every man who has been anointed with the prepared oil. It is quite obvious that in Valentinian Gnosticism there was the same idea that the Primordial Man-Christ had been anointed by God, his Father, with oil from the Tree of Life, and that every Gnostic, like this Saviour, had participated in this anointing. That much is shown by the quotation *C. Celsum* VI 27, where we find also the same identity between the saviour and the saved one as in the *Naassene Sermon* and the *Book of Baruch*. The various elements in baptismal ritual concerning anointing and ablution are ritual expressions of ancient mythical conceptions, associated of old with the Tree of Life and Water of Life.[36] These mythical notions refer us to Mesopotamia as the home of this mythic-ritual pattern, and their local Babylonian colour is further demonstrated by the mention of Euphrates as the living water, flowing through Babylon. On the other hand, the dominant Jewish character of the *Book of Baruch* is incontestable, and in the *Naassene Sermon* it is certainly impossible to subtract the Jewish component from the text, as modern research has proved.[37] Above all, however, we observed that the mythic interpretation of the Gnostic's ascension was adapted to various details of the ancient Israelite-Jewish ritual of enthronement.

It calls for notice that in our texts the *hieros-gamos* motif is absent. This does not mean that it is completely absent from Gnostic texts. Indeed, to the contrary, it is a common idea that the Gnostic ascended to heaven, where he consummated a 'spiritual marriage'.[38] But in Jewish-Christian Gnostic texts the motif does not play any role, as far as I can see.

NOTES

1 For what follows I refer to a Swedish article of mine, *Nathan Soederblom-sällskapets Årsbok*, V (1946), 28–61, the first section of which is presented here in a revised form.

2 This subject is treated by me in the Hooke-Festschrift, shortly to be published. A summary of my views was published in my *Sakrales Königtum im Alten Testament und im Judentum* (1955), 49–53.

3 Cf. *Nathan Soederblom-Sällskapets Årsbok*, V (1946), 29.

4 For the time being cf. op. cit., 38–50.

5 Cf. Reitzenstein, *Poimandres* (1904), 82–102, and contrast *Studien zum antiken Synkretismus aus Iran und Griechenland* (1926), 105.

6 Cf. Haenchen, *ZfThK*, 50 (1953), 123–58. I cannot enter upon a discussion of the problems of the *Book of Baruch* touched upon by Haenchen.

7 Cf. Jonas, *Gnosis und spätantiker Geist*, I, 2nd edn. (1954), 348 ff.; Leisegang, *Die Gnosis* (1924), 112 ff.

8 Adam has played an important role in Jewish-Gnostic systems as both the Primordial Man and Saviour, cf. Kraeling, *Anthropos and Son of Man* (1927), 47 ff., 151 ff.

9 The Greek text has *εἰκόνες*. For the general implications of this term cf. Larsson, *Christus als Vorbild* (1962), where, however, there is no reference to our passage.

10 For the term *archontes*, cf. Widengren, *Mesopotamian Elements in Manichaeism* (1946), 37 ff.

11 For the place of Ps. 24:7 in the Israelite festival of Yahweh's enthronement, cf. Johnson, *Sacral Kingship in ancient Israel* (1955), 64 f., 72.

12 For this notion cf. e.g. Reitzenstein, *Hellenistische Mysterienreligionen*, 3rd ed. (1927), 338 ff.

13 For this notion cf. Reitzenstein, op. cit., 39, 47, 262, 270 and Dey, *Palingenesia* (1937), compared with the observations in Widengren, *Handbuch d. Orientalistik*, 1, 8:2, 59, 74–76, 79.

14 Here the text has: *ἡ πύλη τοῦ οὐρανοῦ*.

[15] Here the text has: *διὰ τῆς πύλης τῶν οὐρανῶν*.

[16] For the idea of 'the true gate' cf. Widengren, *Mesopotamian Elements*, 27 f. The use of the qualification 'true' indicates association with gnostic circles in Syria and Mesopotamia where the notions *kuštā*, truth, and *kuštānā*, true, have played a great role, cf. Schweizer, *EGO EIMI* (1939), 35 ff.; Jonas, op. cit., 243 ff.; Widengren, *Mesopotamian Elements*, 174; Sundberg, *Kuštā* (1953).

The remarkable expression 'silent oil' Kraeling, *HThR* 24 (1931), 224, wants to interpret as 'referred to derogatively' as a contrast to the *ὕδωρ λαλοῦν* of which Ignatius speaks, Letter to the Romans 7:2. But the context shows it to be something quite positive.

[17] For 'living' as a synonymous expression to 'of Life', cf. Widengren, *Mesopotamian Elements*, 17, 154.

[18] Cf. Drower, *The Thousand and Twelve Questions* (1960), 29:88 (Text) *fraš ellāiā*, which is properly the 'upper' Euphrates (but not 'celestial' as Lady Drower translates it).

As to the association between the third gate and baptism we may refer to the language used by ascetical and mystical monasticism, cf. e.g. the following statement: 'Baptism again is the gate of the world to come without which it is impossible to enter into the kingdom of God', Rignell, *Briefe von Johannes dem Einsiedler* (1941), 16* (Text), 40 (Transl.). Here the idea is transferred from a mystical-sacramental experience to an eschatological sphere.

We also meet with the expression 'the gate of Life', cf. Widengren, *Mesopotamian Elements*, 28, applied to the saviour.

[19] For the name 'the Good One', cf. Harnack, *Marcion* (1921), 160 f.; Hilgenfeld, *Die Ketzergeschichte des Urchristentums* (1884), 322, 349, 358, 527 f.; Leisegang, op. cit., 86, 158 ff., 261, 278.

The baptism in 'living water' is mentioned also in the Ps. Clement. writings, e.g. Diamartyria 1, 2. For the *ἀναγέννησις* mentioned in this passage, cf. the expression *ἀναγεννηθῇ* (Hippolytos, V, 8, 21), above p. 207. The underlying idea is a very realistic one: one is reborn, gets a new life, thanks to the baptism in 'living water', *ζῶν ὕδωρ*.

[20] Cf. Bousset, *Die Himmelsreise der Seele* (1960), 31, 43.

[21] Cf. Ps. 117 (118):19, quoted here in a slightly different form.

[22] Cf. Ps. 117 (118):20, quoted here in a slightly different form, but in this case the underlying Hebrew text is the same.

[23] The same quotation—in a slightly different form—is found in Lidzbarski, *Mandäische Liturgien* (1920), 77:7 = Drower, *The Canonical Prayerbook of the Mandaeans* (1959), 41. For this expression cf. Lagrange, RB 37 (1928), 11.

[24] Cf. the Syriac text in Bedjan, *Acta Martyrum et Sanctorum*, III, 275, cf. Reitzenstein, *Das iranische Erlösungsmysterium* (1921), 261.

[25] Cf. Johnson, op. cit., 116 ff.

[26] The quotation from Ps. 109 (110):1 agrees with the LXX text.

[27] The term *τελεῖσθας* indicates him who has been initiated into the mysteries, has received the *τελετή*, and therefore is made perfect, *τέλειος*, cf. in general Reitzenstein, *Die hellenistischen Mysterienreligionen*, 338 f., where it is shown that baptism functions as *τελετή*.

[28] For the background of this saying, cf. Bauer, *Das Johannesevangelium*, 2nd edn. (1925), 65, where references to gnostic literature are given.

[29] Cf. Jonas, op. cit., 102, 322 ff.; Reitzenstein, op. cit., 61, 179, 226, 263 f., 353; Widengren, *The Great Vohu Manah* (1945), passim and especially 49 ff., 76 ff.

[30] Cf. Segelberg, OrSuec, VIII (1959), 24 f.

[31] Cf. for the Mandaeans Segelberg, *Maṣbūtā* (1958), 115 ff., where the original place in ritual is demonstrated.

[32] Cf. Renan, *JA*, V, 2 (1853), 453.

[33] Cf. the discussion in Doelger, *Sphragis* (1911), 89 ff. and cf. also Migne, PG 83, 360 ff. The word 'light' seems to indicate the heavenly origin of the oil in question.

[34] The intricate questions of authorship and sources cannot be discussed here.

[35] In monastic circles a parallel is drawn between the Christian, who is anointed for a spiritual kingship, and Solomon, who received an unction for his earthly kingship, cf. Rignell, op. cit., p. 26* (Text), 47 (Transl.). Another parallel, this time between David and the Christian who is anointed after his likeness, *d^{e}mūttā*, is found p. 36* f. (Text), 56 (Transl.). As is well known, monastic circles inherited many gnostic and obsolete Christian ideas.

[36] Cf. Widengren, *The King and the Tree of Life* (1951).

[37] I have already stated above that Reitzenstein had to abandon his former position, cf. *Studien zum antiken Synkretismus*, 105.

[38] Cf. such passages as Irenæus I 13, 3, 6; I 21, 3; III 15, 2.

XV

SALVATION IN THE MAHĀBHĀRATA

by
R. C. ZAEHNER

'SALVATION' is perhaps a misleading word to use in connection with Hinduism since it has a specifically Christian ring and implies a whole series of Christian doctrines that are not relevant to Hinduism. It is, however, a word frequently used to translate the key Hindu concept of *moksha*; and this is, of course, perfectly permissible if we are quite certain at the outset in what sense we are using the word. It does not, of course, mean salvation from sin though it must include that too: it means, rather, salvation from the human condition itself in so far as it is limited by space and time and the whole active life we lead in space and time. To the Western mind the whole concept often seems void of content and sterile, since it tends to nullify all moral distinctions and to set a premium on complete inactivity. Moreover, the Hindus themselves, though they agree that the 'liberated' state is one of supreme bliss, find it extremely hard to define in what this bliss actually consists.

In the Upanishads the figure of deep, dreamless sleep is frequently used to symbolize the state of the liberated man, but even this is felt to be wholly inadequate, and the *Māṇḍūkya* posits a fourth state beyond those of wakefulness, dream, and dreamless sleep which it describes as follows:

It has cognizance neither of what is inside nor of what is outside, nor of both together; it is not a mass of wisdom, it is not wise nor yet unwise. It is unseen; there can be no commerce with it; it is impalpable, has no characteristics, unthinkable; it cannot be designated. Its essence is its firm conviction of the oneness of itself; it causes the phenomenal world to cease; it is tranquil and mild, devoid of duality. Such do they consider this fourth to be. He is the Self: he it is who should be known.

All that this passage states positively is that the state in question is one of total oneness and of tranquillity: from it the phenomenal world and the empirical ego with all its desires and responsibilities are totally excluded: for the liberated man these simply do not exist. This state is presumably what the 'introverted' as opposed to the 'extraverted' mystic actually experiences. According to the nondualist Vedānta it means that the soul realizes its complete identity with the Absolute One; according to the Sāṁkhya, on the other hand, it means simply that the soul realizes only the unfractionable unity of *itself*, for in this system each soul is totally distinct from all other souls, and there can be no communion between them. If this is the true interpretation of the experience, then, one would have thought, this could scarcely be *ultimate* bliss, so barren and 'selfish' does it appear to be.

In the Upanishads, however, and in the Mahābhārata the two extreme positions—complete monism on the one hand and complete pluralism on the other—tend to be avoided, and the analogy with dreamless sleep is not found satisfying. In a celebrated dialogue between Indra and Prajāpati in the *Chāndogya* Upanishad in which the former appears as pupil and the latter as preceptor, Prajāpati says: 'Now, when one is asleep, composed, serene, and knows no dream, that is the Self: that is the immortal that fear cannot touch. That is Brahman.'

Indra is very far indeed from being satisfied with this description of Brahman which is, by definition, absolute bliss. He says: 'Such a man has no present knowledge of himself (*ātman*) [so that he could say:] "This I am", nor for that matter [has he any knowledge of] things around him. He becomes as one annihilated. I see nothing enjoyable in that' (ChU. 8, 11).

As we have seen, in the *Māṇḍūkya* Upanishad the author, after describing the state of deep, dreamless sleep, goes on to describe the fourth state characterized by absolute oneness. The *Chāndogya*, however, describes something quite different. In the sequel to the passage just quoted the soul, on liberation, severs its links with matter and therefore knows neither pleasure nor pain that contact with matter must inevitably entail. In its liberated state it is not only serene but is said to be serenity itself; but this serenity is a *personal* serenity in which the soul does not lose its individuality (*svena rūpena*). 'He is a "highest person" (*uttama purusha*). Thus he goes around, laughing, playing, enjoying himself with women or chariots or friends, remembering nothing of this body which was appended to him.'

This emphasis on personal survival in the liberated a-temporal state is rare at this stage of Hindu thought, and, as here presented, it appears a little crude, but it must be seriously considered. The soul that survives is not the ego, for even in the earlier Upanishads a distinction is made between ego (*ahaṁkāra*) and self (*ātman*), while in the Epic the liberated soul is time and again referred to as *nirmama*, *nirahaṁkāra* and *nirdvandva*, 'devoid of all sense of "I" and "mine", beyond the opposites'. It must then refer to the *ātman* or 'self', and this *ātman* is here seen as one among many: it has its own 'form' (*rūpa*) and cannot therefore be identical with the 'Supreme Self' (*paramātman*) which we meet with elsewhere.

In the Epic rather more than half of the huge twelfth book is devoted to the subject of liberation, but much of it is inconsistent and confused because the subject always tends to get mixed up with cosmogony, so inextricably interconnected are the macrocosm and the microcosm in Hindu thought. The setting of this vast didactic portion of the Epic is this. The war between the Pāndavas and Kauravas is now over. The Pāndavas have won, though the carnage on both sides has been terrific, and the hero, Yudhishthira, himself a convinced pacifist, is wellnigh inconsolable. He is, however, persuaded to approach the aged Bhīshma who is still lying on a bed of arrows, in order to learn of his wisdom before he dies. For hundreds of pages Bhīshma discourses on the subject of *moksha*, but his discourse is so ambiguous that Yudhishthira becomes increasingly perplexed: he is not at all clear whether the liberated soul is actually identical with the Absolute, whether it is merely part of it, or whether it is simply isolated in its own eternal essence as in the classical Sāṁkhya.

The Epic, however, like the Upanishads, rarely adopts a neatly Sāṁkhya or an extreme non-dualist Vedānta position. In general it admits of a Supreme Being (called either 'Person' or 'Self' or 'Brahman') who emanates and re-absorbs both matter (*prakṛti*) and souls (*purushas* or *ātmans*): between world-cycles these are re-absorbed into the Supreme Being, and this state is thought to be analogous to that of liberation because, there being then neither time nor action, there is only perfect rest: there is no consciousness of duality. Yudhishthira, however, is *dharma-rāja*, the 'king of righteousness', not the king of *moksha*. He is, then, primarily concerned with right action *in* the world, not in escape *from* it. To him all this talk about 'liberation' is disquieting, for it seems to attach no importance to the distinction between right and wrong. He therefore presses Bhīshma to be a little more precise. Bhīshma does his best.

Bhīshma has just described what happens to the soul when it is liberated. After passing beyond the heavens and beyond the spheres of the three *guṇas*, *sattva* (the *guṇa* or inherent quality of pure goodness) leads the individual soul (*ātman*) to 'the highest (*para*) Lord Nārāyana. The pure-souled Lord himself (*ātmanā*) carries him on to the Supreme Self. On reaching the Supreme Self [these souls] become the stainless dwelling-places of that [Supreme Self]; they are conformed to deathlessness, nor do they return [to the phenomenal world] any more. This is the ultimate goal of those great-souled ones who transcend the opposites' (MBh. (critical edition) 12, 290, 74–5).

Here, quite plainly, a plurality of souls is assumed, and the liberated soul is indwelled by the Supreme Self from which it had originally proceeded. What the relationship of Nārāyana, the personal God, to the Supreme Self is, however, is not made clear and cannot detain us here, since it is not this that worries Yudhishthira but the apparent discontinuity that exists between the soul when yet in the phenomenal world and the same soul when released from it.

When [he says] these persons, firm in their vows, have reached this highest state [and] the Lord, do they remember their former lives or do they not? . . . In the state of liberation this is a great defect that sages who have achieved perfection must experience, if indeed they are immersed [completely] in the highest knowledge; [for] I consider that the highest form of righteousness (*dharma*) must bear the marks of activity (*pravṛtti*). What could be more painful than to be submerged in this highest knowledge?

In other words, what is the relationship, if any, between liberation and morality, between *moksha* and *dharma*?

Yudhishthira has a passion for righteousness which sometimes leads him to ask awkward questions, and Bhīshma admits that this is a matter which confuses even the wise. He does, however, attempt to answer. Liberation in some ways resembles dream, and the senses operate though in a different milieu. The individual soul (*kṣetrajña*) is pervaded by the Supreme Self (*sarvātman*) and also by qualities (*guṇas*).

The [Supreme] Self approaches the individual soul and the good and evil deeds [that accompany it] while the senses approach him as pupils [do a Guru]. After transcending matter [the individual soul] goes to the imperishable Self, the supreme (*para*) Self of Nārāyana which is beyond matter and transcends the opposites. Released from good and evil it enters the Supreme Self which is devoid of all imperfection (*anāmaya*) and all qualities (*aguṇa*), nor does it return [to the phenomenal world]. There is a residue of both mind (*manas*) and the senses, and at the proper time they approach [Nārāyana like pupils] seeking instruction from a Guru; and in a short time the liberated soul, trained and of trained understanding and interested [still] in distinguishing characteristics (*guṇas*), can attain peace.

What this passage seems to mean is that even in the liberated state something corresponding to mind and sense remains. There is room for something akin to personal relationships, for the soul retains the pupil-teacher relationship it formerly had with God. The Supreme Self is here not identical with God, but God is the 'form' of the Supreme Self which is itself formless and devoid of qualities (I. 101). It is true that Bhīshma does not give a straight answer to Yudhishthira's question as to whether or not memory continues to exist in the liberated state, but he implies that it does. What he seems to imply is either that the liberated soul can lose itself in the Absolute or Supreme Self which is devoid of qualities, or that it can emerge from trance into a state which still retains links with the phenomenal world.

In the Mahābhārata the state of liberation is sometimes compared to the condition of a gnat in a fig or a fish in water,—a state that is neither complete unity nor complete dissociation. This simile appears three times in the twelfth book and once in the *Anugītā* in the fourteenth. It is, however, not always clear whether the fig and the water represent the Absolute or the phenomenal world. The passages in question are MBh. 12. 296, 303, 313 and 14, 48.

Of these four passages 12.296 is more than usually obscure. Use is made of the twenty-five *tattvas* of the Sāṁkhya system, but in addition we have a twenty-sixth which appears to represent the Supreme Self or Person and which seems to correspond roughly to the 'Lord' of the *Yoga-sūtras*. The individual soul on liberation quits the 'unmanifest' (which here means matter in its undifferentiated state) and becomes 'devoid of qualities'. 'Then the soul whose nature is solitude (*kevaladharma*) unites with the Alone (*kevala*); liberated it lays hold on the Self'—and this Self is the twenty-sixth *tattva* which is yet beyond all *tattvas* and the essence of which is consciousness (*cetana*). This the soul meets and thereby attains to Oneness because both he and it are one thing,—consciousness.

Though attachment is its very nature it becomes really unattached (*niḥsangātman*); it meets the really unattached, the twenty-sixth, the unborn. . . . Unity-in-multiplicity must be seen in this way. Just as there is a difference between a gnat and the fig [in which it lives] and between a fish and the water [in which it swims], so must we understand difference here. So must we realize the unity-in-multiplicity of these two [the individual soul and the Supreme Self]. This is liberation. . . . Just as one who is pure in nature becomes pure by meeting another who is pure, or a wise man becomes enlightened (*buddha*) by meeting an enlightened man, so does one who has liberation in his nature become liberated on meeting a liberated man.

The identity, then, would appear to consist in the transcendent consciousness that each enjoys, but difference of personality remains.

The second passage in which the simile is used is wholly dualist: it is one of the very few passages in the Epic in which a purely 'atheist' Sāṁkhya position is adopted. On the one hand there is a plurality of changeless and timeless souls who remain untouched by *karma*, on the other there is matter which is forever changing. There is, therefore, neither unity nor unity-in-multiplicity, only duality. The same similes, however, are used, but they are used to illustrate a different thesis. The gnat is now no longer regarded as being so closely identified with the fig as to be scarcely separable from it, nor is the fish regarded as being at one with the water which is its natural element: this is ignored, only the difference is emphasized. 'The gnat is to be known as one thing, the fig as another, for the gnat is not defiled (*lip-*) by its connexion with the fig. The fish is said to be one thing, the water another. The fish is not in the least defiled by its contact with the water.' Here follow two more similes, that of a fire and a brazier, and of a lotus and water. It seems strange that these similes which are really helpful in explaining a relationship of unity-in-multiplicity, should also be used to illustrate a complete difference in nature. But, then, there are many things far stranger than that in the Mahābhārata.

In the third passage the simile of the water and the fish is alone used. Liberation is described, as it is in the Bhagavad-Gītā, as 'seeing the Self by means of the [? individual] self, and the Self in all creatures and all creatures in the Self. Contemplating thus the soul is not defiled as a fish [is not defiled] in the water'—the water here representing the phenomenal world.

This particular passage is also interesting in that it explains the relationship between liberation and the institution of the system of the four classes and the four stages of life. These were instituted as the normal stages by which liberation could be won; their ultimate aim is to detach men from the world and thereby bring the world itself to an end. 'This *dharma* was practised by the men of old for the destruction of the worlds, for the destruction of [all] actions.' This is the goal, but on the way to the goal good deeds are recommended,—deeds, that is, that are in accord with the *guṇa* of *sattva* which is itself akin to *moksha*.

It is often said of Hinduism that its ideal of 'liberation' tends to make nonsense of morality; but this is only partially true, for the normal means laid down for the attainment of liberation are largely moral, benevolence to all creatures being almost as important as detachment itself. This comes out most clearly in MBh. 14, 48 towards the end of the *Anugītā*. Here the *guṇa* of *sattva* (usually translated as 'goodness') is very nearly identified with *purusha*, the eternal soul: without it liberation would be impossible. This is what the *Anugītā* says:

> *Sattva*, when it rises superior to the unmanifest, becomes conformed to immortality. Seers declare that there is nothing higher than *sattva* in this world. We know the *purusha* who resides in *sattva* only by analogy; thus it is not possible to reach the *purusha* in any other way. Patience, steadfastness, refusal to do any injury, even-mindedness (*samatā*), truthfulness, honesty, wisdom (*jñāna*), and renunciation are prescribed as *sāttvic* conduct. Wise men think in accordance with this analogy [between *sattva* and *purusha*]: '*Sattva* and *purusha* are one, there can be no doubt about it.' Other learned men well grounded in wisdom, however, say that the alleged unity between *purusha* and *sattva* does not meet the case. It cannot be disputed, they say, that they ever exist separately: their separate existence must be recognized as being inherent in them in the very nature of things. But the position of the [truly] wise is that there is union-in-multiplicity. In the case of the gnat and the fig both unity and diversity can be observed. Though a fish in water is different [from the water], there is nonetheless an intimate connexion between them just as there is a close bond between drops of water on a lotus petal and the petal itself.

It would be absurd to maintain that the didactic portions of the Mahābhārata present any consistent view of the nature of liberation, and the different use made of the same similes shows how great the divergences are, but it can be said that on the whole they tend to avoid the extremes of both the non-dualist Vedānta and the fully dualist Sāṁkhya. Their general tone, like that of the Upanishads, can only be described as 'pantheistic theism'.

INDEX OF NAMES AND SUBJECTS

(References to the notes are shown in brackets)

LIST OF SUBSCRIBERS

R. F. Aldwinckle, 52 Kingsmount North, Hamilton, Ontario, Canada.

The Rev. Professor C. G. Baeta, The University, Legon, Ghana.
A. L. Basham, School of Oriental & African Studies, University of London.
E. G. Bassett, The Training College, Milton, Portsmouth.
C. F. Beckingham, The University, Manchester.
J. Benemann, 28a Polstead Road, Oxford.
Haralds Biezais, Box 34, Uppsala, Sweden.
Beatrice Blackwood, Pitt Rivers Museum, Oxford.
Miss D. L. Bodell, Philippa Fawcett College, 94–100 Leigham Court Road, London, S.W.16.
H. Bourgy, La Sarte-Huy, Belgium.
G. J. F. Bouritius, St. Joseph's College, Kerkstraat 65, Nijmegen, Holland.
Mrs. I. A. Brandon, 18 Woodvale Road, Knutsford, Cheshire.
Miss Theodora Brown, Heathfield House, Chudleigh, Devon.

L. J. Cazemier, Burgknappertlaan 140, Schiedam, Holland.
John H. Chamberlayne, 19 Petts Wood Road, Petts Wood, Kent.
Norman Cohn, 20 Brandling Park, Newcastle upon Tyne, 2.
E. F. Coote Lake, 5 Hurst Avenue, London, N.6.
The Rev. K. R. J. Cripps, The College, Ripon, Yorkshire.
The Rev. Dr. F. L. Cross, Christ Church, Oxford.

The Rev. Leslie Davison, 1 Central Buildings, Westminster, London, S.W.1.
V. A. Demant, Christ Church, Oxford.
Miss Celia Driver, Didsbury Training College, Manchester, 20.
Heinrich Dumoulin, Sophia University, Kioicho, Chiyoda-ku, Tokyo, Japan.

Mircea Eliade, The Divinity School, University of Chicago, Illinois, U.S.A.

Robert Etienne, Faculté des Lettres, The University, Bordeaux, France.

Stanley B. Frost, Faculty of Divinity, McGill University, Montreal 2, Canada.

Arthur F. Giere, Law Offices, Galesville, Wisconsin, U.S.A.

Victor R. Gold, Pacific Lutheran Theological Seminary, 2770 Marin Avenue, Berkeley 8, California, U.S.A.

J. Gonda, van Hogendorpstraat 13, Utrecht, Holland.

D. W. Gundry, University College, Ibadan, Nigeria.

Raymond J. Hammer, Central Theological College, Tokyo, Japan.

The Rev. W. Charles Heiser, S.J., St. Mary's College, St. Mary's, Kansas, U.S.A.

K. D. D. Henderson, Spalding Trust, Orchard House, Steeple Langford, Nr. Spalding, Wiltshire.

A. S. Herbert, Central House, Selly Oak Colleges, Birmingham, 29.

F. H. Hilliard, University of London Institute of Education, Malet Street, London, W.C.1.

Miss Christina Hole, 292, Iffley Road, Oxford.

Canon Frederic Hood, 1 Amen Court, London, E.C.4.

Miss I. B. Horner, 30 Dawson Place, London, W.2.

Edward M. Hughes, St. Augustine's College, Canterbury, Kent.

J. H. Hutton, New Radnor, Presteigne, Co. Radnor.

Agnes Jess, 355 Marburg/Lahn, Bismarckstrasse 24, Germany.

Aubrey R. Johnson, 207 Cyncoed Road, Cardiff.

Sherman E. Johnson, 605 Woodmont Avenue, Berkeley 8, California, U.S.A.

A. A. Kampman, Hoge Rijndijk 10, Leiden, Holland.

The Rev. F. Kenworthy, The Unitarian College, Victoria Park, Manchester, 14.

The Very Rev. Frederick E. Klueg, O.P., St. Rose Priory, Dubuque, Iowa, U.S.A.

The Rev. Professor R. Buick Knox, The United Theological College, Aberystwyth.

M. M. Kraatz, Am Hasenküppel, Marburg/Lahn-Marbach, Germany.

Mrs. H. A. Lake-Barnett, 5 Hurst Avenue, Highgate, London, N.6.
Günter Lanczkowski, 69 Heidelberg, Liebermannstrasse 45, Germany.
Stewart Lawton, St. Deiniol's Library, Hawarden, Near Chester.
O. H. Lehmann, 45 Portland Road, Oxford.
Trevor Ling, 36 Headcorn Road, Thornton Heath, Surrey.
The Right Rev. the Lord Bishop of Llandaff, Llys Esgob, The Green, Llandaff, Cardiff.
Evald Lövestam, Bredgatan 23, Lund, Sweden.

The Rev. C. S. Mann, St. Jude's Old Vicarage, Springall Street, Peckham, London, S.E.15.
Maurice Mehauden, Rue du Noyer 282, Brussels 4, Belgium.
E. Michael Mendelson, School of Oriental & African Studies, University of London.
Horst R. Moehring, Department of Religious Studies, Brown University, Providence 12, Rhode Island, U.S.A.
J. A. M. van Moll, Verena, 10 Lymbourne Close, Belmont Rise, Belmont, Surrey.
Margaret Murray, Forge Cottage, Ayot St. Lawrence, Welwyn, Herts.
E. C. B. MacLaurin, Department of Semitic Studies, The University, Sydney, Australia.
D. G. MacRae, London School of Economics, Houghton Street, Aldwych, London, W.C.2.
Thomas McPherson, Department of Philosophy, University College, Bangor, North Wales.

Mr. and Mrs. Peter Opie, Westerfield House, West Liss, Hampshire.
The Right Rev. the Bishop of Oxford, Cuddesdon, Oxford.

Maurice P. Pariser, 31 King Street West, Manchester, 3.
Alfred L. Parry, Woodlands, Brislington, Bristol 4.
W. S. F. Pickering, St. John's College, University of Manitoba, Winnipeg, Canada.
E. des Places, S. J., Pontificio Istituto Biblico, 28 via Pilotta, Rome, Italy.
J. P. M. van der Ploeg, O.P., Driehuizerweg 145, Nijmegen, Holland.
J. R. Porter, Queen's Building, University of Exeter.

Karl H. Pressler, Grosse Bleiche 16, Mainz, Germany.

Lord Raglan, Cefntilla Court, Usk, Mon.
Ian T. Ramsey, Oriel College, Oxford.
Ernst Thomas Reimbold, Rodenkirchen (Rh.), Haupstrasse 1, Germany.
Karl Heinrich Rengstorf, Munster (Westf.), Melcherstrasse 23, Germany.
The Rev. C. R. Renowden, St. David's College, Lampeter, Cards.
John Reumann, Lutheran Theological Seminary, 7301 Germantown Avenue, Philadelphia 19, Pennsylvania, U.S.A.
I. A. Richmond, All Souls College, Oxford.
Edmond Rochedieu, 7 Rue de Beaumont, Geneva, Switzerland.
Miss M. F. C. Rogers, 65 The Close, Salisbury, Wiltshire.
The Rev. Raymond G. Rowland, 22 Lime Tree Avenue, Peterborough.
H. H. Rowley, The Field, Cowle Road, Stroud, Gloucestershire.

Mohan Singh, P. O. Khalsa College, Amritsar, India.
J. B. Skemp, 9 St. Nicholas Drive, Whitesmocks, Durham.
Ninian Smart, University of Birmingham, Birmingham, 15.
D. Howard Smith, Department of Comparative Religion, The University, Manchester.
The Rev. H. C. Snape, Whalley Vicarage, Blackburn, Lancs.
Kurt Stalder, Bern, Switzerland.
Miss Marjorie H. Sykes, 142 Parkville Road, Manchester, 20.

E. O. G. Turville-Petre, The Court, Old Headington, Oxford.

W. C. van Unnik, The University, Utrecht, Holland.

The Rev. Dr. J. J. Vincent, Champness Hall, Rochdale, Lancs.

The Rev. N. Walker, 300 Chessington Road, West Ewell, Epsom, Surrey.
The Rev. Arthur Marcus Ward, The Field House, Richmond College, Surrey.
The Rev. W. R. Weeks, Sheppey House, Stone Street, Faversham, Kent.
R. J. Zwi Werblowsky, The Hebrew University, Jerusalem, Israel.
Kurt Wilhelm, Värtavägen 6, Stockholm, Sweden.
Miss Violet Wilkinson, 3 Garford Road, Oxford.

The Rev. C. G. Williams, 38 St. Isan Road, Heath, Cardiff.
James Wood, 3 East Savile Road, Edinburgh, 9.

Margaret W. Young, 51 Heaton Road, Withington, Manchester, 20.

LIBRARIES

Aberdeen, The University Library.
Andover Newton Theological School Library, Newton Center, Massachusetts, U.S.A.

Bristol, The University Library.
College of St. Matthias.
British Columbia, Canada, The University Library.

Cardiff, The University College of South Wales and Monmouthshire.
Columbia University Library, New York, U.S.A.

Durham, The University Library.

Eden Theological Seminary Library, Webster Groves 19, Missouri, U.S.A.
Edinburgh, The University Library.
Erlangen, Universitätsbibliothek, Germany.
Seminar für Religions-und Geistesgeschichte an der Universität, Germany.
Exeter, The Roborough Library, The University.

The Folk-Lore Society, University College, Gower Street, London, W.C.1.
Fourah Bay College Library, The University College of Sierra Leone.
Frobenius-Institut Bibliothek, Liebigstrasse 41, Frankfurt am Main, Germany.

Glasgow, The University Library.
Trinity College Library.

Handsworth College Library, Friary Road, Birmingham 20.

Helsinki, Finland, The University Library.
Hull, The University Library.

Katholisch-theologisches Seminar, Johannistrasse, Münster, Germany.

Leeds, Brotherton Library, The University.
London, King's College Library.
Royal Holloway College.
School of Oriental & African Study Library, The University.
Louvain, Belgium, Bibliothèque de l'Université.

Manchester, The Dean of the Faculty of Theology.
Marburg, Germany, Religionskundliche Sammlung.
Montreal, Canada, Faculty of Theology Library, The University.

Nottingham, The University Library.

Oregon, U.S.A., The University Library.
Oxford, All Souls College Library.
Mansfield College Library.
The Oriental Institute Library.

Paris, Collège de France.

Queen's University Library, Kingston, Ontario, Canada.

Institutionen för Religionshistoria och Religionspsykologi, Uppsala, Sweden.
Rome, Libreria Editrice dell'Universita Gregoriana, Piazza della Pilotta 4, Italy.
Royal Anthropological Institute, 21 Bedford Square, London, W.C.1.
The Royal Library, Stockholm, Sweden.

St. Andrews, The University Library.
Sheffield, The University Library.

Sion College Library, Victoria Embankment, London, E.C.4.
The Steiner Memorial Library, Åbo, Finland.

Tyndale House Library, Selwyn Gardens, Cambridge.

Woodstock College Library, Woodstock, Maryland, U.S.A.

Zentralbibliothek, Zahringerplatz 6, Zurich, Switzerland.